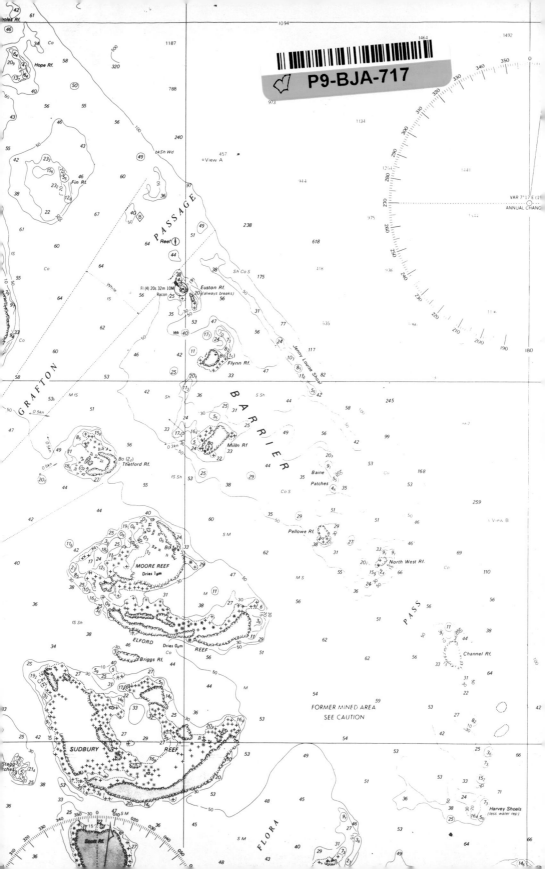

P9-BJA-717

To Rex
from
Capt. Arthur *[signature]*
on his 100th year

LIVERPOOL BUTTONS
&
HOMEWARD-BOUND STITCHES

PORTRAIT OF A MASTER MARINER

[signature]

CAPTAIN OTTMAR FRIZ

1896 - 1996

Cypress House
Fort Bragg, California

LIVERPOOL BUTTONS AND HOMEWARD-BOUND STITCHES:
PORTRAIT OF A MASTER MARINER

Copyright © 1993 by Ottmar Friz

For information, contact:
  Cypress House
  155 Cypress Street
  Fort Bragg, CA 95437

Library of Congress Cataloging-in-Publication Data
Friz, Ottmar, 1896-
   Liverpool buttons and homeward-bound stitches / Ottmar Friz.
   p. cm.
   ISBN 1-879384-22-1
   1.Friz, Ottmar, 1896-   . 2. Ship captains—United States—Biography.
I. Title.
VK140.F75A3 1993
387.5'4044—dc20
[B]   92-82992
                                                            CIP

Author's photo on front flap of dust jacket by Kevin Charles Olson

  Photos on pages 86 and 91, courtesy of the Grueland collection.
  Photo on page 112, courtesy E. C. Forner.
  Photo on page 184, courtesy Moses Cohen photo collection.

Manufactured in the U.S.A.

My last command.
Master, USNS GENERAL N. M. WALKER

DEDICATION

TO
CAROLYNE
AND
OUR PROGENY

AND
THE VALIANT YOUNG MEN
OF
MY GENERATION
WHO BRAVED THE RIGORS
OF STORMY CAPE HORN PASSAGES
IN SEARCH OF FAME AND FORTUNE

THE SEA AND ME

The mournful sound of foghorns
Lures me to the sea.
On a chilled misty morning,
No one's there but me.

I follow the tracks of the shore birds
While gulls above roam free
Shrilly calling to each other
To enjoy the fruits of the sea.

What has washed ashore from afar
Are treasures for all to see,
Shells and agates all ground round
By the surf now assaulting my knees.

I bend to find a polished stone,
Storm carved driftwood, rusting key,
A shining shell, once a creature's home
Kelp from the restless sea.

The foghorns drift into silence;
Gray mists roll away.
Sunlight glints on myriad wavelets,
As the morning becomes day.

Georgia Friz Rousseau

FOREWORD

For years children and grandchildren have urged me to record the outstanding events of my personal and professional life.

The original concept was the publication of a limited edition, solely for distribution to family members and friends and not for sale to the public.

However in the process of writing this history, spanning nearly a century, 1896 to the present, so much material of historical significance as well as anecdotal material surfaced that we decided to go public.

Throughout the years I kept accounts of noteworthy incidents, wrote articles while dabbling in freelance writing and kept records of activities, private as well as professional. All these elements and a retentive memory served in producing this book.

NOTE: The explanation of "Liverpool Buttons" was handed down to me by my shipmates. Others may have different explanations.

ACKNOWLEDGMENTS

Credit is due my wife Edna who scrutinized my handwritten material for errors in spelling and punctuation and whose unfailing support helped me to carry on.

My thanks to C. Cameron Macauley and David C. Miller of CCM Associates for their interest and professional advice as well as their transcription and editorial services furnished through The Topgallant Press.

Introduction

Here is the life story of a man who has done it all, and is still around to write about it! Around the Horn on a square-rigger at age 15, jumped ship in Chile, interned as an alien in Hawaii, labored on a Maui sugarcane plantation, sailed the West Coast in lumber schooners, involved in San Francisco's BLOODY THURSDAY seafarer's labor strike, operated ferries on San Francisco Bay for the 1939 Golden Gate Exposition, progressed from Deck Officer to Master on U.S. Army Transports while plying the Southwest Pacific during WWII, Master of troop transports during the Korean War, including an around-the-world trip repatriating United Nations troops to their homelands, Port Captain for MSTSPAC/MSCPAC until compulsory retirement at age 70, participation in the restoration of the Cape Horn windjammer BALCLUTHA, currently on display as a museum on San Francisco's Embarcadero, cross-country skiing at age 76, and last but not least, finding time at age 96 to write his memoirs.

Captain Friz weaves a fascinating narrative of personal experiences in faraway places, much in the manner of Joseph Conrad or Herman Melville. Melville also jumped ship to live in a foreign land while, like Friz, Conrad rose from deckhand to Captain. All three lived through extraordinary adventures in remote corners of the world, far beyond the wildest dreams of a non-seagoing individual. Captain Friz demonstrates remarkable skill in brilliantly describing the dangerous and often violent existence on a sailing ship in the early 1900's. His story is spliced with anecdotes covering at times the dull, unexciting routine life at sea then turning to dramatic images of the harsh realities and often borderline inhumanities inflicted upon the seamen by their oppressive officers.

This is a delightful combination of part travelogue, part adventure story, and part personal history of a unique nonagenarian who devoted most of his life to the sea. Any mariner who has sailed the waters of the world, either then or now, will enjoy Friz's description of his WWII experiences with Army and Port Officials in Australia and other Southwest Pacific Areas. Similar incidents as stevedores looting the cargo, senior officer with a fondness for the bottle, inept personnel who cannot be repatriated, etc., still exist today as they did then and are easily recognizable.

Captain Friz tells the story of working on a pipeline in the Chilean Atacama Basin in 1916, and having a young Bolivian co-worker who would often feel his bicep and mumble "Muy Gordo, muy gordo" ("Very husky, very husky".) During Friz's recent visit to New Orleans, I had occasion to feel his biceps, and I can tell you, it's as firm today as it was in 1916.

This was a book I read page by page and finished without putting it down. One can't help but wonder what he has up his sleeve for us when he becomes a centenarian-but I hope it's another book.

Richard B. Hosey, Master (Ret.)
MSTSPAC/MSCPAC, Captain USNR (Ret.).

Preface

We didn't call him Ottmar; we called him Harry.

I first encountered him when the Maritime Museum was restoring the full-rigged ship *Balclutha* in 1955. Jack Dickerhoff, master sailing ship rigger and a legend in his time, had skillfully "made" (the professional term) the rigging for the ship in the Moore Drydock Co. loft, but by reason of a shipyard strike (and also the inability of our poverty-stricken museum organization to pay shipyard rates) the completed rigging was not being installed. The restoration of the old ship was a volunteer effort growing out of a telephone call to my office (one of the two best telephone calls there in forty-four years—the other was from Bill Roth's real estate chamberlain to say that Bill had decided to buy Ghirardelli) from a labor union man named Don Shannon. He had read that the museum had bought the near derelict vessel and thought perhaps the Boilermakers, Iron Shipbuilders and Helpers, Local #9, could help us restore her. Oh, could they! Shannon put me in touch with Mario Grossetti, head of the union, who brought in the whole Bay Area Metal Trades Council. On Saturdays the ship hummed with volunteers bringing her back to life.

As the year wore on (it took a year) the journeymen and helpers from the union movement welcomed volunteers in general. Capt. Bill Dodge, from Matson, organized a detail to install the completed rigging. Enter Harry Friz. He tells about it on Page 255. As I met him he was a man of above medium height, taciturn, neat, approachable. His efficiency came easily, plainly springing out of years of exposure to the seamanship craft.

In conversation with Harry, I was taken with his years in the Cape

Horn ships *Obotrita* and *Blankenese,* and the unusual circumstance of carrying cargo in one of Matthew Turner's late-surviving brigantines, the *Geneva,* in 1917. Subsequently, the maritime historian, Harold Huycke, and I went to Friz' comfortable home in Piedmont and tape recorded narratives from his sea experience.

We could not hope to preserve more than fragments of the long life set down here. It is fortunate that he chose to do this. It is an important account. It reveals an individual up against difficulty again and again, and the story is threaded through historic times. As life's pitches come at him, Harry is at the plate, ready. He pauses for introspection but he doesn't wallow. He writes like an angel, in the old expression, but an angel who has a task to do, get down on paper with quiet eloquence the log of a whole life.

Harry turns to poetry easily, with a sentence or two to burnish a scene. He is German, and romance and order could be said to vie with each other on these pages. The format is spacious; the book was originally conceived as something to put in the hands of some hundred members of the family and the photographs of father and mother and relatives attest to this early plan. Wisely, it was later decided to "go public," as Harry puts it, and a good thing for the public. Or I should say that part of it that likes an unfolding, true tale of a sailor's progress. There are a few books like this by 18th Century seafaring men—John Nicol, Mariner comes to mind— but this will likely be the last one spanning homeward-bound stitches and the coming of radar.

The book is a *progress* in the dictionary sense of a "gradual better- ment." Except that the process is rocky, rather than gradual. And therein lies the story's tension. After Cape Horn and South American adventures (fascinating!), Friz came to America in the four mast schooner Columbia and, unknowingly, embarked on the continuation of his sea career on a roller coaster. Shipping conditions along the Pacific Shore wildly fluctu- ated for half a century.

And Harry, who had set his mind early on rising through the ranks to become a captain, rode the roller coaster. "Through the years I had ac- quired the habit of doing a full day's work," he says (pages 118-119). He was undoubtedly a "steady man" from the employer's standpoint. But the times were hard for shipping, and he seems to be always looking for a job. He reports the process in detail, and we are right there with him. He is skilled at describing the gritty reality of the San Francisco waterfront.

In Oakland, there's the morning "shape-up" outside the gates of Moore Drydock Co. where he can work for a day if he's selected from the crowd. Meanwhile he steadily advances his ticket by spurts of seafaring and navigation school attendance.

> "Any luck today?" [his wife asks]. "Why do you look so glum?"
> "Yeah, I have a job."
> Her face lit up. "Wonderful, tell me about it."
> "I have just been promoted from chief mate in deepwater ships to deckhand on a ferry boat."
> She caught her breath. "Did you take it?"
> "I sure did, honey. It was an offer I couldn't refuse."

But Harry, in his ineffable way, soon learns the difficult art of docking a ferryboat across the tide on the far side of the Ferry Building, and before long he is First Officer in a desirable profession for the seafaring man—a steady job and home every night.

And he describes what San Francisco Bay ferryboating was like as he describes everything else. Important maritime history.

Liverpool Buttons and Homeward-Bound Stitches is the story of a non-privileged man (in a formal sense), privileged as a result of steadily acquired professionalism. It is a pleasure to watch him learn. Harry ("Ottmar" seems to have been less used than "Henry" and Henry turns into Harry) had to give up his schooling in Germany—which he loved— at the age of 15 because of familial financial circumstances. He fastened on the sea as a career after a glimpse of the "segelschiffhaven" in Hamburg.

Germany for Harry was an idyll; the home he left was in a valley in the northeast corner of Bavaria where his parents had leased an inn:

> So like the American scene described in Leatherstocking Tales, this enchanting woodland became my playground during the most impressionable years of my boyhood.
>
> The local inhabitants were of peasant ancestry, farming the stony soil. The clatter of weavers' looms was heard, producing textiles in a cottage industry. With limited contact to the outside world, the valley had remained hidden for centuries, unsung and unheralded in the chronicles of the past.

In the golden days of summer vacation I roamed the forest, mastering every trail, hideout and viewpoint. Clearings offered an abundance of wild strawberries, raspberries, blackberries, blueberries and cranberries. The swift little river Selbitz, boiling through the rocky valley, harbored trout and pike in shadowy pools, ready to take the angler's bait. Following the first heavy fall rains various edible mushroom poked their heads through the thick pineneedle carpets in the cool forest...

Harry was already entangled with America as was many a German boy before him. He had got a translation of James Fennimore Cooper for Christmas. With his playmates he acted out The Deerslayer, Chingachgook, and Uncas in the German forest. Two generations before, my Great Uncle Max, another romantic, "had read a number of very fascinating western stories and the *Leatherstocking* books." He came to this country in his teens in 1869 and roamed the American west. Born in 1889, Capt. Fred Klebingat,[1] like Harry Friz, came up to the Pacific Northwest in an American schooner. He writes in one of his memoirs: "But here was a cowboy just as I had encountered them in Karl May's stories of the American West which I read as a boy back in Germany. I read them in the classroom, concealed in an algebra book, when the teacher turned his back to solve a problem on the blackboard."

It was a wrenching business for Harry Friz in later years to make the separation: he had "a soft spot in my heart for the land of my birth. To feel otherwise would be unnatural. I knew Uncle Sam would understand and think no less of his adopted nephew." But he now took the oath of

---

1   Capt. Klebingat, who also was going strong in his '90s, supplies an identification of the master of the brigantine *Geneva* in his booklet *Memories of the Audifired Building and the Old City Front*. The "tail, lean Scot" would almost certainly be "Blackbird" Ferguson. Klebingat encountered Ferguson on the vessel three years before, south of Harrison St. on the San Francisco waterfront. "The *Geneva* surely was cut down—the boom was cut off even with the transom, and the main topmast had been shortened so it was even with the fore." Ferguson had reason to be leery of an over-rigged vessel. For years, he engaged in the "contract labor" trade among the Pacific Islands. Sailors called it "blackbirding." He had recruited 270 laborers in the Gilberts for the coffee plantations in Guatemala. They were aboard the *Tahiti,* another Matthew Turner-built brigantine, under a captain in Ferguson's employ. The *Tahiti* was found floating bottom up off Mexico, no survivors.

citizenship and declared that he did "absolutely and entirely renounce and abjure all allegiance and fidelity to any foreign prince, potentate, state of sovereignty of which I have hereto been a subject or citizen...."

He was emotionally drained by the process. In later years a guest at his wedding was flippant about it. "I was about to suggest to her that a reading of this awesome document might clarify a few things.."

Adjustment to life in my new country became an ongoing process. I found the people to have an extraordinarily well developed sense of humor. Trivial as well as serious events of the day were habitually discussed in a droll and frivolous fashion, frequently interspersed with wisecracks.

And...

It was my first experience with the innate fairness of the American character, of which I had heard much. Someone, within the vast bureaucracy of a great nation at war, bothered to ponder the fate of a handful of individuals of no significance in this time of turmoil.

(This when the American brigantine *Geneva* arrived at Honolulu from Chile with a few Germans in her crew in the month that the United States declared war on Germany. They were interned in the Immigration Station, but a better solution was sought—work on a sugar plantation—because they had performed well on the vessel.)

And...

Another peculiarity was the universal usage of calling people by their first names immediately following introduction. Total strangers became "first name friends" at once. It was not easy for me to accept this custom, coming from a country where daily contact even with close associates was governed by a formality...in certain middle class circles it had attained the ultimate level of freakishness, and wives were addressed by their husband's titles of office: Mrs. Teacher, Mrs. Postmaster, Mrs. Stationmaster, etc.

And...

Visiting with newly made friends, I was impressed by the opulence of the daily dinner table even in the most modest of homes. Following the main dish of meat, potato and gravy there was always

dessert of fruit and cake, every day. I came to understand the meaning of "The great American dream." By contrast, at home a full
dinner was served only on Sunday—perhaps a goose or a rack of
venison...

So Harry settles in. It is not the purpose of this Preface to give all the
twists and turns. He marries the owner's daughter. Thirty-three years
spent aspiring for the pinnacle are finally reached, and he becomes a ship
master. The wild swings of the seafaring profession as found on the
Pacific Coast (our viewpoints differ on the turbulent '30s) become steady
with the need for competent mariners in war time.

Harry becomes a senior master in the Army Transport Service—no
more grubbing for a job in a lumber yard to make ends meet. Voyage
after voyage in the largest kind of ship, chockablock with troops...and no
incidents.

Earlier, in his first command:

> I had him (the second mate) read the night orders out loud. When
> he read the part ordering the course change, I stopped him and asked,
> "Why did you not change course, as directed?"
> He looked puzzled. "I guess I forgot."
> Right then and there, I took a solemn vow: No one, but no one,
> would ever have the chance to wreck my career.

It was an oath to vigilance as only the master of a moving ship can
know it. An oath to sleeplessness. Harry Friz's long career in the transports had it as a cornerstone.

In "Sailing the Waters of Australia and New Guinea" (Chapter 18), he
brings it all back. I sailed as second mate and mate under an equally
unerring captain, Elmer Malanot, in the transports Lorinna and San Anto-
nio, and in the latter vessel we threaded the Great Barrier Reef and
shuttled to the same ports across the Coral Sea. We encountered Harry's
first command, the Will. H. Point, from time to time but it didn't transpire
that I met her master.

In the end, in San Francisco, Harry is made Port Captain —"the peak
of a career at sea." He was thought capable of being in charge of everything.

I have indicated that this is a different kind of book; it moves at a
different pace, leisurely, expansive, because of its original premise as a

memoir for the family. Scenes and incidents that caught his fancy are dropped in. I thoroughly enjoyed this aspect. The tautening hand of an editor doesn't loom over it and it becomes a better record for that reason.

He examines retirement in clinical and extended fashion, for instance, as he examines everything else along the way. Harry, being Harry, is different. When he was obliged to retire at the age of 70, he still had— has—more than a quarter century to go!

Karl Kortum, 1993

Founder, San Francisco Maritime
National Historical Park

CONTENTS

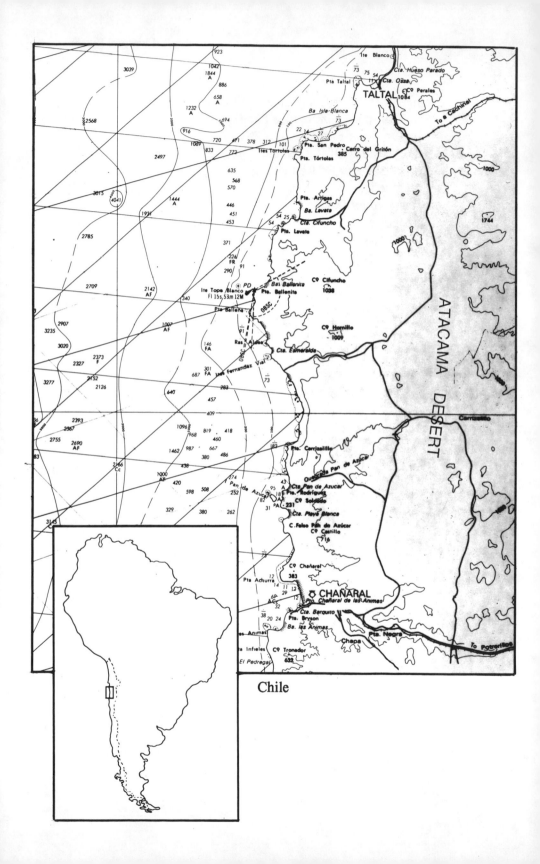

Chile

WORLD WAR I

Deeply laden with a full cargo of coal, the full rigged ship BLAKE-NESE lay at anchor in the Hunter River estuary in Newcastle, New South Wales, Australia. At her staff in the setting sun fluttered her national colors—horizontal stripes of black, white and red—the flag of Imperial Germany.

Awaiting crew replacements, departure was scheduled at first light the following day. Our destination was Chañaral, Chile, from there to a saltpeter port, and then return to home port: Hamburg. A year ago in late 1913, I had joined the ship as an ordinary seaman, my second voyage under sail in a planned career in the merchant marine. I had taken over the midnight anchor watch and, as I paced the deck, I thought of the future. One more voyage as able-bodied seaman would fulfill the mandatory requirement of four years service before the mast in square-rigged ships, then it would be good-bye to Cape Horn windjammers and on to a more comfortable berth in steamships.

In the silence of the night, the muffled sound of an approaching motor drew my attention to the rail in the waist of the ship. Over the bulwark appeared two large dark eyes in a pale face, followed by an arm and hand clutching a partly consumed whiskey bottle. A seaman's bag landed on deck with a thud. I helped the newcomer over the side as the sound of the motorboat receded in the distance. He was a small man and very drunk. "My name is Patrick," he mumbled as he fished in his pockets for his papers. "Just call me Paddy," he croaked as he passed out. With the help of one of the men, we deposited him on an empty lower bunk in the fo'c'sle.

The weather turned ugly during the night, but the familiar sidewheel tug appeared at daybreak and towed us out to sea. Well clear of the land, he signaled to let go his line and departed with the customary "Farewell" of three blasts on his whistle. It was the 28th of June, 1914, my mother's birthday. Under a leaden sky and drizzling rain, the ship wallowed in a heavy swell as we struggled to make sail, getting little help from the new hires.

The mate, surveying the scene, growled, "Where is everybody?" Looking through the fo'c'sle door, he discovered a human form in a lower bunk. He grabbed it by the scruff of the neck and seat of the pants and bodily threw a screaming Patrick out on deck. On the receiving end of a few well-directed kicks, the bewildered Paddy struggled to his feet and feebly attempted to join us in our labors.

It was a rough start, weatherwise. The ship remained in the southern latitudes to run before the westerlies and pick up the wind near the coast that would take her to her destination. Deeply laden, the decks awash in a following sea, the men not at the wheel or lookout were employed under the fo'c'sle head, making chafing gear such as Sennet out of small stuff, or canvas matting to fit over blocks aloft.

Paddy, fighting off a case of delirium tremens, kept to himself. He was not allowed to take the wheel or stand a lookout trick. I often observed him, off watch, stretched out in his bunk and by the light of a stubby candle, reading in a small blackbound book. Not a good reader, he formulated the words with his lips. One morning, as I called the watch, I found him asleep with the open book on his chest. I could not avoid seeing the title, "The Keys to Heaven," a religious tract.

A few days later, coming off the evening watch, I observed Paddy standing at the foremast shrouds. A full moon above, drifting ragged scud illuminated the forward deck. His head tilted back, gazing skyward, he nodded at the moon as I heard him mumble, "Yes, I'll be there, wait for me, I am coming, I'll be there." When he saw me, he smiled and said, "Just greeting some of my friends up there." I helped him over the high sill of the fo'c'sle and turned in to get some rest myself before the midnight watch.

At the sound of seven bells, 3:30 a.m., I went forward to call the watch. Stumbling over the high sill, I fell with my outstretched hands landing on the fo'c'sle deck, which seemed wet. Lighting a match, I saw my hands covered with blood. Near the door lay Paddy, his seabag filled with his belongings serving as a pillow. A gaping wound was at one side of his throat, his razor on the deck beside him. Although he had missed the jugular vein, he had lost a lot of blood. A light cut across his throat and beyond indicated that he was unable to finish his attempt at suicide.

I lit the lamp hanging in the skylight and aroused the watch, then sprinted aft to tell the watch officer. The skipper and mate came forward to see what had happened. They ordered Paddy placed on the mess table. Mumbling incoherently and resisting feebly, his hands and feet were tied to the four uprights supporting the table. Following an examination, the second mate, having applied some medication, proceeded to close the wound, wielding a curved surgical needle and silk thread.

In his delirium, Paddy struggled and protested. It was finally understood that he, as an Irishman, was being pursued by two Englishmen out to kill him. Ironically, among the new hires were two English seamen, but we knew that it was all a figment of Paddy's imagination. The watch about to go on duty sat on their seachests and drank coffee. It was a macabre scene.

Paddy was transferred to a two-bunk room that served as a sickroom. We had to secure his hands, because he made several attempts to remove the bandage. Three of us, an ordinary seaman, a deckboy and myself, were detailed to stay in the room and keep a watch on him. Paddy was clearly insane.

I was very uncomfortable, sitting in that room day in and day out, enduring his unwavering, baleful stare in silence. At times I would cover his face with a towel. The second mate looked in on us occasionally and was then questioned by the skipper in his own unique fashion, "How is the Irish Jesus today?"

When it was thought necessary to remove the stitches that could not be absorbed, Paddy was carried out and laid out on the main hatch. We stood by and watched the operation. The cut was only partially healed, and nothing else could be done but to cover it with a sterilized bandage. We discontinued the round-the-clock watch and only served him his meals. Meanwhile, the skipper had to confront the greater problem of landing a foreigner with a case history of insanity.

We had now been at sea better than two months. One morning, entering the sickroom, I was astonished at the change I saw in the patient. His eyes were bright and clear as he greeted me with a smile. "I want to thank you for the care you have given me," he said. "I cannot repay you, but I want you to have this present from me."

With that, he handed me a pair of bellbottom trousers, made of soft white duck. The garment was handmade with sailtwine, and the even stitches would have been envied by a seamstress. I protested, but he insisted that I keep it. Unfortunately, I could not wear it, as it was much too small for me. He had made it for himself in better times.

Several days later, the coastal mountain range of Chile arose above the horizon. In the dusty haze we discerned the buildings of a small village, nestled on the narrow flatlands. It was the fifth of September, sixty-eight days out of Newcastle N.S.W. to Chañaral, Chile.

As we approached under reduced sail, we could see the outlines of a large ship, her gray painted hull blending in with the background. She turned out to be the German bark NEREUS. No sooner had we anchored in the open roadstead when we saw a small boat under oars leaving the NEREUS. When he was within hailing distance, the captain rose in the sternsheets and hollered, "Germany is at war with the world." He came aboard and disappeared into the cabin.

With no radio communication on board, this was news to us. We devoured the German language newspapers the NEREUS' captain had brought with him. Some were printed in Chile. Their screaming headlines related the successes of the German armies whose lightning advance into Belgium had effectively demobilized the armed forces of that country.

We read how artillery fire of the Krupp cannons, notably one called the "Big Bertha," had reduced the formidable fortress of Liege, in Belgium, to rubble, before the commander of the fortress had realized what had happened.

It was the undivided opinion on board that this war would end in about six weeks and we could all go home. Little did we know what was in store for us and for the whole Western World.

AT ANCHOR

Chañaral, Chile. A forlorn coastal outpost near the southern end of the Atacama Desert. An outlet for a French copper mining concern.

The contract for delivery of coal had been initiated long before the outbreak of hostilities in Europe. In line with prevailing business practices, the cargo and the freight were insured and the freight money deposited in a bank.

Chañaral as a port was nothing more than an open roadstead, exposed to the strong northwesterly wind. The only facility for landing was a jetty, an iron framework extending from the shore, far enough to clear the surf. It had a wooden deck at street level and stairs leading down to the water. To negotiate the stairs from a small boat required considerable agility. A second jetty with railroad tracks served to load or receive cargo in open railroad cars.

The ship's cargo gear had been rigged. Heavily constructed launches, each manned by two men operating long sweeps came alongside.

The main hatch was served by a winch with a noisy one-lung motor using kerosene as fuel. It took the ship's blacksmith to start and operate this contraption, first to prime the motor, then to turn the engine over.

It took time and effort for the motor to catch the spark, only to cough and die. The skipper rolled his eyes heavenward, shook his head and looking around as if to say, "You see now the trouble I am having all the time?" He turned to address the blacksmith, "You think you will ever get this thing going?" The blacksmith paid him no attention; he just kept turning over the flywheel until the motor finally caught on and kept running. It took a month to discharge the coal.

Dispatches from Europe began to refer to Great Britain, France and Russia as the Allies. Germany, Austria, and Italy became known as the Central Powers. Italy, for the time being, remained neutral. The German and Austrian armies continued to score military successes until winter rains and snow turned the battlefields to seas of mud, forcing major operations to come to a standstill.

In anticipation of a prolonged layover away from the home port, all cargo gear was dismantled and stowed below decks. All sails were taken down and stowed in the sail locker. On deck, routine maintenance—scaling, priming and painting the main deck and hull—was the order of the day. The wooden poop deck was hosed down daily to keep it from drying out.

Any hope we had of the war soon ending proved forlorn.

Foodstuffs we had obtained in Australia for the homeward bound passage that did not need refrigeration were now kept in reserve. A contract was negotiated with local merchants to provide meat, potatoes and vegetables on a daily basis.

During the first few weeks, the cabin boy and I rowed the skipper to the landing every afternoon. I then accompanied the captain to fetch provisions. The trip to the boat landing was easy enough, running before the wind and a following sea.

The return trip was always against a strong wind and a choppy sea. The gig was a small boat with a transom stern. We rowed singlebank; that is, I used the stroke oar on the portside, the cabin boy the oar on the starboard side. The captain, in the sternsheets, steered, using a tiller-yoke and tiller ropes. Against wind and sea, the small boat pitched violently. Occasionally, the stroke oar would "catch a crab"; that is, the blade would not clear an oncoming whitecap and send spray over the sternsheets. It became our duty to always have the skipper's oilskins aboard.

He soon tired of the daily trip and it became my job to make the rounds of the butcher, greengrocer and the general merchandise storekeeper. Beef, goatmeat or mutton was produced locally; vegetables and potatoes came up from the south on a weekly steamer, as did Argentinean butter, round balls in salt-encrusted pig bladders that soon turned rancid. Chiloe potatoes grown on an island by that name had a disagreeable taste, probably from large black spots on the skin.

The year 1914 came to an end. Christmas was not celebrated in the customary fashion. Usually we had a Christmas tree made out of old broom material and painted green. Not this year. In view of the dismal atmosphere on board, no one even considered the custom of trooping aft to serenade the cabin occupants with our homemade band instruments. New Year's Eve was ignored. The year 1915 promised no change.

One afternoon, being out of earshot on the foredeck, Wilhelm the deck boy approached me and said, "I will no longer put up with the abuse from the mate. I am going to leave as soon as I see an opportunity." I sympathized with him and, sensing his firm resolve, made no attempt to dissuade him. I wished him luck.

In the beginning, we would visit on Sundays with the crew of the NEREUS. Their captain had a liberal attitude in that he allowed his men to go ashore at will. Some had made friends ashore and even found occasional employment. Our captain, afraid that some of this might rub off on us, disallowed further contact with the men on the NEREUS. It was on our last visit that Wilhelm joined some of the NEREUS men for a look at the village and did not return.

It was only a matter of time before others decided they had had enough and somehow managed to leave. The young second mate informed the skipper that he would leave to join some auxiliary units of the German Navy still operating off the coast in international waters. The captain's comment was, "Yeah, they need you to win the war!" The next to go was the sailmaker, perhaps the only one to be paid off, because of illness requiring hospitalization.

As the year progressed, we settled down to a routine of "make work," performed without enthusiasm. Eventually, the stock of materials for maintenance and repair was depleted. The daily call of "Turn to" became just a formality. Scaling rust off the deck and hull plates continued. With primer and paint no longer available, a coat of boiled linseed oil was applied to the surfaces.

For me, the daily run to the village for provisions was a relief from boredom. In my contacts with the local merchants, I acquired a working knowledge of Spanish. From the people ashore, I learned the pronunciation of words. In the ship's library, I had found a book written by two German professors, designed for self instruction. A daily study of this book enabled me to form sentences and converse with citizens of the village in everyday Spanish. I received many compliments on this achievement, and they began to call me "Mayor Domo."

Aside from the French interests, there were offices of American mining concerns. The manager occasionally donated cigarettes and pipe tobacco. Eventually, this source dried up. The skipper still had some British plug tobacco in the slopchest. It was hard as rock. We shaved it paper-thin, rolled it in the palms of our hands and used it for pipe tobacco.

Another foreigner in the community was a lone Englishman. A Dick Tracy type with a snap-brim hat and a straight-stemmed pipe clenched between his jaws, he was always present when any of us were on a rare shore leave. He marched along in a purposeful fashion, looking neither right nor left, at a pace indicating an important errand elsewhere, yet he somehow managed to keep us in sight. I was conscious of the fact that he shadowed me on my daily visits. There being no British establishment in town, we believed him to be an agent of the British Secret Service.

An occasional break in the daily routine came when large schools of fish, sardines and herring, entered the shallow bay. Their presence was heralded by swarms of gulls, pelicans and other seabirds hovering aloft. Diving in unison with folded wings from a height of several hundred feet, they always got their prey. The mass of fish was so dense that, seen from a distance, the upper layer seemed a mass in turmoil, struggling above and disturbing the surface of the sea as the school headed for the beach, where it came to a standstill. This was the signal for many of us to crowd into the gig and head for this bonanza.

To get a catch was simple. Instead of bait fishing, the shanks of three medium-sized fishhooks were tied together to form a small grapnel. The dense mass of fish could be seen below the bottom of the boat. By gently lowering the hooks, the fish would part and close again around the line. A sharp jerk would hook the body of a fish, sometimes two. In about an hour, the boat was half full and down to the gunwhales. It was time to return to the ship.

Smoking the catch was accomplished using a fire of hardwood shavings, mostly ash from old broken oars. The fish were strung on wires laid across an open large tub. The shavings were lit in the bottom of the tub, and several layers of gunny sacks were laid across the tub, reducing the fire to a dense smoke. The smoked fish were delicious and a welcome change to our one-sided diet.

Eventually, our shipboard supply of water ran out. Upon request, a tankcar filled with fresh water was positioned on the railroad jetty. We loaded our two lifeboats with wooden barrels that had formerly contained salt meat. Water was transferred by means of a hose. At the ship, the barrels were hoisted on board and the water casks on deck and the tank below deck were filled to capacity. It was a two-day job and hard work, but a welcome relief from monotony.

In general, the health of all hands had been good. It fell to my lot to come down with what seemed to be an intestinal infection that failed to respond to any medication available in the ship's medicine chest. A local doctor advised hospitalization.

The hospital was a one-room affair with six beds. Besides myself and a crew member from the NEREUS, there were two local men. The hospital staff consisted of an elderly individual serving as nurse and cook. He served a roll and a mug of tea for breakfast, a thin watery soup of indefinable ingredients for lunch and dinner.

There was nothing to read. The man from the NEREUS and I told each other the stories of our lives. It developed that he had attended a conservatory of music in Berlin, studying the piano. He did not want to talk about why he went to sea. He earned some money giving piano lessons to the children of two local families who possessed pianos. Occasionally, he played at the local hotel.

The days went by and turned into weeks. No one at the hospital followed the basics of medical practice, such as taking a pulse or temperature. The doctor walked through the room occasionally, stopping at each bed, saying, "Como esta, hombre, how are you?" That was his treatment. More often, a representative of the Anglican Church stopped by to inquire about our well-being.

Attempting to rise one morning, my knees buckled and I fell.

Throughout civilized lands, it was the fashion for physicians to make house calls to treat and heal the sick at home. Difficult cases were handled in hospitals. In certain circles, call it superstition or not, hospitalization was a last resort. Many regarded it to signal the end.

With this terrifying thought in mind, I slept little that night. By daybreak, I had resolved it was time to leave the place to avoid a slow death by starvation. In the morning, fortified by the usual roll and tea, I dressed and crept out on all fours until I reached the street.

Supporting myself along the houses fronting the sidewalk, I reached the jetty. The boat approached and, by sheer coincidence, the captain was aboard for one of his rare visits to the village. I stood at the top of the stairs as he walked by me and gave no sign of recognition. I called out to him. As he turned around, I could see by his expression that he did not believe his eyes as he saw this apparition, a bundle of garments draped over a skeletal frame. He instructed the boat crew to take me out to the ship and return to pick him up later.

With the help of one of the oarsmen, I managed to ascend the accommodation ladder. Reaching the top platform, I was met by the mate. He ordered some of the men on deck to help take me down to the fo'c'sle. Observing my ghostly figure as I passed the galley, the cook came out with a cup of coffee and some food left over from lunch.

There being no full-length mirror available anywhere, I could only guess at my appearance as I observed the mixture of astonishment and solicitude on the faces of my shipmates. Following several days of rest, I was assigned light duties.

Within days, the recently hired cook decided to leave. By now, the crew had been reduced to the able seamen, ordinary seamen and the cabin boy. His name was Karl and he was appointed to be the cook. I was detailed to his cabin job and to help him in the galley. It was easy enough, for the fare remained one-sided, meat, potatoes and onions, and the occasional fish. To my regret, because of this dual assignment, the job of fetching the grub was left to the ordinary seaman who had relieved me during my illness. It was a severe blow to my morale.

The ship had now been riding to her anchors for better than two years. At the waterline where air and water meet, the hull was encrusted with a dense marine growth of mussels, barnacles and a variety of hard shells. Someone jokingly remarked, "If there were a handhold, we could walk around the hull on the shelf of marine growth." The anchor chains were similarly encrusted with a collar of marine growth.

One day it was discovered that the starboard chain was hanging vertically at the end of the hawsepipe, a sure sign that the chain had parted. A first attempt to heave the chain in came to a halt when the massive marine growth came up to the hawsepipe. Being larger in circumference than the hawsepipe opening, it had to be cleared, a task that took many hours.

A cargo barge was obtained and positioned over and near the anchor. Using a grapnel, a device with four hooks radiating from a common shank, the loose chain was located on the bottom of the bay and brought up to the barge by means of a three-sheave rope purchase. When retrieved, the two ends were connected with a patent link the ship had in stock. It was grueling work.

No sooner had this been accomplished when orders were received from the local port authority to move the ship further out. We never learned the reason for this.

There being no towboat available, the answer was sailpower. The forestaysail was hauled out of the sail locker and bent to the forestay. For the first time in two years, it was again "All hands on deck" to carry out the move, using the early land breeze.

The capstan was manned and the anchors hove up to the forefoot. The skipper at the wheel and the gentle land-breeze filling the staysail, the ship moved out slowly. As soon as steerageway had been obtained, the sail was dropped. The ship was allowed to drift to her newly assigned anchorage, now about a mile and a half from the beach, practically in open waters.

As a precaution, a kedge anchor had been lowered over the stern on short scope to serve as a drag. The port anchor was dropped. In response to the rudder, the bow was canted to starboard and the starboard anchor was dropped. The spread between the two anchors would prevent the chains from crossing, should there be a change in wind direction.

The bow anchors were kept on short scope until the regular sea breeze came up in late forenoon when both chains were eased out simultaneously to the desired scope, both chains leading well forward. Meanwhile, the kedge anchor had been retrieved and suspended from the bow of the barge. The mooring chain was coiled in the barge, the end belayed to mooring bitts on the poop deck.

The final act in the day's work was to move the barge well astern and drop the kedge anchor to steady the ship in the strong northwesterly winds. An exhausted crew slept well that night.

Without song and dance, we once again had slid into a new year. It was 1916. The shocking truth dawned upon me that I had been on board for nearly three years and was still an ordinary seaman. Combined with my previous employment in the bark OBOTRITA, I now had seen service in square-rigged ships close to five years, well in excess of the obligatory four years. Even so, there were still two years' service as able-bodied seaman ahead. Why not ask the skipper to grant us a promotion.

I discussed it with the other two ordinary seamen. They thought it a good idea. Because of the various assignments I had undertaken in the past, I had inadvertently become the go-between for the men before the mast and the men in the cabin. It was thought only natural that I should be the one to explore the possibility of advancement.

Procrastination having never been one of my vices, I saw the captain that very afternoon on the poopdeck and laid our request before him. He looked past me, took his pipe out of his mouth and shook his head. Without uttering a word, he turned around and walked away. I got the message.

News from the war zone no longer reported great successes by the armed forces of the Central Powers. Italy had abandoned neutrality and entered the war on the side of the Allies, tying down Austrian forces in the rugged terrain of the Alps. For more than two years now, the armies of both camps had been locked in mortal combat. The Battle of Verdun dominated the news from the Allied sector, the news always ending with the famous phrase attributed to General Petain, defender of Verdun, "They Shall Not Pass."

Greatly reduced issues of German-language newspapers reported see-saw battles on the western and eastern fronts. Spanish language papers carried screaming headlines of great sea battles in the North Sea.

None of this was designed to support our earlier opinion that the war would last only a few weeks. Our spirits sank to a new low at the appalling prospect of many more months, even years, of stagnation in this forsaken backwater.

We were acutely aware of the fact that many of our compatriots were dying by the hundreds of thousands, while we were spared the horrors of a slaughter that was destroying the youths of nations on both sides of the conflict. I recall my mother saying in later years, "In a way, I was glad you were not here. Knowing you as a go-getter, you would not have survived the war."

THE ESCAPE

The atmosphere in the fo'c'sle of the Blankenese had turned to hope-less resignation as the straw in our mattresses turned to dust. The tongue-and-groove wooden lining now harbored bedbugs that came out at night to feed on our bodies. No chemicals were available to control the pest. Some of the men took to sleeping on deck. Everyone began to grumble. Trivia became crisis.

I heard one man exclaim, "If we only had a football, we could go ashore on Sundays to kick the ball around and get some exercise."

I lost no time in bringing this to the attention of the mate. The follow-ing day the skipper went ashore and returned with a leathery object. Inflated with lung power and tied with laces, it was the nearest thing to a football we could get.

The following and succeeding Sundays we went ashore and kicked the ball around in an open field. Residents of the village came out to watch and local youths joined us to our mutual enjoyment.

Rather than take part in the game, I sometimes went to the village plaza. It was the focal point of social life. From a small bandstand, a three-piece brass band played a tune that was the rage of the day, *Soy Una Chispa del Fuego* ("I am a Spark of Fire").

After Mass, following a time-honored custom, rows of village maidens in their Sunday finery paraded around the bandstand in one direction, their eyes demurely downcast, although shyly venturing an occasional sideways glance. Local swains, going in the opposite direction, boldly ogled the maidens and commented to one another about the various degrees of pulchritude they observed.

On one such occasion, I met one of the men from the NEREUS. He had found some employment ashore and lived in a boardinghouse. He invited me to dinner, which was served at noon. For the first time in years, I enjoyed a "home-cooked meal" of meat, beans, and rice. Seated at a round table, I listened to and conversed with other guests about local matters, studiously avoiding anything about the war. I thanked my host and the landlady and left in time to join my shipmates returning to the ship.

In spite of these occasional diversions, the shipboard environment was depressing. The corrosive demoralization resulting from enforced idleness frequently caused raw tempers to flare, ending in violent quarrels, destroying what little harmony was left. There was no sanctuary to which one could retreat.

The dreary days grew into weeks and months. Secretly, I nourished the hope that I might again be detailed to fetch the provisions, but, with the passage of time, I gave up hope in despair. I found the situation more and more intolerable and the conviction grew in me that to save my reason a change, any change, would be better than the miserable existence which had become my lot.

Then, one Sunday, I was walking through the village, when my friend caught up with me.

"I am glad to see you again," he said. "The folks at the boarding house enjoyed your company and hoped you would come again. The landlady called you 'Un hombre muy simpatico.'"

I was pleased to hear this. It strengthened my belief that only a change of scenery and different lifestyle would help me to retain my sanity. I began to plan my escape, waiting only for an opportunity.

It came near the end of the year, when I learned that the captain would soon travel on business to Caldera, a port city to the south. It was now or never.

Along with others, I had drawn some money. I increased my funds by selling a white turtleneck sweater to the butcher's wife, who wanted it for her young son. I had built a model ship, and I sold that to a member of the American community.

I made every effort to keep my plan a secret. Surreptitiously, I thought,

I examined from time to time the meager contents of my sea chest. However, I was observed by a shipmate, an ordinary seaman whose bunk was next to mine. He said, "I know what you are up to. I understand and wish you luck. I have nothing to give you but this pack of cigarettes. Take it and enjoy it on your way." I thanked him. I was profoundly moved.

What I had not foreseen was that young Karl, the acting cook, also sensed what I had in mind. "I am going with you," he yelled. "You are not going to leave me here!"

I tried to talk him out of it, to no avail. He cried, ranted and raved, begged and implored me to take him along. I closed the galley doors, lest the clamor of his protest be heard by the mate. The more I remonstrated, the more adamant he became, "I am not going to stay here, I am going with you," he declared.

I had wanted to go alone, to disassociate myself completely from the dreary past. Now, this. I could not stop him from going ashore to play ball. He was crazy enough to follow me when I left the group. I had no choice but to resign myself to this unexpected situation.

This was not the first time nor would it be the last that others would latch on to me for guidance and comfort because they lacked the inner resources to cope with the problems of life.

I agreed to take Karl under certain conditions. I would endeavor to teach him what Spanish I knew, to enable him to shift for himself, foreseeing the time when circumstances would demand that we come to a parting of the ways.

The weekend the captain was going away soon came. Knowing he was traveling south, our plan was to go north. We filled some empty beer bottles with water. For food, we had some biscuits and cans of sardines and clams we had bought. We stowed it all in gunny sacks fashioned into rucksacks, and we managed to get them into the boat unobserved.

That Sunday, immediately upon landing, we left the group. We made our way north, keeping close to the backs of the buildings, skirting the beach. In late afternoon, we came across the ruins of what seemed to be an abandoned copper smelter. Now that we were out of sight, we took a rest. I made one last attempt to dissuade Karl from tagging along.

"You still have a chance to turn back if you want to. Stay in the village overnight and return to the ship on the afternoon boat." I detected a moment's hesitation, but he decided to stay with me. There were no sandy beaches to the north, only a rugged, rocky coast as far as the eye could see. We turned inland and followed what seemed to be a trail until it got too dark to see. We slept on the bare ground under an open sky, brilliant with myriad stars. The mystery of the unknown beckoned to an unaccustomed freedom.

It was a cold night and daybreak didn't come soon enough. The trail soon disappeared, and we wandered through open country without distinguishing features or signs of life. In late afternoon, we saw a small wooden building. We approached cautiously, fearing it might be an outpost of the carabinieros, the rural mounted police, a rough lot with an unsavory reputation.

As we neared, a middle-aged woman appeared in the doorway. We doffed our caps by way of greeting as we came nearer. We sighted a row of telephone poles and concluded this was a way station for communications.

The woman did not seem apprehensive as we approached. From a safe distance, I asked for directions to the nearest settlement. She pointed north and mentioned Taltal. We had no intention of going there, but I did not say so. We knew that a company ship, the GLÜCKSTADT was there, and we had deemed it wise to avoid the place.

Having broken the ice, I asked if she could give us something to eat, which we offered to pay for. She hesitated briefly, then invited us in. As she prepared some food, we explained to her that we were German seamen in search of employment. She was fully at ease and told us her husband was a maintenance man patrolling the telephone line.

She served us each a bowl of soup into which she had broken an egg. We ate slowly, enjoying the comfort of chairs and table. In time, we rose to go. I handed her some money which she did not accept. I offered her some cans of clams, which she took.

To fill our water bottles, she directed us to an abandoned mine shaft. We filled our bottles, using a bucket on a rope. We waved a last "goodbye" and continued our journey until nightfall. We lay down on pebbly ground, knowing we would not sleep. We had reached a higher elevation with a dense cloud cover.

Arising at daybreak, we saw several small plants hugging the ground. The leaves were fleshy and covered with fine white hair. At the end of each hair hung a tiny drop of water, deposited during the night by the wet fog. This was the plants' principal means of survival in the rainless landscape.

Shivering in the cold morning air, we washed down a few biscuits with swallows of water from our bottles. A rising sun caused the drops of water on the plants to scintillate. We shook the small plants gently, gathering the drops in our hands to wet our faces. We considered that, in an emergency, if we ran out of bottled water, we might be able to gather enough to drink. Fortunately, the need for this extreme measure did not arise.

We marched along in the cool of the morning. I did not know how my companion felt about it, but I had never enjoyed a greater feeling of exhilaration as I experienced hiking through that barren but colorful landscape. Neither heat of day, thirst, hunger, the cold nights, nor the discomfort of sleeping on the bare ground without blankets, shivering under our jackets, could dampen my spirits and the pleasure of at last being free of any restraints.

A rising sun accentuated the vivid hues of the mountainside. As the sun rose, the heat increased. In the flat landscape below us, the rolling hills above, and the sun directly overhead, no shady place could be seen anywhere. In the far distance, in the shimmering heat, mirages of water and greenery danced before our eyes. We knew them to be mirages, but our hope persisted that eventually they would turn out to be the real thing.

We stumbled on until darkness and fatigue called a halt. During the night, I heard a train whistle, or was I just dreaming? No matter. We were on our way at daybreak. Our food was gone; the water bottles yielded their last few drops. Far away, the train whistle sounded. In late afternoon, we came upon two shiny ribbons of steel. We were sure it was the feeder line from Taltal to the mainline in the interior. As we learned later, the main railway ran from the northern border due south through the center of this skinny piece of land called Chile. It was called "The Longitudinal" with feeder lines to every coastal community along the way.

Just beyond the track, we observed a bluff. A depression below it seemed to contain water. It was covered with algae. We had some tea left and, with our empty sardine cans, we dipped up some of this water, thinking there would be no harm drinking it if we first boiled it. Along the track, we found small pieces of wood from lumber cargoes that had fallen off the trains. We built a fire and boiled the water in the sardine cans, adding a generous amount of the tea, and drank it. It was awful but it was moist.

We decided to make camp at this spot for the night. We heard train whistles that seemed far away. As we sat around discussing what to do, the bark of a dog wafted our way on a light breeze. The dog was certainly much closer than the train whistle. Where there are dogs, I concluded, there must be people. We decided to follow the railroad track. Rounding the spur of the bluff, we came upon a small wooden building. It turned out to be a train station.

The station master informed us there would be a train to the interior at 4 a.m. In my best Spanish, I negotiated for the train passage, some food and a place to sleep. We paid the train fare, thirty-five pesos. We received no tickets, neither did we learn the name of our destination. We didn't care.

The station master gave us some tea, a piece of dry bread and some cheese. He made up a bunk for us in a corner of his office. He went about this in a matter-of-fact manner that led us to believe that we were not his first customers and might well not be the last.

Being exhausted, we lost no time bedding down and slept soundly until the whistle of the approaching train awakened us. It was a freight train. We took our leave of the station master as he directed us to board an open gondola, several cars behind what passed for a caboose. Not at the end of the train, but behind the engine.

It was a windy day and we cowered under the sides of the open car to escape the swirling drafts of the wind stirring up the coal dust of the last cargo carried.

At a waystop, one of the train crew came back with a pot of hot tea and told us that the next stop would be our destination. He called it *Aqua Fresca* ("Sweetwater"). We expected to see an oasis with water and trees but found only a dusty shack in the dusty landscape.

It was now noon. The train crew pointed to a smokestack in the distance, partially hidden behind low-lying hills. They told us it would be a place for us to find work.

Perhaps the name "Agua Fresca" alluded to a large open tank about the size of a gondola. It was filled with water. Our reflection in the clear water revealed two faces, black with coal dust from the open gondola. We drank thirstily, then removed our clothes. We scooped out some water and luxuriated in a complete washdown.

We took a bearing on the distant smokestack and started walking in that direction. There was no trail on the open land and we hiked along, keeping the smokestack in view. We had expected to reach our goal in about an hour. It was sunset when we finally reached the settlement. Not reckoning with the undulating landscape, it had taken four hours to walk the distance.

The establishment consisted of an open pit mine flanked by a stamp mill and associated machinery designed to separate the saltpeter from the rock called "Caliche." There were rows of one-story wooden buildings, used for housing the employees. It was a large spread.

We wandered around for awhile, not knowing what to do. It was dark and sleeping one more night on the bare ground was an appalling thought. We had some dry tea left and thought to beg some hot water. The tea would sustain us and we would find a place to sleep in the outskirts, then return in the morning to look for work.

We approached a house with light streaming out through a half-open door outlining the silhouette of a young woman. I asked her if we could have some hot water. From a gruff voice inside, "Who's there?" The girl said, "Two strangers are asking for hot water." From the gruff voice inside, "Tell them to come in."

In a chair behind a round table sat the massive figure of a man. His strong face topped by a thatch of gray hair would have tempted any portrait painter. He did not ask why we were there. He knew.

There was instant rapport between him and me. It was mealtime, and he invited us to stay. Once again, we enjoyed a meal of beef, beans, and rice. During the meal, we learned that his name was Pinos, chief boiler-maker. As a highly respected member of the community, we heard him addressed as Maestro Pinos by his co-workers.

Following the meal, he took us up to the manager's office to see if there was any work for us. We learned that we had landed in one of two establishments called Oficina Chile and Oficina Alemania, respectively, with a German firm as concessionaire. Standing at his desk, the manager looked at us sideways, "You fellows were crazy to come up here. There is no work for you up here," he said. "What skills do you have, if any?"

"Only those we learned on board ship," I replied.

"Can you splice wire rope?"

"Yes sir, I can."

"Well, come back in the morning, there are some damaged wire ropes to be spliced," he said.

This exchange took place in German, perhaps not understood by Maestro Pinos. The latter was told to take us to the fonda. It was a large hall

used for gambling, but also had some sleeping rooms. Nightly, the pamperos and their women came to try their luck at cards or dice. It was a
noisy scene. When the old boilermaker left us, he said, "If you hear any
commotion in the night, even shooting, pay no attention, stay in your
room." With this comforting thought, we rolled into the mattresses on the
floor and slept soundly.

In the morning, following breakfast of sorts at the fonda, we reported
to Maestro Pinos' house. The old man said, "You heard the manager say
there would be three or four days' work. You can eat the evening meal
here with us. When you get paid, you can pay me." We were delighted
with this arrangement, knowing that the food at the fonda would be less
palatable.

Our place of work turned out to be behind the stamp mill. Following
the extraction of saltpeter from the caliche, the residual material, mud,
was hauled out in small dump carts, traveling on a narrow gauge track
and dumped in the pampa. This practice had been followed for many
years and had created a pile visible in the flat pampa for many miles. It
was locally referred to as *La Montaña* ("The Mountain").

On top of the mountain was a shack housing the winch used in hauling
the dump carts up by means of a wire cable. The winch operator pointed
to a pile of wire cable, coiled up in a corner of the shack, broken ends
sticking out. The wire had been laid aside in the expectation that some
hapless sailor would lose his way up there and be put to work to repair the
cables by means of long splices.

Theoretically, I knew how to make a long splice. Actually, I had not
done it. As an ordinary seaman, it was not required of me, but I had
helped older seamen do it. I had learned to make a long splice in a
three-stranded manila rope and intended to apply this method to the six-
stranded wire. The winch operator watched us struggle with the task and
helped us occasionally. Within three days we had finished the job and
reported to the manager.

"That's all the work we have here for you, but as laborers you can join
a gang further up in the pampa to repair our water system."

At the paymaster's office, we were paid off in company money, brass
coins, called "fija," some very large, to be exchanged for Chilean pesos at
the termination of our employment.

We paid a last call on Maestro Pinos and his family. We spent the
evening discussing world affairs. The maestro read from a local paper

called *El Obrero* ("The Workman"). His eyesight was poor; he read through a thick piece of glass that looked to me like the bottom of a Coke bottle. He was a socialist with many good ideas and I enjoyed our conversation. Silently I vowed, should I have the opportunity in the foreseeable future, to make him a present of a magnifying glass. Alas, that opportunity never came.

It was nearly midnight when we took our leave. As we shook hands, I sensed he had something on his mind. Hesitatingly, he said, "Do you have a picture of yourself?" I gave him one of two photos I had left, taken when I was seventeen at the end of my first voyage in 1913. I never saw him again. Throughout the years, I thought of him often. He was a true gentleman.

Following a last night's sleep at the fonda, we boarded a small tracked vehicle drawn by mules which carried us to our destination and a new world.

GOOD-BYE CHILE

The various mining establishments in the vast Atacama Basin, with its harsh desert climate, received water, that indispensable commodity, from the mountain range in the east, known as the Cordillera de los Andes. Along the crest of the Cordillera ran a zig-zag border between Chile and Argentina, at elevations from 14,000 to 22,000 feet, with volcanoes perpetually covered in snow.

A double pipeline laid on top of the desert floor for hundreds of miles, covered with sand to a height of about four feet. It was a striking trait in the otherwise featureless landscape. Not only a conveyance for water, it also served as a trail to travelers.

It was late in the afternoon when we arrived at our destination, a small mining establishment operated by the concessionaire of the Officinas Alemania y Chile. Along with a group of local laborers, we were housed in circular tents supported by a center pole. As a preliminary to the seasonal task of repairs to the pipelines, a row of 2.5-inch used pipe twenty feet long, were laid out for many miles to be cleaned and connected.

Along with one of the natives, Karl and I drew the job. Cleaning was accomplished by walking along a length of pipe, striking it with sharp blows of a five-pound sledge hammer to loosen up the rust and other waterborne sediment. Upending each pipe to allow the debris to run out, they were then connected, a formidable if not to say delicate task.

At the connecting end was the third member of our team, at the other end were Karl and I, holding the pipe resting in an iron bar, curved in the center to accommodate the size of the pipe. Our teammate having lubricated the threads in the sleeve and at the end of the pipe employed a chain wrench and motioned with his free hand, right, left, up or down until the threads were matched and the connection made.

It was a difficult job that left us exhausted at the end of a ten-hour day. The final act in the day's work was to cover the new pipeline with a two-sided pyramid of sand about four feet high.

At the end of each day, we made camp. Our tents, bedding, food, tools and firewood followed us in a canvas-covered cart with two enormous wheels, drawn by six mules. The driver, a wizened old desert rat, rode one of his mules. His name was Francisco, but everyone addressed him respectfully as Don Pancho.

The first day out, we were served an evening meal of sirloin steaks about an inch thick. The driver built a fire and cooked them on the blade of a shovel and we ate them off the bright and shiny blades of our shovels, which had been scoured clean in the process of covering the pipeline with desert sand. It was the only fresh meat we saw during the whole trip. To water the mules and provide us with drinking and wash water, Don Pancho's helper and assistant cook exposed the active pipeline and, with hammer and punch, made a tiny hole. Arching under tremendous pressure, the water was caught in a bucket held by one of the men about ten feet away. The hole in the pipe was then closed with a wooden plug. It was a procedure used every day while we were in the desert.

We estimated the daytime temperatures to range from 70 to 80 degrees Fahrenheit, but the nights were bitter cold, as we were soon to find out.

Each tent, supported by a center pole, held from four to six men. Sleep came swiftly. It was interrupted regularly in the small hours of the morning as the tent collapsed under the force of a strong wind blowing from the glaciers in the east. While others snuggled deeper in their blankets and offered no help, Karl and I would attempt to erect the tent again. Under a cloudless, starry sky, chilled to the bone by the icy wind, we managed to raise the tent only to have it collapse again within a short time. The desert soil was poor holding ground for the tent pegs.

It was near daybreak when I crawled back under my blankets. Chilled to the bone, I could not sleep. Staring into the darkness with wide open eyes my thoughts turned to the bewildering events of the recent past. I began to wonder how it came to be that I was in this strange land, among strange people, working at tasks I had never before thought of. At first, the pay of five pesos a day sounded good. In time, I found it was below subsistence level. Some of the Andean Indian workforce were openly hostile. I could tell from their conversation that they resented our presence, taking away jobs from the natives. I had met the project engineer, a Peruvian. In our casual conversation, he dropped the remark, "You are a different class of people." I got the hint that he didn't really want us on his crew but, being subordinate to the concessionaire, he had to keep us.

Although we had upheld our share of the workload, the men kept muttering, casting hostile glances in our direction. One young fellow, a Bolivian whom I had believed friendly, sometimes confronted me to feel my biceps. He would turn away mumbling, *"Muy Gordo, muy gordo."* ("Very husky, very husky.") Perhaps it was his way to warn others not to try any fisticuffs.

I lay thinking of my early youth and the carefully laid plans I had made for a life utterly different from that in which I now found myself.

At the end of the desert rose the mountain range, the source of the water supply. There were only three months in the year when the catch basins were clear of the snowpack at the ten-thousand-foot elevation.

Our mode of transportation had changed; pack mules now carried our bedding, tools and food supplies on narrow trails along the steep mountain sides.

Most of the work consisted of clearing the many shallow catch basins, built at the end of gullies, of debris and replacing rusted-out pipes. Starting in small dimensions and increasing in size, the end of the pipeline reached twelve to fourteen-inch pipes at the settlements, where the enormous pressure was controlled by massive valves. At first, the thin air at the high elevation slowed us down until we became accustomed to it and could uphold our end of the work.

The daily fare now consisted of rice and beans cooked in a large iron pot over a wood fire and flavored with onions and beef jerky. It tasted mighty good at the end of the day's work.

The landscape had changed. There were tufts of coarse grass and gnarled roots of old dead brush which served as firewood. To the east lay the magnificent background of the Andes.

I was intrigued by the abundance of fossils strewn all over the landscape. I believed them to be fossilized giant sea snails of a pre-historic age. They were the size of dinner plates, each weighing several pounds, a phenomenon of interest to anthropologists. Their presence led to the speculation that this lofty terrain, eons of time ago, once lay below the sea.

There appeared to be no wildlife except for a wild ruminant called vicuña! The foreman had a Winchester rifle, which he offered to me one Sunday morning and suggested I might want to do some hunting. I stalked the elusive creatures for the better part of the day without success. I found their droppings, still warm to the touch, but no vicuña, a quarry obviously masterful at concealing itself in a terrain offering few hiding places. And this had been our only free Sunday.

Weather forecasts indicated an early snowfall. The work went on apace during daylight hours. At the first snow flurry, we packed our gear and led the pack mules along the trails to the desert floor, where crusty old Don Pancho awaited us with his cart.

We spent several days covering the new pipeline with sand. Arriving at the mining establishment, we were paid off. At the same time, we were informed that all German nationals were required to report to the nearest consulate. In our case, it was the port of Taltal. The administrator handed us the railroad tickets.

"It is only a matter of registration," he said. "Perhaps you can find work down there; if not, you can come back; we will find something for you to do." I felt he really did not mean it.

We rode by gravity car to the nearest officina and boarded the train at the station nearby. This time, we rode in a passenger coach instead of an open gondola. In Taltal, we engaged a room at a modest fonda. It was our plan to remain out of sight for the time being, to await developments.

In late afternoon, we ventured out in the street, keeping away from the center of town. We were accosted by a man, obviously a sailor, three sheets in the wind and waving a half-empty bottle of Pisco as he steered an uncertain course in our direction.

"You fellows looking for a job?" Before we could answer, he pointed to a sailing craft anchored in the bay, discharging timber. "She needs men," he said. "I am not going back to her; go on out and see the skipper," was his parting shot.

It was still daylight and I hired a boatman to take us out to the ship. At her staff fluttered the Stars and Stripes. At her stern we read the name

GENEVA, of San Francisco, a brigantine.

Upon boarding, we were met by the skipper, a tall, lean Scot. He looked at us quizzically as I stammered in the few English words I knew, asking to be hired. Dressed in garments not usually associated with sailors, we looked like landlubbers to him, dusty and unkempt. Addressing me, he asked: "Are you a sailor?"

"I am," I replied.

He looked at me, and then at Karl. "I'll hire you, but not this kid. He is too small," he said. The 'kid' had a mustache, but he was small, less than five feet.

"You turn to in the morning," he said and went to his cabin. Ever since we had left the BLANKENESE, I had attempted to teach Karl certain Spanish words and phrases to prepare him for the day when he had to shift for himself. I soon knew it to be a lost cause. He had displayed a total lack of capability for learning.

Up to now, he had been a silent partner in my negotiations with the people we had met. I had my doubts that any of this had been of benefit to him. Apparently he had had no formal education. He displayed a doleful lack of interest to even pick up a rudimentary knowledge of Spanish.

I found this combination of ignorance and indifference hard to beat. I now reminded him that, when he insisted on joining me, I had told him I would strike out for myself at the first opportunity.

"Well, Karl, we have come to the parting of the ways. I am sorry the skipper won't hire you," I said. I gave him all the money I had, about forty pesos and wished him luck as he clambered back into the boat. I never saw him again.

I went to the fo'c'sle, a small, square compartment, lined with eight bunks, each containing a mattress, pillow and blankets.

The after-bulkhead bordered on the galley. Individual portions of food were served directly from the galley through a sliding window by the cook, a bearded, paunchy, middle-aged Hollander. His food was better than his disposition. For the first time, I enjoyed an evening meal, the likes of which I had not seen in years.

I was joined by the only crewman on board. He told me he was from Kentucky. He was not a seaman but had joined the ship to see some other parts of the world. An affable fellow, we became good friends. It was a Sunday and most of the crew was ashore.

Monday morning, I turned to. There was no mate. I was directed by the skipper to join a crewman whom he called the second mate. With all cargo discharged, the wooden hull rode high out of the water. Our task was to scrape off the barnacles and other marine growth visible on and below the waterline. We worked from a small boat, hauling it along a line extending half the length of the ship.

The second mate was a taciturn Scandinavian, obviously an old hand of the saltpeter coast. Neither of us spoke much English, but conducted our limited conversation in Spanish. We soon came to the end of the line amidships. While the second mate let go his end, I took the other aft to the poop and belayed it on a mooring bitt with a roundturn and two halfhitches. As I turned around, I nearly bumped into the skipper who, unbeknownst to me, had observed what I was doing. As he turned away, he said, "I see you are a sailor, all right."

As the ship began loading saltpeter, some of the men drifted back. An elderly seaman joined the ship as first mate. Like myself, he was a native of Hannover, and had shipped in the German fourmast barkentine MOZART, now anchored in the bay. He had served many years in British sailing ships and knew the language of the sea. He answered all orders from the skipper with "Aye, Aye, sir." Another young German was hired as cabin boy.

One evening, the mate took me aside and said, "There is a young fellow, Henry, on board the MOZART. We must get him off before he goes crazy. Why don't you, some night, take the boat and get him over here?"

I agreed to do it, knowing from my own experience how Henry must feel.

We were well along in February 1917. From the beginning, I had had good rapport with the Captain. As the loading progressed, he said to me one day, "You know, there seems to be a possibility that the United States might enter the war on the side of the Allies. Perhaps you might want to get off before we sail?"

I did not know whether the other German crew members had been so advised. I weighed the question and came to the conclusion that I could not face a return to the inhospitable saltpeter coast. I hoped at the same time that, perhaps, the war would end before the United States became involved. I told the skipper that I would like to stay. He agreed, and I signed the articles at twenty-five dollars a month, as did all my other compatriots. We were bound for Honolulu.

On a shelf in the foc's'l'e, I found a stack of publications called *The Blue Book,* known as a pulp magazine, because of the rough paper used in printing. Story material was of the American West. Although my English was still limited, I avidly read with comprehension and fascination about cowboys and Indians, cattle drives, buffalo hunters, outlaws, gunslingers, sheriffs, train robbers and the cult of the six-gun. In a few weeks' time, I knew all about America!

It was customary to address the first mate as Mr. Mate; privately, we referred to him as Old John. As time went by, he reminded me occasionally about young Henry on the MOZART. In retrospect, I realized that Henry, an orphan, saw in Old John a father figure, someone to stick with, as Karl had attached himself to me as elder brother.

In a late afternoon, the last slingload of saltpeter was stowed and the hatch closed. Sailing time was set for the following morning. The night was bright with a full moon. At one o'clock in the morning, with the moon below the horizon, I took the boat and rowed toward the MOZART. Under her bow I gave a low whistle. At the break of the fo'c'sle a seabag was lowered, followed by Henry. The GENEVA, now low in the water, made it easy for Henry to clamber aboard. I did not take

Brigantine *Geneva,* 496 gross tons, built in 1892 at Benicia California by Capt. Matthew Turner

him in to the fo'c'sle, fearing someone might make a fuss. I led him forward to the rope locker and told him to stay there until the ship was underway.

At daybreak, with a pilot aboard, GENEVA stood out to sea. I was at the wheel. The pilot seemed curious and asked questions. "Where are you from? How long have you been here? What ship did you leave?" I provided no answers. With the pilot gone and all sails set, I was relieved at the wheel.

As I passed the skipper, he said, "How about the fellow you brought aboard last night? Bring him to the cabin." I was crestfallen but said nothing. I was disturbed at the turn of events and mentioned it to the mate. "Not to worry," he said. "It is customary to help a fellow seaman in distress." As a stowaway, Henry was signed on at twenty-five cents a month.

HELLO HAWAII

Under shortened sail and closehauled in the stiff northeast trade winds, the American brigantine GENEVA stood in towards the Honolulu anchorage to await the pilot and port officials.

The ship had left Taltal, Chile in February 1917 with a cargo of nitrate. Shorthanded, the master had beefed up his crew of Americans, Scandinavians and a Dutch cook with several German seamen, stranded on that inhospitable coast in the early days of World War I.

Along with others, I had welcomed the opportunity to ship out. The passage had been arduous. The combination of seawater entering through the leaky seams and the moisture generated by the cargo had kept us at the bilge pumps for many weary hours. At last the voyage had ended. Furling the last sail aloft I was entranced by the picture of sunlit canefields against rainshrouded mountains and the silhouette of somber Diamond Head. With deep gulps, I drank in the perfume-laden breeze of the subtropical vegetation. What a contrast to the arid and dreary wastes of the saltpeter coast where many of us had eked out a precarious living, human flotsam and jetsam of a remote world in conflagration.

Without wireless, we had been cut off from the world during the voyage. Nobody had talked much about the war in Europe, except to speculate whether the United States would become involved. The boarding party dispelled all doubts with the news of America's entry on the side of the Allies shortly prior to our arrival. Honolulu was still in an uproar. A German gunboat and crew had been interned, as had the crews of several German merchant ships brought in from German Samoa. It was April 1917, the month and the year I reached the age of 21.

Immediately upon mooring, the GENEVA was surrounded by Territorial Guards. Lined up on deck, we were informed that all German Nationals would be removed. The cook provided an amusing by-play as he scuttled about like a fat little cockroach, pointing at various men and telling the officials, "There is another one, and there," after which he returned to his pots and pans, having done his bit to win the war.

The evening found us lodged in the Immigration Station. It was to be our home for many months. The days of tedium were relieved only by the flow of faces which came and went while we remained. Chafing under the enforced idleness, we wondered with increasing anxiety about our future. One day I posed the question to an official, "Sir, can you tell us anything?"

"Well, according to Washington you will not be interned with the others. The fact that you came off an American ship seems to make a difference." There was a trace of exasperation in his voice as he continued, "But they haven't told us yet what to do with you and we don't know when they will."

It was my first experience with the innate fairness of the American character, of which I had heard much. Someone, within the vast bureaucracy of a great nation at war, bothered to ponder the fate of a handful of individuals of no significance in this time of turmoil.

For days we had observed the struggle of a few employees to maintain the grounds around the buildings. Here seemed a fruitful field of endeavor, of benefit to us in terms of improved health through physical activity and relief from boredom.

As a committee of one, I presented the plan to the superintendent for approval. It was granted a few days later, subject to a signed pledge not to leave the grounds nor demand pay for our voluntary work. We signed pronto! As a useful service to our unwilling hosts, we were allowed to act as volunteer gardeners.

The next day found us, with rakes, hoes and spades, venting our long pent-up energies in a wild burst of activity. The cool and fragrant freshness of the morning hours instead of the stale dormitory air was like wine to our spirits. The guard observed our frenzied capers with astonishment.

"Hey, fellows, slow down for the love of Pete, you'll all be dead in a week."

We weren't. The nights were spent in the blessed sleep of exhaustion. This turn of events was duly recorded in the local papers, although not with complete approval. Nevertheless, it was later conceded that the grounds had never looked more attractive.

Perhaps our fame as workers had spread. With the superintendent, there came one day a man who was introduced to us as a plantation owner from the Island of Maui. "Men, you will be paroled to this gentleman who is willing to employ you."

This was good news. The planter spoke: "Well, boys, if you want to work, I will provide transportation, housing and the basic necessities. The pay will be the going rate for field labor."

We were impressed with his direct talk and steady, but not unkindly gaze. Of the round dozen German nationals housed in the immigration station, six accepted the offer. From the GENEVA, only Henry and I were in that group. Old John remained behind, not being employable because of his age. From other ships, there were Paul, William, Herrman, Max and Bruno.

A few days later the little inter-island steamer CLAUDINE deposited us at Kipahulu landing on the island of Maui. The Honolulu press promptly dubbed Kipahulu "the dumping ground for undesirable aliens."

We moved into small, whitewashed, one-room shacks which we shared with tiny pale lizards that scuttled along the walls in search of insects. Mattresses on the floor and tin buckets to wash in were the promised necessities.

The pay turned out to be ninety-six cents per day, plus a daily bonus of around thirty cents, payable at harvest time. Our spirits were dampened by the bleak prospect that these wages were to feed us and buy the necessities of life as well. But, what the hell, we were young, healthy and eager for the things the days ahead would bring.

Daybreak brought the piercing wail of the mill whistle summoning us to our labors. Under the charge of a Portuguese overseer, locally called a luna, we climbed along slippery trails to high-lying fields to cut cane. We arrived there in a state of near-exhaustion before our task had even begun. The unaccustomed work was the more arduous as the day's heat alternated with chilling rain squalls.

Adding to our discomfort in the days ahead were the harangues of the head luna who, ironically, always appeared when we took the brief spells without which we could not have endured. Astride his horse, he would bitterly upbraid us. "What's the matter with you fellows; do you call this working?"

Wheeling his horse without waiting for an answer, he would clatter downhill, muttering curses. At such times, we stood mute, trembling with fatigue, hands bleeding from cuts inflicted by sharp-edged cane leaves, clothes streaked with sweat, often chilled to the bone by drenching rainfall. Despairingly, we wondered how much longer we could carry on. And, poor Joe, our luna! As an aftermath to such encounters, he would vent his feeling in extraordinarily colorful language, not directed at us, but at the bewildering situation in which he, involuntarily, had become involved.

We soon realized that we could never match the daily output of the wiry Filipino laborers, more accustomed to work in this climate and able to subsist on the meager diet of rice and fish that had been the fare of their race for centuries.

Running the plantation was a family affair. The owner-manager had five sons. The eldest acted as head luna and all day was in the field astride a magnificent buckskin horse. The mill was operated by another son, an engineer, usually referred to as the sugar boiler. The third was the bookkeeper who was also in charge of the company store. The younger boys, still in college and high school respectively, were visible only during school vacations.

We laid our case before the owner. He seemed not unprepared for this and quietly said, "Very well, next week you can start at something else." As he mounted his horse for the daily inspection of his domain, we had the feeling that he rued the day he had taken us on, a feeling we had all come to share.

We were assigned as helpers in the carpenter shop and machine shops, the blacksmith shop and the store. We also took over the loading of the weekly steamer, thus freeing the Filipino laborers to work in the fields.

The war effort demanded increased production. More land was cleared of brush and put to the plow. I drew the job as helper to the operator of a caterpillar tractor, which was used to uproot the brush, and I became the operator when my predecessor quit.

Cane was brought to the mill by wagons or teams of pack mules. Henry, assigned to the blacksmith shop, in time became a skilled farrier.

His daily job was to shoe the many pack mules as well as the draft animals.

Our other companions were detailed to work with a surveyor hired to build a transportation system designed to bring in the cane from the newly planted acreage. A long suspension flume was constructed crossing several streams. Tapping waterfalls, the flow of water floated the cane to a low-lying plateau and dumped it into high-sided carts sitting on a narrow gauge track. No longer needed, the tractor was replaced by a draft animal. I was now in charge of a Missouri Mule, a magnificent, powerful animal.

The procedure was to hitch the mule to a cart, using a single chain with a hook at the end. The hook was attached to a structural part of the cart in a fashion ensuring quick and certain release. The heavily laden carts were drawn along a stretch of level terrain to a point where they were allowed to continue by gravity to the mill yard. This required, without fail, the timely disengagement of the hook to free the mule, lest he be dragged along and injured or killed.

I was appalled at the task and vowed never to let this happen to this beautiful animal. For days, I carried on without mishap. I then devised a method designed never to place the animal in jeopardy: I stopped him short of the beginning of the incline and disengaged the hook. Putting my shoulder to the cart, I was able to nudge it to the point where gravity took over. Within weeks after this routine had been established, I was relieved by another man. I showed him what to do. I impressed upon him the need to safeguard the animal, of whom I had become very fond.

Improvements in the sugar mill became mandatory to meet the demand for raw sugar, but also because of the system that each year another mill was required to provide refined sugar to fulfill the needs of all the islands. New machinery arrived by steamer and who was better qualified than this gang of Jack Tars, skilled in the use of rope and tackle, to haul, lift, and set the new machinery on its foundations.

Not everything went off trouble-free. A boiler, tubes plugged and manhole cover tightly bolted down, was floated from the inter-island steamer CLAUDINE to the rocky promontory, serving as a landing. The steam winch and derrick, rated at ten tons, had never lifted such a weight. At the moment the boiler ceased to be waterborne, the winch stalled, the old wooden boom crumpled and the boiler, manhole cover knocked off against the rockwall, filled up and sank in about eight feet of water.

At her next weekly call, the CLAUDINE delivered a heavier wooden derrick by floating it ashore. We parbuckled derrick and boom to the landing platform and, using the stump of the old derrick and the steam winch, we erected the new derrick.

Meanwhile, Herman, a high school athlete and leading member of his school's swimming and diving team, had made several unsuccessful attempts to recover the wire slings we had used, but he found them to be jammed under the boiler resting on the rocky bottom. During his last attempt, a large shark made an appearance, cruising about in an inquisitive manner. Efforts were wisely discontinued.

As I stood waist deep on the boiler to help Herrman out of the water, the open manhole suggested an alternative method. I proposed to the engineer that if a discarded machinery shaft would be found it could be lowered through the manhole and temporarily held in place, to serve as a sort of toggle. The same day, a heavy steel shaft was provided, lowered and held in place inside across the manhole while we passed turns of wire cable around the shaft and through a shackle at the triple traveling purchase block. An auxiliary purchase hitched to the caterpillar tractor provided additional lifting power.

Under the combined pull of winch and tractor, the boiler slowly rose to the surface. Although the new derrick had a 30-ton rating, it was found advisable to proceed with caution. Thus, while still partially waterborne, the plugs were removed from the boiler tubes above the water until most of it was out and the load could be safely guyed in and landed on two flatbed cars on the narrow-gauge railroad track. It led uphill from the landing to the gravel road serving the mill about a mile and a half away. The rails were portable. The tractor hauled the load to the end of the rails, where several lengths were removed from the rear and connected to the front and the movement repeated. It was a cumbersome method, but there was no other choice. It took most of the day of grueling work until the boiler was at the mill.

The year 1917 lay behind us. We had made the necessary adjustments to a new and different lifestyle. By and large, we got along quite well with everyone. We quickly learned to speak pidgin English, a mixture of English, Hawaiian and Oriental words employed as the means of communication between the polyglot of ethnic groups composing the plantation workforce throughout the islands.

We had made friends with local Hawaiian families. Their lighthearted nature, devoid of inhibitions and ever-ready abandon to the pleasures of the moment, the music of their stringed instruments and festive luaus gave brightness to our days. But the free Sundays provided the real high-lights to our existence, for then we swam in a landlocked freshwater pond, fed by upstream waterfalls. It was a deep body of water, separated from the ocean by a narrow strip of rocky beach. A nearby grassy plot, shaded by young coconut palms, was an idyllic resting place. Upstream, groves of mango trees provided an abundance of delicious ripe fruit. Here we recuperated and gathered new strength.

Once again, without solicitation on my part, I found myself in the role of spokesman for the group in matters of mutual concern. Aside from the company store, the local postmaster, a Chinese man named George, oper-ated a modest business, stocking the same type of goods. At the end of the workday, the company store would be crowded to the door, with field laborers buying food for their families, solely on credit.

A single salesperson not only placed the merchandise on the counter, but also recorded in each laborer's book the items and the purchase price, all of which was deducted from their wages on payday. It was our prefer-ence not to participate in this system, but to cover our modest means on a cash basis. Often standing in line for half an hour or more to make a purchase taking less than five minutes, we found it more convenient to trade with George across the street, where there was no crowd.

It did not take long for the manager to ask why we did not patronize the company store. When I had explained the situation to him, he ordered, within hearing of everyone present, that we were always to be served within a reasonable time. The sales clerk interpreted "reasonable" as "immediate." We were not comfortable with this arrangement, but to avoid any contro-versy, made occasional purchases, which seemed to solve the problem.

The erection of a reinforced concrete smokestack was the final phase in mill improvements. Again we bent our backs to the task. We built scaffolding, poured concrete and hoisted forms each day until the prede-termined height of ninety-six feet had been reached. Amidst a cluster of low buildings stood the gray, gleaming column, in sharp contrast to the vivid green of the surrounding countryside. We regarded it with pride as a monument to our labor. The idea that we had, indirectly, supported a war effort directed against our native land may have occurred to us, but it was never discussed.

One day, the mill now having reached a peak load, the sugar boiler invited some of us to see the production. We observed the stream of sticky, dark molasses entering a bank of centrifuges, whose spinning motion converted the molasses into brown sugar, to be sacked and sewn by female labor for shipment. With particular pride, the sugar boiler demonstrated the production of refined sugar, accomplished by leaving raw sugar in the centrifuge until it turned into gleaming white crystals.

The accelerated phase of production brought along a higher degree of prosperity. One Sunday morning, the sugar boiler displayed his latest acquisition, a 1919 Dodge touring car. He took some of us for a ride on the narrow highway leading to the neighboring community of Hana. It was a thrill for us to see the lush growth of trees and flowering plants and waterfalls at every curve in the road, of which there were many.

This combination of occasional favors led us to believe that, in the end, management had come to appreciate our input. I exclude from this the head luna, who never had a friendly word for any of us. Unlike my fellow workers, I had cultivated the friendship of individuals in the community. I had persuaded a young Hawaiian lad, same age as us, to come some evenings to our cabins and play his guitar for us. His name was Henry, but we called him Maka. It was said to be a nickname because he only had sight in one eye. He also taught me the rudiments of guitar playing.

On Sundays, we would congregate at the storefront of the post office where we were joined by other young men and women for an hour of socializing.

Early on, I had been the last in line for payday. One day, the book-keeper came out of his office and handed me a camera. "You may as well have it," he said. "I don't know how to handle it."

"But, Joe, this is a valuable present," I protested.

"Naw, you keep it. Shucks, I never had much luck with it," he said deprecatingly. I thanked him. I had never used one before. One of its features was a circular level with a bubble to ensure that a picture would come out straight. It was a bellows camera of unknown make and had film in it. As I stood in the road, uncertainly fingering the instrument, a middle-aged Japanese stopped by.

"You take picture, I develop and print, yes?"

I was glad to accept his offer. In time, I managed to expose the film but only got four photos worth keeping, the best of it a group picture of four of us at our swimming hole.

Kipahulu, Maui *(O.H. Friz third from left, c. 1919).*

Not to be outdone by the sugar boiler, George, the postmaster, also purchased a 1919 Dodge touring car. For weeks, it sat in front of his store. I had never seen him drive it. One day he said, "There is something wrong with this car. You fix it."

"George," I protested, "you know I am not an auto mechanic. I am a sailor!"

"I know, but you drive the tractor, don't you?"

"I operate it, but the machine shop repairs it."

But he persisted. "You can fix it," he said, and handed me the maintenance manual. Idly, I turned the pages in this richly illustrated booklet. The first illustration was that of the clutch. It was described as a spider clutch, followed by instructions on how to disassemble and reassemble it.

Having no idea what to do with this, or any other component of this vehicle, I felt I had to make a show of it. Under the watchful eyes of a

Maui Revisited—After Half a Century

by Ottmar H. Friz

Ottmar H. Friz is a retired master mariner, now living in Piedmont, Calif. But in 1917, during World War I, he came to Hawaii as a young German national—and eventually was paroled locally; not as a prisoner of war but as an enemy alien. The following are his reminiscences of Maui 50 years ago—thoughts that became again vivid to him after a recent revisit to Maui.

UNDER SHORTENED sail and closehauled in the stiff northeast trade wind, the American brigantine Geneva stood in toward the Honolulu anchorage to await the pilot and port officials.

The ship had left Taltal, Chile, in February of 1917 with a cargo of nitrate. Shorthanded, the master had beefed up his crew of Americans, Scandinavians and a Dutch cook with several German seamen, stranded on that inhospitable coast in the early days of World War I.

Along with others, I had welcomed the opportunity to ship out. The passage had been arduous.

The combination of seawater entering through the leaky seams and the moisture generated by the cargo had kept us at the bilge pumps for many weary hours.

AT LAST THE voyage had ended. Furling the last sail aloft, I was entranced by the scene of sunlit canefields against rain-shrouded mountains and the silhouette of somber Diamond Head.

With deep gulps I drank in the perfume-laden breeze of the subtropical vegetation. What a contrast to the arid and dreary wastes of the saltpeter coast where many of us had eked out a precarious living, human flotsam and jetsam of a remote world in conflagration.

Without wireless, we had been cut off from the world during the voyage. Nobody had talked much about the war in Europe, except to speculate whether the United States would become involved.

The boarding party dispelled all doubts with the news of America's entry on the side of the allies shortly prior to our arrival.

Honolulu was still in an uproar. The German gunboat Geier had been seized, plus crews of several German merchant ships in from Samoa.

THE GENEVA was surrounded by Territorial guards. Lined up on deck, we were informed that all German nationals would be removed.

The cook provided an amusing sight, scuttling about pointing at us, assuring officials, "And there is another one"; whereupon he returned to his pots and pans, having done "his bit to win the war."

That evening found us lodged in the immigration station; to be our home for many months. Days of tedium were relieved only by the flow of faces, coming and going while we remained.

"Sir, can you tell us anything?" I asked an official one day.

"Well, according to Washington, you will not be interned with the others. The fact that you came off an American ship seems to make a difference."

With a trace of exasperation in his voice, the official added: "But they haven't told us yet what to do with you and we don't know when they will."

IT WAS my first experience with the innate fairness of the American character, of which I had heard much.

Someone, within the vast bureaucracy of a great nation at war, had bothered to ponder the fates of a handful of individuals of no significance in this time of turmoil.

We were allowed to act as volunteer gardeners, a relief from the boredom. The cool and fragrant freshness of the morning hours, instead of the stale dormitory air, was like wine to our spirits.

Our fame as workers spread fast. One day a man who was introduced as a plantation owner from the Island of Maui came with the superintendent.

"Men, you will be paroled to this gentleman, who is willing to employ you," we were told.

The planter told us, ". . . If you want to work I will provide transportation, housing and basic necessities. The pay will be the going rate for field labor."

A few days later the little Inter-Island steamer Claudine deposited us at Kipahulu landing.

HONOLULU newspapers promptly dubbed Kipahulu "the dumping ground for undesirable aliens."

We moved into small whitewashed shacks, which we shared with tiny pale lizards. Mattresses on the floor and buckets to wash in were the promised necessities.

The pay turned out to be 96 cents a day plus a daily bonus of around 30 cents, payable at harvest time. Our spirits were dampened by the bleak prospect that this was to feed us; buy the necessities of life.

But we were young and healthy, and eager for the things tomorrow would bring.

Dawn brought the piercing wail of the mill whistle summoning us to our labors.

Under the eye of a Portuguese luna we climbed, along slippery trails, to high-lying fields to harvest cane — arriving there in a state of near exhaustion before our task had begun.

The unaccustomed work was the more arduous as the day's heat alternated with chilling rain squalls.

ADDED TO our discomforts were the harangues of the head luna, who seemed always to appear as we took a breathing spell without which we could not have evolved.

Sitting astride his horse, he would bitterly upbraid us.

Eventually, we realized that we could never match the daily output of the wiry Filipino laborers who were more accustomed to toiling in the climate, while subsisting on the meager diet that had been the fare of their race for centuries.

We laid our case before the plantation owner. Surprisingly, he was not unprepared:

"Very well, next week you can start at something else," he said.

Subsequently, we found ourselves assigned as helpers to the carpenter and blacksmith, the machine shop and the store.

Initially this may have been "made work" but it quickly turned to be a bonanza for the company, as well as for us.

The war effort demanded increased production. Improvements in the sugar mill became a necessity. New machinery arrived by steamer.

And who would be better qualified than this gang of Jack Tars, skilled in the use of rope and tackle, to haul, lift and set the new machinery on its foundation?

A YEAR went by. We had made friends with many of the local inhabitants. Their buoyant nature devoid of

inhibitions, and ever ready abandon to the pleasures of the moment, the music of their stringed instruments and festive luaus sparked brightness to our days.

But it was the free Sundays which provided the real highlights when we swam in a landlocked fresh water pool, separated from the ocean by a narrow rocky beach.

A nearby small grassy plot, shaded by coconut palms, was our idyllic resting place. Upstream, groves of mango trees provided an abundance of delicious ripe fruit.

Here we recuperated and gathered new strength.

The erection of a reinforced concrete smoke stack was the final phase in mill improvements. We bent our backs to the task — built scaffolding, poured concrete and hoisted forms until the desired height of 96 feet had been reached.

Amidst a cluster of low buildings stood the gray, gleaming column, in sharp contrast to the vivid greens of the country surrounding us. We regarded it with pride as a monument to our labors.

IN EUROPE, armies were locked in trench warfare until that monstrous engine of war — the tank — turned the tide in favor of the Allies terminating hostilities near the end of 1918.

Our thoughts turned to the day when we would return to a world from which we had been cut off for a half a decade.

But the days, weeks and months of 1919 dragged on, and no word from Washington.

"How long, Lord, how long?" became our daily prayer.

On a day in early fall the bookkeeper rushed out waving a piece of paper.

"Hey, fellows, you are free to go, it says here."

We sat on the stoop of our shack in the mild evening air, discussing and speculating aimlessly what the future would hold for us.

THE NEXT few days were spent in last farewells. The men shook hands and wished us well. The womenfolk tearfully pressed food on us and we ate in silence.

In the face of unexpected tears, the solicitude of our hosts did little to lift our spirits. We stood about dumbly seeking appropriate last words.

We spent a final night on our hard mattresses. For the last time we boarded our faithful Claudine.

Sailing up the coast, the palis were shrouded in heavy rain. White clothes fluttered from porches of half-hidden dwellings. They were waving a last "Aloha," or were they?

Perhaps it was only laundry hung out to dry.

A DAY LATER we stepped ashore in Honolulu. We dispersed, each preoccupied with his own affairs. Few of us ever met again.

California became my home for 50 rewarding years. Return to my first love, the sea, citizenship, marriage, children, grandchildren and eventually retirement.

Often a visitor to the Islands in the pursuit of my calling, Maui was off the beaten path; but not forgotten. Perhaps, someday . . .

I awoke with a start to a touch on my shoulder.

"You've been asleep, dear," my wife said.

I sat up. The surf pounded the black rocky beach. Shivering in my wet bathing trunks, I surveyed the familiar scene.

THE DEEP POOL fed by small falls cascading over shiny black rocks. On the far side, the cave formed a high arch of volcanic rock.

All seemed the same — but not quite. The water had lost its sparkle. The pool was dark; yellow scum collected in the eddies. The grassy plot — which had been our bed 50 years ago — had been taken over by an impenetrable jungle.

Slowly, my wife and I made our way to the top of the bluff. I cast one long backward glance. From the distance it was still the lovely picture I had never forgotten.

The Kipahulu I had known was no more.

Above the cavernous hollow of the old sugar mill, the stack still stood, weathered and crowned by a turf of grass.

What price nostalgia!

'UNDESIRABLE ALIENS' – This photograph, taken in 1917 or 1918, shows author Friz and three other German nationals at their favorite swimming hole on Maui. Friz is third from left.

Maui Revisited. This article by the author appeared in the *Honolulu Star Bulletin,* Aug. 22, 1969.

crowd of village children, no doubt wondering what this *haole* (white man) was doing, I removed the clutch, cleaned it and replaced it. It had taken the better part of a Sunday. I was not at all sure that I had repaired anything when I told George that this was all I could do. He was noncommittal.

"Maybe, you like some fruit?" he said. I pointed to a tree in his backyard, loaded with large pale yellow fruit. "Oh," he said, "those are Chinese oranges. You pick as many as you like!" I did. The fruit was large, twice the size of an orange. The skin was half an inch thick, the flesh very bitter and unpalatable. I learned later that it was grapefruit. The Dodge remained in front of his store until the day I left the island.

Then there was Juan, a Spaniard. Past middle age, he and his wife occupied a small shack next to the post office. A cement mason by trade, he had put the concrete floor in the boiler room and adjacent centrifuge compartment. When talking, we avoided the plantation lingo, but conversed in Spanish. One day he handed me a letter and asked me to read it to him. I realized then that neither he nor his wife could read or write.

The letter was from their son in Spain. I read it to them without much difficulty. I offered to transcribe a reply that Juan would dictate. It was a service I gladly performed several times. The evening I paid a last call on them, we embraced in a last farewell. As I walked down the road for a last time, I could hear her voice: *"Vaya con Dios, amigo, Vaya Con Dios!"* It brought tears to my eyes.

One day, after working hours, Joe, the bookkeeper, hailed me. "Our father has not returned from his ride," he said. "He is somewhere near the landing where the road ends. He sent word that he could not ride his horse back. We are going to bring him home in the car. I would like you to come along and ride his horse back to the stables."

I climbed into the Dodge. The old gentleman had dismounted and had not been able to get back into the saddle. As I mounted the horse, Joe said, "Let him go slowly; don't try to run him." I promised I had no intention to "run" the aged steed that was more like a plow horse than a saddle horse.

As I rode past the cabins, I was greeted with shouts and laughter by my compatriots. "Hey, look here comes the new boss," one shouted. Others joined in. "Boss, when are you going to raise our wages?" and "Don't fall off that horse; it's a long way down."

One day as I was returning from work I was met by an individual who extended his hand and said, "I am running for Representative of the Territory of Hawaii at the Congress of the United States. I would like your vote."

I did not catch his name. Of stocky build, he was well dressed. Because of his swarthy appearance I judged him to be of pure Hawaiian lineage. I did not tell him that, not being a citizen, I could not vote. I wished him well and we shook hands.

Joe, the bookkeeper had observed this episode. Through the open window of his office he pointed to the receding figure: "You know who that was?"

"I have no idea."

"Well, you just shook the hand of Prince Kuhio, scion of the princely Kuhio family whose ancestral land is the Island of Kauai."

In the evening I related the encounter to my companions. Said one, "So you shook hands with a bigshot, eh. Always looking for the main chance, aren't you?"

"Main chance my foot." I said. "I am not looking for anything; things just come naturally to me." These were episodes that added spice to my life.

In Europe, the armies were locked in trench warfare until that monstrous engine of war, the tank, turned the tide in favor of the Allies, terminating hostilities near the end of 1918. Our thoughts turned to the day when we would return to a world from which we had been cut off for nearly a decade. But the days, weeks, and months of the year 1919 dragged on, and no word came from Washington. "How long, oh, Lord, how long?" became our daily prayer.

Finally, the Lord must have heard us. Or was it perhaps the "Great White Father" in Washington? It was a day in early fall of 1919, when the bookkeeper came running out of his office, waving a piece of paper. "Hey, fellows, you are free to go. It says so right here!"

We were past the point of exuberant rejoicing. We sat on the stoops of our shacks in the mild evening air, discussing and speculating aimlessly what the future would hold for us.

The next few days were spent in last farewell visits. The men shook hands and wished us well. The womenfolk tearfully pressed food on us they had prepared for the occasion. We ate in silence. In the face of unexpected tears, the solicitude of our hosts did little to lift our spirits, as we stood about dumbly, trying to find an appropriate last word.

We spent a final night on our hard mattresses, our few belongings packed. For the last time we boarded our faithful CLAUDINE. Sailing along the coast, the deep gulches called *palis,* were shrouded in heavy rain. White clothes fluttered from the porches of half-hidden dwellings. They were waving a last *"Aloha."* Or were they? Perhaps it was only laundry they were hanging out to dry!

A day later, we stepped ashore in Honolulu. We dispersed, each occupied with his own affairs. I joined Henry in search of Old John. We found him in a hospital ward. We told him we would find quarters for him when he was discharged. He shook his head, "Thank you, boys. I know this is the end." He died the following day.

I had rented a room in a private home on the outskirts of Honolulu. Sitting on the edge of my bed, I tried to think things out. Once again I found myself at loose ends. Nearly penniless, I needed work. The small fleet of Inter-island steamers? Not a chance. They were manned by natives. I had seen them on the CLAUDINE. Big beefy barefoot men in shorts. Having cast off the lines, they gathered at the stern around a large open barrel. One of the men with a broken oar stirred the purplish gooey contents. The men ate with their fingers. One finger poi, two finger poi, three finger poi? I shuddered at the thought.

The only American Steamship Service, Matson Navigation Co. said, "We only hire crews on the Mainland." Shipping in the harbor was dominated by foreign flag vessels, mostly Japanese. Staying in the islands was out of the question. What was I to do? Where could I go?

My thoughts drifted to the distant past. What had become of the carefully laid plans so many years ago of a career at sea? Envisioned as an orderly life, every step had been pre-ordained: Four years of mandated service before the mast in square-rigged sailing ships followed by schooling for a mate's ticket. Service in steamers in all deck officer grades to qualify as Master, then the ultimate goal, the command of a ship.

Tired of making the rounds of the waterfront I was soon asleep. In my dreams, the scenes of early childhood and adolescence played across my mind like a moving panorama.

CHILDHOOD AND ADOLESCENCE

I was born April 9, 1896, the first child of Ottmar and Luise Friz, nee Dörpmund. They resided in Linden, an industrial suburb of the City of Hannover, capital of the Prussian Province of that name, in Imperial Germany.

My father was the eldest of six children of Adolf and Laura Friz. The pronunciation of that name was "FRITZ," but the reason for the spelling without the "t" has never been ascertained. There were two branches of the family by that name, one in the Kingdom of Wuerttemberg residing in the Stuttgart area, the other headed by my paternal grandparents in the Munich area in the Kingdom of Bavaria. They leased and operated hotels and dining rooms at prominent division points of a burgeoning railway system which had displaced the carriage trade in the mid-nineteenth century.

Following graduation from the public school system, my father entered the prestigious Brewer-akademy of Weihenstephan. With these credentials, he served the prescribed term as a journeyman brewer in Bavaria, Austria, Poland and finally in Prussia, where he met and married my mother, the fifth of six children of the Dörpmunds residing in the agrarian area near the villages of Bensdorf and Ahrenfelde in the Prussian Province of Hannover. My father's sister, a staunch Bavarian, initially always

Ottmar Friz, 1898. Age two

referred to my mother as "The Prussian."

My maternal grandfather was a teacher and church organist. He and grandmother came to visit their latest-born grandchild. I was later told that when they left grandfather was heard to say sadly to grandmother, "She'll never raise that boy!" So much for grandfather as a prophet. Rickets, my childhood disease, was a problem that failed to respond to various diets, until a doctor advised, "Never mind the diets, just feed him a little of everything." It proved to be the best advice a medical practitioner had given to anyone. From then on, I grew and grew and grew.

In a nearby village lived mother's sister, Em, her husband Gus, and their three children. Uncle Gus was a teacher and a strict disciplinarian. His children lived in fear of him. When we visited, they would join me in noisy roughhouse play until their father came home. Upon entering the house and hearing the clamor of our play, he would ask Aunt Em, "Is that terrible boy here again?"

My father Ottmar Friz, 1904.

By contrast, Aunt Em was always glad to have me around. As a country woman, she raised ducks, geese, pigeons and chickens in her backyard. On a small plot of land outside the village, she grew vegetables, potatoes, berries, and flowers. As a city apartment child, I was entranced by country life and enjoyed helping collect eggs, grub potatoes, pick berries or rake leaves. None of her children would help her, lest they get

My mother Luise Friz, 1903.

their hands dirty, so perhaps I fulfilled a need she could not get from her own offspring.

Uncle Gus was eventually relieved of my disturbing presence. Immediately following the New Year, father received and accepted an offer as brewmaster in the City of Graudenz in West Prussia. Situated on the Vistula River, Graudenz was a garrison city on the Russian border, hous-

Gathering of the Dörpmund clan, circa 1900. In the center, Grandmother Dörpmund (nee Kramer). Lower right, Luise Friz (nee Dörpmund), my mother. Lower left, the author at age four. In the family I was called Ott'l, in accordance with the Bavarian custom of shortening given names.

ing several regiments of infantry, field artillery, pioneers, and support groups. The brewery was part of a large estate composed of grazing land and a large crop of sugar beets. The estate provided housing with a large ornamental garden and extensive rear yard extending to the property line. I was five years old then. I had no other children to play with because of our location on the outskirts of the city.

Our rear yard bordered on the training grounds of the field artillery and my principal entertainment was to perch on the wooden fence and watch the training of recruits and the horses they were to ride. A well trained band was an essential part of any regiment in the German military establishment. On early summer mornings we were often awakened by the martial music of companies of artillery as they moved in formation past our quarters en route to field maneuvers.

In 1902, at age six, I was enrolled in the prescribed three year elementary school system, known as the *Volksschule,* or the People's School. From the beginning I was an apt pupil, liked by most of my teachers.

Grading of class and homework was by numbers in red ink on the students' work papers, with I being top grade, II good, III passing and IV failing. I generally brought home a I. The sole exception was math, with which I had great difficulty and, at times, failed to achieve even a passing grade. This incensed the math teacher who perhaps saw his own failure in my inability to excel to the same degree as I did in other schoolwork.

Corporal punishment was part of the educational system and the day soon came when I was hauled to the principal's office for the caning he alone was allowed to administer. Overcome by fear, I fought like a wildcat, and it took three grown men—the principal, the teacher and finally the school custodian—to subdue me to administer the punishment.

Other children at times fared likewise, their parents accepting caning, perhaps even approving of it as part of the system. Not so my mother. when she heard of it through gossip in her circle of acquaintances, she confronted me at home, demanding to know why I had not told her. In her wounded pride, her anger knew no bounds as her carpetbeater descended upon me in hot pursuit around the dining room table, her tears of anger mingling with my tears of anguish.

That afternoon she donned hat and coat and was on her way to school. Mother was a handsome person, friendly and amiable, but a formidable adversary when aroused. She sailed into the school corridor at intermission time and, confronting the teacher, berated him in highly audible fashion, until this astonished gentleman sought refuge in the principal's office. The upshot of this was no more chastisement in school without informing the parents before or after the fact. Father, coming home that evening, found me cowering in bed and mother dissolved in tears, no longer in anger, but in chagrin at her actions against the son whom she loved very much, then and forever.

Time passed and had its healing effects. My interest in things around me led me to roam through the brewery grounds, where I watched with fascination the manufacture of wooden beer barrels, from scratch, by highly skilled coopers. Sometimes, I visited father in his laboratory or accompanied him on his rounds on elevated platforms around the giant brewing vats as he dipped a cup on a long handle into the boiling brew to take a sample to his office lab.

A hallowed custom was the Sunday morning *frühschoppen,* or early drink, when citizens gathered at the city hall plaza at eleven A.M. for a stein of the local brew, while a small military brass band provided lively music. Sunday afternoons found most families in a local beergarden, where the women had coffee and cake, and the men quaffed beer and ate sausage and sauerkraut. It was a social event for the grownups, a day of fun for the children. On a large grassy playground, there were swings, slides and horizontal bars. Adults would organize footraces and sack-races. Cartwheels or wrestling were the preferred activities of the older boys.

One Sunday when the family prepared to go home, much to their consternation, I was nowhere to be found. A frantic search of the meadow and adjacent woods and the questioning of other children failed to disclose my whereabouts. Mother was attracted by a circle of grownups and children. Pushing through the crowd, she found me standing on my head, a demonstration generating considerable applause from the bystanders.

Weekly gymnastics were a part of the school curriculum. We were issued white tee shirts, emblazoned with the four capital letter F's in green. They stood for the motto of the German gymnastic club: *Frisch, Fromm, Fröhlich, Frei,* translated as "Brisk, Pious, Joyous, Free."

The winters were severe. Ice-skating was the Sunday afternoon sport for most people. On a frozen pond at the outskirts of the city, men and women clasped hands and skated to the waltz-time tunes played by a small military band. A present under the Christmas tree was a pair of skates. Mother had never skated but Father was accomplished in executing graceful curves and figure eights. On days when I went skating, Mother always gave me ten pfennig, saying I could buy a loaf of bread from soldiers at the infantry barracks. On my way, I passed the Army bakery from which emanated the enticing odor of freshly baked bread. Opposite it were the barracks. At the gates stood soldiers on weekend passes with loaves of that fresh bread, just issued, and glad to exchange one of them for my ten pfennigs, so they could buy a glass of beer. The bread was black and coarse. It was called *Kommissbrot;* perhaps it would have been called GI bread in the U.S. I loved it; it was tasty and nutritious.

With Father's help, I made passing grades in math. I excelled in reading, writing, grammar and spelling. When Mother visited other families, she was often asked to bring me along to help their children with their homework. From the beginning, I was an avid reader, not alone in the mechanical sense, but I also had the faculty of comprehension and reten-

Ottmar Friz in 1900. Age four.

tion. Encouraged by my Mother, I read German and Scandinavian fairy tales and the mythology of the legendary *Nibelungen,* the folk tales that form the basis of the well known Wagnerian operas.

My favorite reading subjects were history and the romantic historical novels relating the life and exploits of Charlemagne, King of the Franks in central Europe and Emperor of the West. Other favorites were El Cid, also known as Cid Campeador, the epic hero of Spain, the champion in the wars against the Moors; and Roland, legendary nephew of Charlemagne and hero of the French epic, "Chanson de Roland" who died fighting the Saracens in the Valley of Roncesvalles.

Social activities in Graudenz were limited, perhaps due to the twelve-hour work day, six days a week. Mother began to chafe under the lack of communication within her circle of acquaintances as well as with the outside world. She complained often, "People are so buttoned-up." She was happy when father decided he needed a change from the large brewery to a smaller establishment with a less demanding workload. He was engaged as brewmaster in Lemgo, a small community in Northern Germany. The city bore a strong imprint of its medieval history, having been a member of the Hanseatic League, composed of free towns whose merchants were engaged in foreign trade by land and sea around the 12th and 13th centuries. The residents of Lemgo seemed to live and work under the aegis of their ancient past. They formed a closed society, dominated by one or two prominent families.

Having completed elementary school, I was enrolled in a college preparatory establishment leading to a university education. In line with this, the dead languages were from the beginning an important part of the curriculum. I took to Latin like a duck to water. I continued to excel in German, reading, writing, spelling, grammar, and other subjects. Once I even surprised the math teacher by solving one of his complicated pet problems in advanced arithmetic on the blackboard, in front of the class, Nevertheless, the time I spent in that school was not a happy one. As the "new kid on the block," I was first ignored, at times subjected to tricks, and always teased about my precise and pure German, a heritage from my Hannoverian background. It was generally known that both City and Province of Hannover were the cradles of the best modern German, although a vernacular known as Plattdeutsch was also in common use.

Lemgo still had the wall and moat of medieval days. The moat was filled with water which froze in the winter and provided the opportunity for skating. Some of my classmates made fun of my skates, of a vintage that still had to be clamped to my everyday shoes. I had outgrown them, but I managed to keep them on with leather straps. They challenged me to a race. I accepted, and much to my surprise and theirs, I beat them by several lengths. By their standards, I was now found acceptable and the word got around that I was, after all, a "regular guy." By that time, I didn't care much, one way or another. I took part in their games when invited and declined when I found interests elsewhere. I believe to this day that these experiences left their mark and conditioned me to deal with life in later days.

Among Christmas presents that year was a German translation of Tales of the Leatherstocking by James Fenimore Cooper. Edited for youthful readers, this fascinating tale opened up a new world to me, not hitherto known or even imagined. Reading these absorbing stories of Indians and Frontiersmen involved in the wars between the French and the British and their Indian allies, fighting for possession of a fabulously rich continent, was strong, rich fodder for my imagination. It is fair to say that these and other accounts I read about America had a profound influence in my life.

At the end of a year in Lemgo, it was apparent that father was not happy. He had never dropped his Bavarian accent and did not feel comfortable in the North German atmosphere, so different from that of his homeland in the South. Came a letter from his parents, informing us that they had retired from the management of railroad hotels and dining rooms. They had opened a small wine restaurant in Munich. It was the typical arrangement of the times that the wife would manage the kitchen and the husband supervise the dining room and wine cellar. Grandmother's reputation as a gourmet cook had followed her and attracted many former customers to the delights of her table, as did my grandfather's knowledgeable selection of good wines, beers, and cigars. The tone of their letter was an unmistakable plea to come and help in their new venture.

It did not take long for Father and Mother to pack up and take residence in the same building downstairs from where my grandparents lived. The wine restaurant was at street level. It was an exciting time for me when mother took me to the English Garden, housing a military museum with an outside exhibit of cannons of the Napoleonic Wars and the equestrian statue of Otto von Wittelsbach, Duke of Bavaria, and founder of the dynasty that ruled and governed the kingdom for nearly eight centuries.

It was summer vacation time, and I spent many days flying kites with other children on the Theresienwiese, that legendary grassy meadow famous for its annual beer bash, the *Octoberfest*.

At summer's end, a letter from Father's sister, Alvina, living in Issigau in Upper Franconia in the extreme northeast corner of Bavaria brought the news of a newly built hotel in a neighboring village. Constructed and owned by a peasant family with no experience in hotel management, the

Hotel König David—Hölle, Bavaria

property was offered for lease. An enclosed photo showed a handsome, three-storied structure with a tower at one corner. With Father's background and Mother's competence as a gourmet cook, which she had acquired while helping Grandmother in the kitchen, it was considered a worthwhile opportunity. At an initial visit, a two-year lease was signed.

The hotel was located in a small village with the intriguing name of Hölle, or Hell. In spite of this forbidding name, I shall never forget my first glimpse of this entrancing place, cradled in a deep and ruggedly beautiful hollow. In a rural countryside, otherwise characterized by lovely green and gently rolling hills, it was the only one of its kind here. Elsewhere it was aptly described as a geological oddity, the result of a prankish upheaval of Nature. I was enraptured by the view of massive rock formations and dark pine-clad hills, so different from the northern plain. So like the American scene described in the *Leatherstocking Tales,* this enchanting woodland became my playground during the most impressionable years of my boyhood.

The local inhabitants were of peasant ancestry, farming the stony soil. The clatter of weavers' looms was heard, producing textiles in a cottage industry. With limited contact to the outside world, the valley had remained hidden for centuries, unsung and unheralded in the chronicles of the past. At last, a slow awakening had taken place as railroads extended hesitant fingers into this backwoods area. Venturesome families built hotels to accommodate weekend visitors from nearby cities. Vacationers came to enjoy the clear and pure air and the beauty of the adjacent Höllenthal, or Hell's Valley.

Advanced schooling was available only in the distant city of Hof. I enrolled in a college preparatory school but later shifted to another school, as my parents could not provide the funds for a university education. The study of French now took the place of Latin in a standardized curriculum leading to the trades or the business world. I also played the violin in the school orchestra. I commuted daily, including Saturdays, to Hof by rail. During the one-hour ride, other students boarded the train at various stops. In the golden days of summer vacation, I roamed the forest, mastering every trail, hideout and viewpoint. Clearings offered an abundance of wild strawberries, raspberries, blackberries, blueberries and cranberries. The swift little river Selbitz, boiling through the rocky valley harbored trout and pike in shadowy pools, ready to take the angler's bait. Following the first heavy fall rains various edible mushrooms poked their heads through the thick pine-needle carpets in the cool forest, a welcome addition to the family table.

Boys my age became my playmates in various games. There were days when we played at being soldiers marching in formation. At other times we were knights with shields and swords, battling imaginary foes. Our favorite game was the reenactment of the scenes of the Leatherstocking Tales I described to my playmates. As the frontiersman called Hawkeye, the Indian Chingachgook, the Great Snake, Uncas the Delaware, and others, we trod the paths in the dark forest above the valley in imaginary pursuit of Magua, the Clever Fox, the treacherous Huron scout who abducted Alice and Cora, daughters of a British officer. We made our toy weapons and our bows and arrows from saplings of wild hazelnut bushes. It did not take long for the parents of my companions to look askance at this intruder from the north who had introduced their sons into this new world of fantasy at a time when they should have helped with the farm chores.

In early autumn, we drove the community-owned herd of chattering geese to the stubble fields to feed on the kernels of grain left by the gleaners. Adjacent potato fields had been harvested and the foliage stacked up in small shocks to dry. They provided a smoky fire in which we roasted left-over potatoes. Their skins turned black and crisp. The mealy interior was delicious. The still evening air of the Indian summer carried the sound of faraway church bells and the lowing of cattle in their stables. Layers of dense white smoke from our fires gathered in the valley, to be dispersed by the mild evening breezes. The charm of the idyllic pastoral scene led to a feeling of reverence and contentment.

The boys drifted away. As the girl and I leaned against a shock of foliage I felt her arm across my shoulder. Her upturned face bore an expression of utter devotion. Her young firm breasts and warm body pressed against mine as our lips met. The natural fragrance of her hair that a gentle breeze had blown across my face was like an aphrodisiac. Her thighs yielded to my groping hands in a rapturous union. The age of innocence faded never to return.

A new member joined our family. Born in 1907, she was named Erika after the low-growing heather found on rocky outcrops above the valley floor. A beautiful child, she was our pride and joy. When taken out for a walk, strangers would stop in admiration and ask her name. A lady of our acquaintance always called her Little Heather Rose. I loved her dearly, carried her and played with her, but there was the age gap of eleven years.

With the care of the new arrival, the task of arising at six every morning, giving me breakfast and sandwiches for lunch and seeing that I made the commute train on time became an exhausting chore for my mother. The universal custom of boarding students from outlying communities with middle-class families in the city was the answer to the problem.

School hours were from 8 a.m. to noon, followed by a two-hour noon recess. Classes resumed in the afternoon from 2 to 4, except on Saturdays, when the afternoon was free. In a fast trot, I made the early afternoon weekend train to my beloved valley, to leave again late Sunday afternoon. The family saw little of me in the intervening daylight hours, for I joined my playmates on the familiar trails in the woods. In 1909, in the tradition of our religious affiliation, I was, at age 13, confirmed in the Reformed Evangelical Church, together with other children of the region served by the ancient church in Issigau.

At Easter recess, we visited relatives in Hamburg. I was intrigued by the bustling activities in this great port, seen from the deck of an excursion steamer. Daily visits included stops at the sailing ship harbor to see and admire the great square-rigged sailing ships, engaged in trade to the far corners of the world. I began to dream of an adventurous life at sea. Books about ships and the sea fired my imagination and awakened a burning desire to travel, to see foreign lands and to emulate the deeds of sea heroes, men of daring who issued orders to their crews in stentorian voices which could not be drowned out by the roar of the gale and the tumult of the raging sea. Subsequent visits in Hamburg during summer vacations strengthened my resolve to seek a career at sea, which offered the prospects of becoming an officer and eventually captain of a merchant ship. My playmates scoffed at the idea. Family members wagged their heads in doubt and disapproval, and prophesied that no good could come from such outlandish notions.

The high hopes we held when the hotel had been leased failed to be fulfilled. The seasonal summer income vanished during the winter months, when heavy snowfall brought beautiful Christmas scenery but no business. Winter sports as a form of enjoyment were known only to the elite few whose wealth permitted them to patronize the prestigious establishments of St. Moritz and Davos in Switzerland. Locally, cross-country skis provided a utilitarian form of transportation only to forest service personnel and rural gendarmes in the pursuit of their outside activities. Within hundreds of miles, I was the only youngster who was the proud owner of skis, which I used to roam the open terrain. Our neighbors viewed such frivolity with disdain but did not hesitate to enlist my services, when a heavy snow cover impeded conventional means of transportation, to fetch a rucksack full of foodstuffs from nearby communities.

In the face of mounting financial difficulties, I quit school at age fifteen, hoping to find some sort of employment. The pressure of applicants against jobs was such that, without a sponsor, young people found it difficult to get a start. My parents did not take kindly to my idea to seek a career in the merchant marine, primarily because it required a term of service in sailing ships, which they considered a dangerous service at best.

Again, fate intervened. At a gathering in Hamburg of family members and acquaintances, a retired sailingship master, hearing of my desire, offered to place me. It was explained that the first step involved a mandatory four-year service before the mast in square-rigged sailing ships, which included but was not limited to a year as deckboy, a year as ordinary seaman, and two years as able-bodied seaman. The latter could include one year as quartermaster (helmsman) in steam ships. Following completion of the required stint in sail, the second step was enrollment in a nautical school, featuring navigation, ship handling, maritime law and ship's business, leading to certification and issuance of the coveted mate's ticket. Having overcome these hurdles, future employment with steamship companies was assured.

To the question of the necessity of sail training when the ultimate goal was service in the less hazardous and comfortable steamship, there is a logical answer. Although the steamship was in the ascendancy and had captured the highly profitable short trade routes between European ports and the principal ports on the American continents, ship owners with a long history and tradition continued to build and operate wind-driven ships, changing from wooden hull to iron and eventually to steel-hulled vessels. These lofty ships, magnificently rigged and equipped, depended entirely for propulsion upon the natural forces of wind, ocean currents and the skills and endurance of the men who manned them. It is safe to say that the prescribed four-year term under sail was designed to assure the operators of a virtually inexhaustible labor pool composed of men with a steadfast purpose to endure the low pay, the low quality of food and the common perils of the sea.

On the long haul from Europe to the east and west coasts of South America and beyond to Australia, these ships encountered everything in the way of weather known to man, from the vicious storms of the North Atlantic to the benign breezes of the tradewinds; from the flat calms of the equatorial doldrums, known as the breeding grounds of destructive seasonal hurricanes, to the short-but-potent pamperos off the Argentine coast, and finally to the incredible turbulence of wind and sea around feared Cape Horn.

Exposure to these elementary forces of nature not only resulted in technical competence but was also thought to be psychologically sound, in that anyone who had weathered this preliminary period of service had also undergone a process of character building that led to such virtues as tenacity of purpose, self reliance, pride in his profession, and the capacity for leadership.

The time was the beginning of the Twentieth Century; the locale, the great seaport of Hamburg in northern Germany, linked with trade by way of the oceans to the ports of the world. It was an era of peace. The freedom of the seas was not challenged, and the trade routes of the world were open to free and innocent passage of ships flying the flags of all nations. The Industrial Age in Europe was in full swing. The wharves of seaports were clogged with manufactured goods awaiting shipment. The countries of South America, notably the republics of Chile, Peru, Bolivia and Ecuador had no industries but offered a wealth of copper, nitrate, tin, hides, and other raw materials, conveniently carried as bulk cargo. They represented a highly receptive field, veritable sponges ready to absorb fabricated goods in unlimited quantities, from sewing needles to pianos, from the industrial nations of Europe, who in turn swallowed up the raw materials available in the vast reaches of the South American continent. Reduced to the simple terms of give and take, one may say that the commercial world had rarely seen a more ideal situation involving an exchange of goods to the benefit of both sides. Against this background my career was launched.

THE FIRST VOYAGE

Riding quietly at her moorings in a remote corner of the harbor in Hamburg lay the bark OBOTRITA. Built in Denmark in 1892 and named FAVORITA, she successively passed into German ownership. Renamed OBOTRITA, she was presently owned by the Eugene Cellier Company. Just out of drydock, her hull had been painted a shiny black. A yellow stripe from the bowsprit at the maindeck level all around the hull accentuated her fine lines. Seen above the waterline was the red boottoping paint, below it a coat of white anti-fouling paint was visible. Her masts and yards were painted a bright buff color. As a bark, her foremast and main-mast was square-rigged; her third mast, or mizzen, was fore and aft rigged.

My silent fascination was interrupted by the voice of my sponsor. "Well, boy, are you ready to ship in her? This will be your home for at least a year, possibly more." I could hardly wait to get to my aunt's house in the city's outskirts where we were staying to impart the good news. Father had left several days ago to look after the family business, and it was left to mother to arrange for the purchase of an outfit. It was an exciting experience to watch the ship chandler, long in the business of supplying seamen, as he hauled the goods from the shelves and piled them on the counter: workshirts, pants, underwear, socks, shoes, head gear, mess gear, blankets, chunks of saltwater soap, a straw mattress and lastly that foul-weather gear composed of oilskin pants and coat, southwester and knee-length leather seaboots.

Trying on the southwester and regarding myself approvingly in a full-length mirror, I heard words of caution from the man behind the counter, a grizzled veteran of the sea himself. "Stow the illusions, boy, better stow them."

The words fell on deaf ears, but they were to be remembered before too long in the face of the realities of the grim business I had embarked upon.

All the purchases were delivered onboard, packed in the sea chest traditionally carried by all seamen. At a last tearful farewell, mother handed me a large bundle containing a featherbed cover, pillow, and also my violin. As a final gesture, she put her hands on my shoulders and said, "Promise me you will never allow yourself to be tattooed."

I was not aware that in the view of landsmen, all sailors were tattooed with images of varying designs, were fond of strong drink and indulged in riotous living when they were paid off at the end of a voyage and had money in their pockets.

It was a fair generalization, but there were exceptions, particularly among those who wanted to see the compulsory sailingship service behind them as soon as possible, to become eligible for the more prestigious positions with the large steamship companies. In this highly competitive calling, it was essential to guard one's personal and professional reputation. I gave the promise and kept it.

After a last embrace, I clambered onboard to be greeted by the sailors with hoots and laughter. "A featherbed? Wait 'till the salt air gets on it, it will never dry out," they said.

On a dark, rainy November day in 1911, OBOTRITA, loaded, provisioned and crewed, cast off her lines and in tow of a smoke-belching tug started down the River Elbe. Her decks were a jumble of mooring lines and running gear, the former to be coiled away, the latter to be sorted out and suspended from their assigned belaying pins.

The crew worked silently in the chilly drizzle, without benefit of the sea chanties commonly used to lighten the labor of hauling and pulling. At her gaff fluttered the German merchant ensign, horizontal stripes of black, white and red and below that her call letters: RJMS.

Arriving at Cuxhafen at the end of the day, the tug was cast off. It departed, sounding the traditional farewell, three blasts on the steam whistle as it disappeared in the murky gloom. Because of a rising northerly wind and a falling barometer, the skipper decided to anchor to await better weather. Buffeted by a strong wind and choppy sea building up across the roadstead open to the North Sea, both anchors were dropped on a long scope. At daybreak, with the wind near hurricane force, multi-sheave relieving tackles were set up on the anchor chains, lest the anchor windlass, under heavy strain, be torn from its moorings. The voyage had gotten off to a poor start.

The third day, with a break in the lead-colored sky and the wind abating, the call went out: "All Hands On Deck!" Some of the men went aloft to loosen the sails, others started heaving up the port anchor. I drew the job of stowing the anchor chain in the chain locker, a five-by-five-foot square wooden box reaching from the maindeck to the bottom plate. Following a few brief moments of instruction by the second mate, that worthy left me with the stern admonition to properly coil the chain to reach all the corners lest the locker would prove too small to take all of it.

I clambered down the iron rungs at the rear bulkhead. I could hear the tramp of the men manning the capstan bars. I guided the slowly incoming chain, link by link, into the corners of the locker. At the lowest depth it was not too difficult; by the time the locker was half full, it took all the strength I had. When the locker was three-quarters full, my efforts were in vain. As I watched in horror, the links piled up in the center, almost up to the spillpipe. In a last desperate move, I kicked the pile with my boots to see it slide off, a maneuver I continued until all the chain was in. I emerged from the locker in a state of exhaustion and hid for awhile behind a coil of rope in a small room called the bos'n's locker. Wet and mud caked, I looked out and saw, with relief, one of the ordinary seamen entering the starboard locker.

With the anchors clear of the bottom, OBOTRITA got underway on a westerly course. Fortunately, a stiff easterly breeze held, until the ship, scooting along under shortened sails, passed the coasts of Holland and Belgium and entered the English Channel. Emerging several days later at the Lizards and clearing the Scilly Islands, OBOTRITA went her way, closehauled against a rough sea into a fog shrouded North Atlantic.

En route, the crew had been divided into the notorious two-watch system, called in the articles, "watch and watch": four hours on, four hours off. The watches relieved each other for the evening meal on a split watch. These were known as the Dog Watches. Although various other systems prevailed on other ships, the end result was the same: much work and little sleep. To my relief, I had landed on the second mate's watch. At sea, every day at 4 p.m., all hands, including the day workers, mustered at the break of the poop for a head count, at the conclusion of which the mate would intone: "Watch on deck, stay on deck, Watch below, go below."

This last expression was a leftover from the days when seamen slept below decks. Merchant ships needed the decks below for cargo. Seamen were moved up to the main deck underneath a short superstructure over the bows known as the forecastle, then and forevermore known as the fo'c'sle, no matter where its subsequent locations might be. In retrospect, a more lamentable area to house human beings could not possibly be found, considering the fact that the limited space was further encroached upon by the anchor windlass, the bos'n's locker, paint locker and that abominable amenity known as the "head" in the English speaking world, and latrine or more descriptive appellation elsewhere.

This impractical arrangement was soon found to be a deathtrap. In head-on collisions with ships or other objects, seamen were killed or severely injured. The law stepped in and decreed a radical change in accommodations on all ships built after a certain date. Fortunately, OBOTRITA had come under this new law.

A large deck house, constructed abaft the foremast, contained the new fo'c'sle and other spaces. Seamen were now quartered in one large room. A table and benches for messing were in the center; the bulkheads fore and aft and athwartships were lined with upper and lower bunks, in front of which the owners' sea chests were the only seating arrangements.

Not provided by the company, each bunk had a homemade curtain, to ensure some degree of privacy. Anyone finding time to read did so by the feeble light of a wax candle on a small shelf.

Near the center of the fo'c'sle, a narrow door on each side provided exit or entry across a high sill designed to keep out the seawater in bad weather. There were no heating facilities. A single oil lamp from the overhead provided a dim light. A small skylight with hinged windows admitted some daylight and air. Hanging from a short lanyard was a bucket of drinking water and a communal long-handled dipper.

The place was "home" to the watchstanders composed of Able-bodied Seamen (A.B.), Ordinary Seamen (O.S.), and Boys, one of whom served as Cabin Boy to Captain and Mates.

Across the forepart of the house were two small rooms. The carpenter shop was on the port side. On the starboard side was a four-bunk room where the carpenter, blacksmith, and sailmaker bunked. Although day workers, they were required to assist the crew on deck when working the ship. Across the afterend of the house was the galley. The cook was quartered aft. Since he was on a schedule of his own, when in the galley the cook traditionally was responsible for the single task of handling the sheet of the foresail through a single sheave in the bulkhead, conveniently located across from the galley doors, when the ship underwent the maneuver of changing her tack.

In the fo'c'sle, the pecking order was from the Able Seamen through the Ordinary Seamen, with the Boys at the bottom. Having drawn the fo'c'sle duty, my daily routine included fetching the grub from the galley, rain or shine, washing all the mess gear, scrubbing table and benches several times in the week, sweeping the deck and, most ignoble of all tasks, the daily feeding of two obstreperous, squealing hogs. The hogs were the standard addition to the ship's cuisine and would eventually be slaughtered in the cold latitudes, refrigeration then being unknown. In fair weather, in the trade winds and the equatorial calms they were often given the run of the deck, and who was to follow with broom and shovel to "police" the area? You guessed it.

Ah, those beautiful illusions I had been warned against by the old ship chandler. How quickly they were dispelled in the face of the demeaning daily routine. It was a time when the shiny image of brass buttons and gold braid was further tarnished by the powerful combination of homesickness and seasickness. Still a child, I rued the day I had embarked upon a seagoing career. In the shelter of my bunk, I shed bitter tears and vowed that, once ashore, I would never set foot again on any deck.

But the die was cast. The ship, committed to her appointed tasks, was on the high seas, cleaving a westward path into the setting sun, inexorably carrying me away from the carefree childhood to which there was no return. Time and the compelling force of coping with the daily workload, which aside from a demeaning routine would eventually include "going aloft," "learning the ropes" and acquiring the skills of seamanship essential in a profession demanding the utmost in physical and mental stamina.

Posted inside the sailors' quarters was a document called the Fo'c'sle Card. It contained a statement giving the voyage's estimated duration, pay-off port, legal rations (food and water) and the Master's name, stamped by the shipping commissioner. The daily food allowance consisted of hardtack, with emphasis on the "hard." It could be eaten only when soaked in tea or coffee. Margarine in tins was an evil-tasting spread, referred to by all hands as "axle grease." Coffee came in the form of bricks, labeled Crew Coffee. Broken up in boiling water, it was a black and bitter tasting brew. Brown cane sugar was in sacks as it came from the fields. Lumpy and sticky, a teaspoon or two added to tea or coffee produced an unappetizing concoction. Breakfast consisted most of the time of a cereal known as Burgoo, obviously an international term. It had the consistency of wallpaper paste. Because of its purplish color it was called by German sailors, "Blauer Heinrich" (Blue Henry). Mixed with a generous amount of brown sugar and washed down with coffee it still took courage to swallow it. The main part of the daily whack was salt beef and salt pork. Packed in barrels and preserved in rock salt, the contents were first transferred to large wooden containers, called harness casks. They were located on the forward corners of the poopdeck, beef on the starboard side, pork on the port side. The casks were made of hardwood, highly varnished. They were held together with broad, polished brass hoops and closed by a hinged lid. Their outwardly ornamental appearance belied the odor of the contents, brisket of beef or sowbellies.

Every afternoon, the second mate weighed out so many pounds per man using a hand-held scale. I soon learned to stand on the weather side of the open cask to escape the pungent odors assailing my nostrils as the meat was transferred to a large dish to be delivered to the galley. There was an occasional issue of dried fruit, such as apples, prunes, and raisins.

Water rations were also dispensed daily. Every crewman lined up with a bucket to receive his allowance. Most of it was given to the cook, some to the drinking-water bucket suspended from the sky light. The rest was for washing hands and face. This last water was transferred daily to a second bucket which, when full at the end of the week, served either to take a bath or wash clothes, a matter of individual choice. In spite of these restrictions, personal cleanliness rarely became a problem.

Seamen, by the very nature of their calling, are resourceful and inventive. To relieve the one-sidedness of the daily servings and create something more pleasing to the palate, a home-baked sheetcake was prepared. Every man donated a hardtack as the basic ingredient. Placed in a canvas bag and pounded with a sledgehammer on top of a mooringbitt, the contents were reduced to a meal. This was kneaded to a dough, filled with dried fruit and spread out on a baking sheet, then brushed with margarine and lightly sprinkled with brown sugar. Our obliging cook placed it in the oven to bake, whence it was removed some hours later to be enjoyed by all hands.

And then there was "labskaus" (or "lobscouse") whose name and ingredients were a matter of many different opinions. It took the form of a hash, mainly composed of leftovers of salt beef, pork, crumbled hardtack, and other indefinable foodstuffs, causing it to be referred to as "mystery of the galley." In time it became a specialty, mostly served near the end of a voyage. It was a dish known and appreciated only by deepwater men. Many an old-timer was known to roam the docks on a nostalgic visit, sniffing the familiar aroma emanating from the galley of a just-arrived ship. There was always hope there might still be a dish of "labskaus" for him, for old times' sake.

Any self-respecting dietician would have regarded with disfavor the nutritional value of the daily fare consumed during a voyage of a year or more. But we throve on it in spite of the hoary tales of beriberi and other symptoms of malnutrition. German shipowners followed the practice of the British by issuing rations of lime juice to prevent scurvy.

CHAPTER

8

STRIKE UP THE BAND, HERE COMES THE SAILOR

The recorded history of men and ships has dwelt on the perils of the sea, the vagaries of the human element on board, and how shipmasters and their officers dealt with the problems peculiar to their calling.

Throughout the ages, seamen were held in low esteem. They were exploited by their employers, working for low pay and poor food under adverse conditions. Historical novels contained florid tales of profligacies as men, freed from the constraints of shipboard life at the end of a long voyage, suddenly found themselves in an environment welcoming them to the tune, "Strike up the Band, Here comes the Sailor."

With money in their pockets, some embarked upon a lifestyle whose principal ingredient was the proverbial "Wine, Women, and Song." Exploited by unscrupulous boardinghouse keepers and hangers-on, their money was soon gone, as well as their welcome. Their hosts treated them to a few beers on the house and advised them strongly to ship out. Whether robbed ashore or brutalized on board ship, seamen had little redress in the courts.

It was left to influential church groups to counteract the machinations of the shadowy denizens of the world's waterfronts. They established rooming houses where men, between ships, could stay at a modest price, and missions to cater to their spiritual needs. Their representatives visited arriving ships and invited seafarers to take advantages of these facilities.

The missionary zeal of religious organizations was eventually felt in the courts. The judiciary established rules and regulations to protect seamen against cruel corporal punishment on board ship and harassment ashore. Grievances were heard in consular offices abroad, or in admiralty courts in the homeport. In the United States, cases involving shipping matters were tried in district courts where seamen, perceived as poor and friendless, had the status of wards of the court.

Within the American judicial system the protection of "poor and friendless" seamen eventually reached the height of absurdity. A seaman fell off a barstool breaking his leg. His ship was $3\frac{1}{2}$ miles from the accident. The seaman sued the owners claiming that, although he was on leave, he was in the service of the ship. He sued for maintenance and cure and full care until his recovery. Another case involved a seaman who broke his leg when he tumbled out of a dance hall window. Apparently, he won his case when the court expanded on the doctrine of seaworthiness to make the ship owner liable for a seaman's own negligence.[*]

Improved conditions attracted youths of various levels of society to a profession where initial hardship in low-paying jobs were the norm. The expected rewards were promotion through various grades to the final goal: the command of a ship. Thus, I found myself in a fo'c'sle with an assortment of young men in their late teens or early twenties. They were intent upon a career in which the average term of service from deckboy to Master was considered to be thirty years.

The North Atlantic presented a most inhospitable scene, a condition which did nothing to enhance morale. Proceeding under reduced sail, the watch frequently manned the braces, with sea water sloshing around their legs, to bring the ship about on another tack. These tacks were usually scheduled at the turn of the watch to have all hands on deck for the hazardous maneuvers.

Early on in a voyage, men begin to observe and evaluate each other by the only yardstick carrying weight: performance under stress. The sharp eyes of the men before the mast soon had the cut of the jib of the officers,

---

[*]   "Torts: Admiralty Happy Wards," *Time Magazine,* April 2, 1965.

their strengths and weaknesses. The captain was a graybearded veteran of many Cape Horn passages. Experienced, he was at ease with all the problems inherent in long voyages. To the crew, he was "The Old Man."

The first officer was a handsome fellow sporting a spade-shaped beard, always neatly trimmed. A widow's peak gave him the appearance of Mephistopheles. Easily excitable and in a perpetual state of agitation, he was soon in the bad graces of all hands. Habitually sarcastic, it was discovered before long that he was not quite sure of himself. His voice would rise and crack as he shouted orders he expected to be carried out before the last word had left his lips. Watching the men move about, he had a nervous habit of playing a tattoo on the seams of his pants, a quirk that earned him the nickname of "The Piano Player."

The second mate also had a fine brown beard. The rich brown coloring was due in part to a steady flow of chewing tobacco juice. Reared in a family-owned fishing boat, he had become a seaman before entering his teens. Leaving the strenuous family business to seek his fortune in off-shore trade, he was a stolid individual who knew his business. Esteemed by the men on his watch, he was referred to good-naturedly as "Herring Tamer."

Harsh corporal punishment now being prohibited under the law, "haz-ing" was introduced as another method of discipline. It was practiced in two forms, psychological and physical, and had the advantage of leaving no outward visible signs. In the early stage of the voyage, I was informed by several able seamen (A.B. for short) that, in their opinion, the ship was severely undermanned. I was admonished that every hand counted and that everyone (meaning me) was expected to do his utmost to ease the state of short-handedness.

I swallowed it hook, line and sinker. I was elated and imbued with a sense of pride to be regarded as a useful member of this august group of sailormen. I vowed to myself that I would, without hesitation, undertake any task, however difficult. This feeling of pride and belonging was rudely injured when the watch officer, the second mate, berated me as the most useless article he had ever encountered, an imbecile, stupid and a total loss. The smooth delivery of this harangue seemed proof that others before me had received the same treatment. He would conclude his rant-ing with: "When I order the watch aloft, I want you to be the first one up."

I came to regard all this as standard procedure. I thought that my quiet acceptance and bland expression, showing neither fear nor resentment, infuriated him, but I carried on as best I could from day to day.

The physical side of discipline included sending the offender over the top three successive times. A senseless form of penalty, it had the beneficial result of body building. At other times, I was sent up to the main crosstrees for an hour. Approximately a hundred feet above the deck, it was not a comfortable place to either stand or sit. It was discontinued when I failed to come down to relieve the helmsman or lookout. A seaman, sent up to investigate, reported that I had secured myself with a piece of rope and was sound asleep.

No work was performed on Sundays or during hours of darkness, save for the wheel and lookout tricks, but the watch was required to remain on deck. In fair weather, it was the custom of the men to stretch out on the hatch for a nap, while I was required to remain awake and alert. This custom was known as the "whistle turn." In the event the mate blew his whistle, I was to respond on the double to learn his wishes and arouse the others to whatever task was at hand.

After finding a seat on a spar near the lee bulwark, the murderous two-watch system took its toll. Soon I succumbed to the slumber that, as a growing boy, I was unable to resist. Aroused by vicious shaking, and still half asleep, I stumbled in the direction of the poopdeck. Because I had not responded to the watch officer's whistle, I was ordered to shoulder a heavy capstan bar like a musket and march up and down on the leeside of the poop.

Following several repeat performances, this eventually took on the aspects of a comedy. Out of the corner of my eye, I could see the watch officer on the weather side. His face bore an expression of uneasiness and concern. He would avert his face and avoid my glance in his direction at the turn of my walk. At times he came over to talk to me. I would stand, stock-still, staring straight ahead in silence.

Eventually, both he and I tired of this farce. He ordered me to replace the bar in its rack and, laying his hand on my shoulder, said, "When you go down, step into my room and fill your pipe from my tobacco can."

When my next whistle turn came, he handed me a length of marline, a light rope, and said, "Sit down at the break of the poop and tie this end to your hand. I will secure the other end up here on the taffrail. Instead of using my whistle when I want you, I will give the rope a yank to alert you." When the men heard of this arrangement, they howled with derision, calling it crazy. I did not share their sentiment. Throughout the years, I always remembered this kind and compassionate man.

The fore and main masts each carried five sails. Counting from below, they were named foresail, mainsail, lower topsails, upper topsails, galant sails, and royals. The mizzenmast carried two sails, the spanker and gaff-topsail. Between the masts were from two to three staysails. From the foremast to the jibboom were the fore staysail, inner jib, middle jib and outer jib. The squaresails were attached to crossmembers called yards. They were stationary at the mast except the upper-topsails yards and the royal yards which were hoisted by halyard purchases.

The masts were secured in their upright positions by strong wire ropes. They led forward from the mizzen to the mainmast and from the foremast to the jibboom. Others led aft in support of the masts. At each side, from the masthead to the deck, a set of heavy wire ropes provided lateral support. Usually there were seven or more. They were crossed by iron bars, wooden staves or small ropes called ratlines. This assembly was named shrouds and served as ladders. All of this was known as the standing rigging.

The running rigging included halyards, downhauls, buntlines, clewlines and staysail sheet ropes. Halyards were generally single whips. Certain yards and their sails were hoisted or lowered by halyard purchases.

Teakwood rails ran along inside the shrouds and around the foot of the masts, containing a number of belaying pins. Each rope of the running gear was made fast to its iron pin. When instructed in this procedure, the emphasis was on belaying a named rope to the same belaying pin without fail. In this manner, ropes and their assigned pins could be identified by touch in total darkness. By frequent inspection, I could soon distinguish each rope and the purpose it served.

Buntlines and clewlines served to haul a squaresail up to the yard to be furled. Buntlines were rove through a single block well above the yard, led forward down to the foot of the sail. When a sail was set, the buntlines were overhauled to hang in a small bight below the foot leech to prevent chafing of the canvas. For the bight, the buntline was stopped off with sailtwine at the jackstay. When it was to be furled, a sharp tug from the deck below broke the stopper. This was not a very efficient method, and it became my daily job to renew stoppers that had broken during the night.

The next requirement was learning to "box the compass." Boxing the compass was a method of committing to memory all the points on the compass card, down to quarterpoints. It was not a difficult task. In a day's time, I was able to recite from memory all the points from North to East, to South, to West, and back to North. Having taken this hurdle, it was suggested that I would soon learn how to steer the ship. I thought the men were trying to play a joke on me, but I was soon convinced that grooming the youngest to become a helmsman was an accepted practice. I was advised that the Sunday watches, when no other work was performed, was the time to try it.

With the consent of the watch officer, I was allowed to put my hands on the wheelspokes and follow the moves of the regular helmsman. He would instruct me how to keep the course, how to outguess a lively compass card and to anticipate and compensate for the ship's tendency to luff to windward or fall off to leeward.

When contrary winds prevailed, the compass was ignored. The ship was closehauled and the helmsman ordered to steer "by the wind." It involved the squaresails to be trimmed in the shape of a fan. The lowest sail was at a sharp angle to the fore and aft line, others gradually less so until the highest, the royals, were almost square. The trick was to bring the ship close to the wind until the weather royal sheets, that is the lowest corners of the sail, were beginning to shiver. This allowed all other sails to draw and some headway was achieved. When it was desired to cover more distance, the course was "full and by." Still closehauled, the ship was sailed close to the wind with all sails full and drawing. In either case, it demanded the closest attention of the man at the wheel, who stood with his head tilted back and eyes glued to the royals.

One morning, a rising sun tinting fleecy clouds, the wind changed and steadied. A warm air no longer carried the sting of the North Atlantic. All hands turned to with a will to trim the sails to a lively quartering breeze. The ship had fetched the Northeast Tradewind. With very little change in the wind, as to force and direction, it was necessary only before nightfall and at daybreak to routinely set up on the sheets, halyards and braces. It left the daylight hours to the never-ending tasks of scrubbing the deck, scaling and painting, varnishing teakwood rails, and polishing bright-work.

To each mast an A.B. was detailed to work aloft. He carried a ditty bag slung over his shoulders, filled with the tools of his trade: marlinspike, pricker, spunyarn, marline and ratline stuff to overhaul shrouds, blocks and running gear. Footropes were sent down to be overhauled or replaced against the day when they must safely carry the weight of men straining to fight ballooning and flapping canvas in a rising gale.

I learned to worm, parcel and serve the wire footropes. "Worming" means to wind a thin rope to follow the lay of the wire. Parcelling was done by winding a narrow strip of burlap around the length of the wire secured by marline hitches. Following a liberal application of stockholm tar, serving was the final step. It involved wrapping spunyarn tightly around the whole by means of a serving mallet.

It was also a time for me to stand wheel watches to free the more experienced for the work on deck. The day I was first allowed to take the wheel on my own on the regular two-hour trick was a never-to-be-forgotten thrill. Still a stripling, I was overcome by an indescribable feeling of exhilaration as I stood behind the wheel and handled the ship, this winged wonder, as she heeled to a stiff breeze, her stern rising and falling, her bow yawing under the push of a quartering sea. But this most pleasant aspect also had a down side. It developed that the connivers on the watch managed to weasel out and stick me with their Sunday wheel tricks.

Ships, on long voyages, carried two full suits of sails. The first and better one for stormy weather. The second suit of older sails was used in the milder region of the tradewinds and exchanged again in preparation for the tempestuous Cape Horn passage.

Beginning at daybreak, it was again "all hands on deck." One watch hauled sails out of the sail locker to be stretched out on deck. The other watch was aloft, unbending sails and lowering them down by means of a gantline (single whip). It was a full day's work, sometimes ending by the light of a full moon. Each watch being assigned to a mast, it became a sporting event, both watches competing to finish first.

The days were now sunny and warm. Squaresails, staysails, jibs, spanker and gaff-topsail, every rag was set and drawing. The ship bowled along through the whitecaps with a bone in her teeth, while schools of porpoises, albacore and bonitos raced along under her bows.

It was flying fish weather. Men sat in the jibboom rigging with hook and line. A hook was covered with a white rag to resemble a small fish. Dancing just above the bowwave, a hungry bonito would leap out of the water and take the bait. Occasionally, a windborne flying fish, escaping a pursuer, would land on deck and, along with the bonito, wind up in the cook's frying pan. It was a welcome change to the one-sided ship's diet.

One day a snatchblock was rigged to the vertical stock of the starboard anchor. The end of a line led to a hand-held harpoon in the hands of the mate. Sitting in the jibboom netting, he hurled the harpoon into a surfacing porpoise. It took the whole watch to haul the big fish on board. The harpoon having penetrated the ribcage, the catch was dead before it was landed on deck. The skin and its underlying inch of white fat was rendered for its oil. Among German seamen the porpoise was known as pigfish because of the reddish color of the flesh. It was served to us on alternate days, boiled, fried, breaded and finally pickled in vinegar. Everyone was glad when it was over.

In this temperate weather, the sailmaker was perhaps one of the busiest men on board. Sitting on his sailmaker's bench, he was engaged in making a new lower topsail. I was detailed to work with him to learn the rudimentary skills of sailmaking. My first job was to apply stockholm tar to a skein of sailtwine. It was done by coating the palms of my hands with tar and rubbing it into the twine. The tar served as a lubricant and preservative.

From a roll of canvas, the sailmaker cut the required lengths of the material. The piece of canvas was called a cloth. Made of closely woven hemp, it had a pale beige color. Along the sides of the cloth ran a single blue thread perhaps an inch and a half wide. Overlapping cloths were sewn along the blue thread, first on one side, then turned over to be sewn on the other side.

The instruments of sewing canvas are palm and needle. The palm is a leather strap fitting around the hand with a hole for the thumb. In the center is a metal disk with a number of indentations to keep the needle from slipping as it is pushed through the canvas. The needle is a sharp, three-cornered instrument.

I learned to sew canvas, even stitches along a straight seam with no fewer than seven stitches to the length of a number fourteen needle. Thanks to the patience of this old-time sailmaker, I acquired skill in handling the palm and needle. It was to come in handy many times before the voyage ended.

Engaged in other activities, I had no part in finishing the sail. The final steps involved sewing the canvas, reinforced by lateral strips, along the top and bottom to the leeches, ropes acting as a frame. The upper leech was called the bolt rope. It served to attach the sail to the jackstay on top of the yard.

The ropes on the sides were called standing leeches. Along the bottom it was called footleech. Both sides and bottoms were made of light wire to withstand winds of gale force. This final act of "framing" demanded consummate skill as well as strength. A much larger palm and bigger needle were used, the eye of the needle large enough to take several thicknesses of sailtwine. Pushing the needle through several thicknesses of canvas and hauling the thick twine through the hole was done with the help of the sailmaker's pliers whose jaws were rounded and smooth lest they cut the twine.

One day the wind slackened to a light breeze, followed by the baffling calms, stifling heat, and sudden rainsqualls of the equatorial doldrums. Again it was "all hands on deck" to a weary round of manning the braces to trim the sails to every little puff of wind shifting maddeningly around all points of the compass. Exhausted and ill-tempered, the men grumbled and muttered under their breaths. But they knew full well that this breeding ground of the feared West Indies hurricanes was no place to linger. They bent their backs to the relentless task.

There was, however, the compensation of an abundant, if temporary supply of fresh water, dumped on the ship from rain-swollen clouds. It was a welcome opportunity to fill the empty water casks, rinse out salt-caked clothes and prance around in our birthday suits, luxuriating in the sting of the pelting rain.

Partly drifting as well as catching every little errant breeze, the northern limits of the Southeast Trade Winds was eventually reached. The words "watch below, go below" was music to our ears. Routine work and watch duties were resumed.

However, having escaped a hurricane, Father Neptune was not to let things slide that easily. He shook out of his bag of tricks a "Pampero," that ferocious land wind blowing seaward from the Argentine Pampas.

A wall of impenetrable black clouds, illuminated by bolts of lightning, appeared in the west. A warm wind carrying the aroma of a lush countryside increased rapidly in force. Some exotic birds, driven from their habitats and borne by the wind landed in the rigging or on deck, among them several large grasshopper types with scarlet bodies and green wings. The even tenor of the trades thus rudely interrupted, both watches laid aloft to take in sails to meet this unexpected emergency. Because of the increasing force of the wind, all canvas was reduced to the fore and main lower topsails. Shortly, they were further reduced by the process of "goose-winging." It was accomplished by furling half of the sails, from the weather yardarm as far as the masts. A strong canvas belt, called the middleband, was wrapped tightly to further secure that half of the sails. This left only a triangular part of the sails on the leeside It was hoped that some steerageway and control would be possible. It was only a step away from being under "bare poles."

During the length of the disturbance, I stood two wheeltricks. It was an awesome sight as the ship was being tossed about from deep troughs to towering, white-crested seas and back again. Rolling and pitching, she shipped tons of green water, the scuppers and freeing ports in the bulwarks barely able to clear the deck before another load came on board. In this hellish cauldron of mountainous seas, OBOTRITA was a fragile plaything at the mercy of a cataclysmic force. Although a life line had been stretched along the deck, we were ordered to stay on the poopdeck, out of harm's way. In our oilskins, we huddled in the lee of the charthouse, without sleep or warm food, for the galley was tightly secured, pots and pans on deck and no fire in the stove.

The pampero passed as quickly as it had come. Within days we reached the southern limits of the Southeast Trades. Again, it was time to change sails, the second suit, somewhat battered, came down to be replaced by the better suit. Meanwhile the new lower topsail had been completed and was bent to the mainyard. Sheeted home, it was a perfect fit. Filled by a strong wind, in the rays of the rising sun, the golden tint of the canvas was accentuated by the seams in which every stitch of the dark twine was visible. It was a beautiful sight.

In appreciation of our escape from Father Neptune's present and under full sail again, we were told to stand by to "Splice the Main brace." The expression is a euphemism for the special occasion when every man is treated to a jigger of strong drink. I was at the wheel when the captain doled out a shotglass of liquor to each man. At the end he turned to me with the question, "I suppose you want one, too?" I answered in the affirmative. A shot of gullet-scratching Holland gin warmed my innards for the remainder of the watch.

THE FIRST
CAPE HORN PASSAGE

A favorable wind carried us into the South Atlantic. The warmth of the sun was tempered by a crisp and cold air. It was a chilly Sunday morning when I was relieved at the wheel. Descending from the poop-deck, I was stopped by the first mate at the mainmast. He ordered me aloft to overhaul the buntlines on the royal tight against the canvas. They had been stopped off in the days before, but had carried away in the night, not an unusual occurrence.

To reach the hoisted royalyard, it was necessary to step off the topgallant shrouds to a single ratline, called a rider, stretching to the royal backstay. The wire was cold to the touch as I shinned up to the royal yard. Expecting stronger winds during the night, I used a ropeyarn instead of twine for a stopper.

On deck again, I was confronted by the mate, pointing to the buntlines tight against the canvas and no bight. He ordered me up again. The wind had turned colder and a feeling of frost was in the air. I could barely get a grip on the wire backstay with numb fingers.

When I came down again, the mate told me I had not done a proper job. "Up again," he snapped. I told him I would not go up again because I could not maintain a grip on the icy backstay with cold fingers. With a malicious grin, he said, "Go in and tell that to the captain."

I entered the cabin door. I met the captain in the passageway and told him what I had said to the mate. Perhaps he had observed the incident through a porthole. "You need not go up again. Go back to the fo'c'sle and get warm."

I passed the mate without a word. "Where are you going?" he shouted, grabbing my arm.

"To the fo'c'sle. The captain told me not to go up again."

Muttering, he turned around and, went back to his quarters. Arriving forward, the sailors confirmed my suspicion that he had deliberately broken the stoppers each time I was descending. What had motivated the mate in this act of hazing? Pure malice, I thought. I had committed no offense and was not on his watch.

In the fo'c'sle, the topic of the daily conversation centered around the rigors of the Cape Horn passage. Everyone was prepared for the usually foul weather of contrary westerly gales and heavy rolling seas, forcing us further and further south. The long reach close to the Antarctic Circle before a turning point could be arrived at would lengthen the voyage by many weeks.

Contrary to all expectations and the dire predictions notwithstanding, it turned out to be a rare and remarkable passage under full sail. In the gray dawn of a cold morning, the bleak headland of Cape Horn, usually fog-shrouded, appeared on the starboard bow. A moderate easterly wind held fair while the Cape remained in sight all day, to disappear as night fell. The following morning the ship changed to the tack which was to carry her along the entire length of the west coast of South America.

One hundred and eight days out of the home port, the ship dropped anchor in the open roadstead under the yellow bluffs of the Peruvian port of Mollendo. It was an early Saturday morning arrival. After all sails had been furled, a security night watch was set. It left most of the men free to get a taste of the first shore leave over the weekend. I joined the group, dressed to go ashore, at the break of the poop to get a draw on our wages. The captain handed each man his allowed sum. As the last in line, he looked at me sternly. "So, you want to go ashore with the sailors?"

"Yes sir, I do," I said confidently.

"Well, I don't know whether I should allow that, a young fellow like you." I stood in silence, feeling that this was not a time to plead or argue. Following a lecture on the evils of debauchery, including consorting with females of questionable virtue, most of which was over my head, he handed me some money with the words, "You be careful, now."

I promised.

We were rowed ashore in one of our lifeboats. For the first time in my life, I set foot on foreign soil. We climbed wooden stairs leading to the top of the bluff and wandered around to get our bearings. There was a small park with a bandstand in the center. With the afternoon waning, we secured rooms at a hotel and exchanged some of our money for pesos. At a sidewalk restaurant, we had a few cold beers.

Strolling through the park, street venders offered their wares. Mostly Indian women, they were dressed in voluminous, colorful garments. All wore some kind of a high-crowned derby hat. From an elderly woman, I bought a folded pastry I thought was filled with fruit. Disappointed, I found it contained meat of questionable origin. When out of sight, I disposed of it in a potted palm container.

For a Saturday, it was a quiet evening. Stores were open. In the dimly lit interior of a grocery store, shelves were lined with brightly labeled canned goods. We chose several cans of peaches, chocolate syrup and condensed milk. Dinner at the hotel was the bright spot of the evening. Our labors, which had begun at daybreak, followed by the excitement of shoreleave, had left us exhausted. No one was in the mood for any further adventures. Sleep in the comfortable beds came quickly.

The luxury of sleeping late came to an end at the sound of nearby church bells. We enjoyed a late Sunday morning breakfast and checked out of the hotel. Our goal was the bright yellow sand beach, stretching for miles along the coast. The desire for a swim and for frolicking in the surf was quickly abandoned as we observed the heavy breakers and felt the strong undertow washing the sand out from under our bare feet. We had the clean beach to ourselves and enjoyed relaxing in the sunny day.

Mid afternoon, we observed the boat leaving the ship to pick us up. We were met at the head of the accommodation ladder by the mate and an observant captain at the poopdeck railing to ascertain that our packages did not contain any strong drink. So ended my first shoreleave in a foreign land. By the reputed standards of behavior of seamen on the loose, it was an experience that could be described only as respectable, if not dull.

And what was done with the canned goods? All of us shared the delectable peach halves in heavy syrup with our shipmates. I followed the example of others and pierced the lids of the chocolate syrup and condensed milk with opposing small holes to ensure a free flow. Coming off watch, the first thing I did was take a swig of the tasty contents. To preserve and guard against spillage, wooden plugs closed the small holes.

Everyone turned in early Sunday evening, anticipating the heavy workload of discharging the cargo. We were rudely awakened at daybreak by the nightwatch. Hot coffee and hardtack was the usual early fare. Soon the burly figure of the mate darkened the fo'c'sle door. "Turn to," he bellowed in the usual invitation to the day's work.

Some men uncovered the hatches, others were engaged in rigging the cargo gear aloft. A single gin block was centered high above the hatch opening at the end of gantlines between the fore and main masts. A heavy rope through the gin block served as cargo fall. One end led to the drum on the cargo winch, the other end to the cargo hook plumbing the hatch opening. The hand-operated cargo winches consisted of a wooden frame on heavy footing, anchored to the deck by sandbags. Two handles on the sides were manned by four men, two to each side.

Two heavily constructed launches or barges were observed leaving the beach area, propelled by two men manning heavy sweeps. We knew it would take some time to arrive at the ship's side, enough time for us to partake of a hasty breakfast of the usual mush, hardtack and coffee.

A variety of manufactured goods were handled through a daily ten-hour period. A weary crew welcomed the hour when operations ceased for the day. With bitter humor, the men called the winches "bone mills," alluding to their aching bones at the end of the day. The work was hindered at times as the ship rolled in the unprotected open roadstead. As a slingload came up, it was occasionally necessary to stop, lest the load smash against the hatch coaming, damaging some of the goods. These delays caused the captain to lengthen the workday to twelve hours. The men protested loudly and demanded overtime pay, to which he replied with unaccustomed sarcasm that he would pay no more than ten cents an hour.

Because of the small hatch opening in the forepart of the ship, unloading progressed slowly. The mate harangued the men to speed things up. In his usual "bull in the china shop" fashion, he decided to show them. He ordered the men to stand clear while he, single-handedly, would quickly hoist a load. The load this time was a single, fairly large barrel. Not constructed to hold liquid, the barrel staves were of light material held together by split willow branches. He brought the load up, heedless of the ship's roll. The barrel smashed against the hatch coaming and broke, spilling its contents, an assortment of small toys, into the lower hold. Without a word, he left the scene. We never found out what passed between him and the captain, except that the latter withdrew his threat of a twelve-hour day.

Our next port of call was Salaverry in Peru. A dusty little village nestling against barren hills, its anchorage was an unprotected open roadstead. With little cargo destined for this port, our stay was brief. At daybreak, favored by a land breeze, OBOTRITA stood out to sea, seeking the wind of the northern limits of the Southeast Trades to take her to Guayaquil, the principal port in the Republic of Equador, our final destination on the South American Continent.

Being close to the equatorial doldrums, the wind was gentle and slackening from day to day. When we entered the Gulf of Guayaquil, it died out altogether. To seaward, a glassy sea blended in with a cloudless sky. To the east lay the land mass of the continent. Instead of the arid dusty coasts of Chile and Peru, the countryside of Equador was lush with a dense green jungle. In the dead calm, all sails remained set except for the fore and mainsails which were clewed up and hanging in the buntlines to keep them from slapping against the masts as the ship rolled gently in a barely perceptible swell.

It was soon apparent that a current was setting the ship toward the coast. The land mass, earlier shrouded in mist, now appeared in greater detail. A single, brilliant white line of surf crashing against a narrow strip of yellow sandy beach was backed by the brooding, impenetrable jungle. It was a color combination worthy of a painter's palette. I was standing my early morning wheeltrick. Drifting about, the ship no longer answered the helm. In the quiet morning hours, the only sound was the creaking of the dry rigging and the gurgle of water around the stem and the rudder post.

An age-old sailor's superstition held that whistling on board ship would bring unwelcome strains. Anyone heard whistling on deck was quickly told to knock it off, but there was the exception called "whistling for wind," when a ship lay becalmed. The captain, a worried frown on his face, paced the deck restlessly, his well-browned meerschaum pipe clenched in his teeth. He took it out frequently, scanning the horizon with anxious eyes and whistling softly for the wind that, perversely, seemed far away. In desperation, he suddenly stopped in front of me.

"Boy, can you make wind?" he asked.

I was startled and taken off guard, but, sensing the "Old Man's" anxiety, I brashly replied with the supreme and foolish confidence of the young, "Yes sir, I can."

"Well, you better hurry, and if you do make wind, I will give you a carton of cigarettes." Naturally, I did not for a moment believe what he had said, but, no sooner had this exchange taken place, when, miraculously, a thin dark line on the distant horizon indicated the approach of wind. Within a short time, the welcome squeaky sound of the running gear tightening around cleats and belaying pins became audible as a lively breeze filled the sails and the ship clawed seaward and away from that menacing stretch of wilderness.

Relieved from the wheel, I returned to the fo'c'sle and triumphantly related to all hands the incident of windmaking and the captain's promise of a carton of cigarettes. The listeners were amused and skeptical, but seeing a chance for some fun, one said, "Well, are you going back for those cigarettes?"

"I don't think I should. He really didn't mean it."

"Didn't he? He made a promise, didn't he? So, go back and remind him."

"Aw, come on now, fellows, this isn't right."

"Look, you made wind, didn't you?"

"Yeah," I said, reluctantly.

"So, what's holding you back? Go ahead, I'll bet he'll give them to you."

Realizing that this prodding would have no end, I trotted back to the cabin, while the sailors watched with amusement and expectation to see me come flying out of the cabin door with the skipper's boot in my backside.

"Captain, you promised me a carton of cigarettes if I could make wind." He eyed me as I stood before him, literally shaking in my boots.

"Hmm, I guess you did make wind, and I did promise you those cigarettes." His face was serious, but there was a twinkle in his eyes as he handed me a box containing one hundred cigarettes. He said, "You tell those comedians forward I am still selling them in the slopchest."

Such were the humorous incidents that provided a welcome relief from the daily grind. The cigarettes were elegant in appearance, ovals, with a gold mouthpiece. They were very dry and the paper had tiny holes in them, caused by insects, and therefore were no longer salable. In the end, the skipper had kept his word.

The following morning, the ship anchored off Puna Island, at the mouth of the Guayaquil River to pick up a river pilot and engage a tug boat. In contrast to the dry air of the saltpeter coast, the atmosphere now was hot and humid in this port, close to the equator amidst a steaming tropical jungle.

Because we were now in the Tropic of Cancer, the workday for seamen was reduced to eight hours, by law. Being in this debilitating climate, native labor was employed to unload the vessel, leaving the crew to perform the less arduous ship's work. We deposited the goods on the open wharf and covered them each night with corrugated iron sheets against the rain. To prevent thieving, several large arc lights illuminated the area at night. Unfortunately, the brilliance of these lights attracted swarms of bugs, locusts and other flying insects, setting up an unceasing clatter during the night as their singed bodies fell and bounced on the iron sheets. Restful sleep was impossible. Mosquitoes carrying malaria took their toll of the crew. Giant cockroaches invaded the living quarters and storerooms. Torrential rains failed to relieve the oppressive heat. To keep the sails from rotting, they were unfurled from time to time to dry while hanging in the buntlines. It was a disagreeable task to go aloft and shake out the bugs, bats and other strange creatures from the folds of the canvas.

Although it had been half expected, diversion to Australia for a cargo of coal destined for Chile put a damper on the men's spirit, for it meant another six or eight months tacked onto the voyage. But, "more days-more dollars," was a compensation. Also, Australian ports were known to offer more pleasant diversions than the drab little communities visited up to now. In addition, there was the welcome prospect of fresh provisions to replace the daily one-sided fare we had been served in recent months.

Following the last draft of cargo out of the hold, shifting boards were installed fore and aft to the height of the tween decks. A cargo of clean sand was loaded as ballast. To further reduce the dangers of shifting, tween deck boards were used to cover the sand. Mooring chains crossed the planks to further stabilize the ballast. It was obvious that a rough passage was expected. Disabled crew members had been replaced with beachcombers only too glad to leave this port.

Whether for economic reasons, or because the low-powered tugboat could not have kept ahead of the ship borne on the swift river current, the unique method of using both anchors alternately to control speed and direction was employed. Leaving the wharf, the ship was allowed to drift, stern first, on the current's maximum strength. The greater depth of water was always found on the inside of the stream leading into a bight. To prevent contact with the shore, the anchor on the opposite side was dropped on a short scope of chain, causing the ship to veer away from the shore.

Once clear, the anchor was hove up again. The natural river channel had many turns, and steering the ship by alternately dropping the anchors was an exhausting procedure, further aggravated by the need of simultaneously bracing the yards on opposite tacks, lest the gear became entangled in the dense jungle growth overhanging the river banks. All maneuvers were executed by manpower. Fortunately, it was a bright night with a full moon. At daybreak, and clear of the river, sails were set. Except for the helmsman, the crew was given a spell to recover from the man-killing hours.

Once clear of Puna Island, it was "Turn to" again to wash down the decks and clear the scuppers of jungle debris. Shovels full of dried shells of giant cockroaches were cleared out of the living quarters. I opened my seachest to find my woolen clothes full of holes, occasioned by the voracious appetites of the now dead and dried-out insects.

As expected, the crossing of the Pacific was rough. One of the Aussies who signed on in Guayaquil to gain passage to his homeland died and was buried at sea. A crossing of sixty-eight days brought us within sight of land. A powerful sidewheeler tug boat guided us into the Hunter River estuary of Newcastle, New South Wales. The estuary was a solid forest of masts of windjammers of many nationalities, awaiting a berth under the coal-loading chutes.

Immediately upon arriving, a boarding party of a customs officer and doctor came aboard. Lined up on deck, the doctor in passing made eye contact with each man. I learned later that the purpose was detection of insanity. In accordance with local law, the customs sealed all provisions on board ship, including the captain's slopchest carrying clothing and tobacco products for the crew. All hands assembled in the fo'c'sle were required to surrender tobacco and cigarettes, to be returned upon departure. To tide us over the first few days, we were allowed some pipe tobacco and one hundred cigarettes for each man. The dual purpose of this law was to prevent the importation and clandestine sale of merchan-

dise and to bring money into the local economy, as the ship was required
to purchase local provisions while in port. Needless to say, we were in
total agreement with this latter arrangement.

For the first time in months, we reveled daily in such luxuries as real
butter, fresh bread, fresh meats and vegetables. With all formalities completed, the skipper doled out several pound notes with the admonition that
this would have to last for the expected layover of six weeks.

The other deckboy and I lost no time in heading across the river to the
nearest pub, only to be told that, since we were minors, we could only be
served lemonade. This was a heinous insult to a couple of lads practically
raised on beer, which we regarded as food. However, amendments were
made at another establishment where a buxom motherly barmaid slid a
couple of beers in our direction, well into a corner away from the open
door, thus assuaging the hurt to our pride.

The next day, Sunday, found us in town again to sample the local life,
only to discover that the place was shut down tight, the streets dark and
deserted, windows shuttered and doors tightly closed. In the face of the
utter darkness of the scene, our hearts sank. We had never heard of "Blue
Laws," having come from a country where Sunday was indeed a holiday
in the fullest sense of the word. Darkness had descended and, disconsolately, we weighed the advisability of returning to our ship, when, "Hey,
what's this?"

Out of the gloom appeared a large, nondescript building. A ray of light
fell across the steps through a partially open door and the sound of music
and singing was heard. As we peeked in cautiously, we were promptly
hauled in by a frock-coated gentleman and, without further ado, found
ourselves seated. Several ladies handed us hymnbooks and, somewhat
bewildered, we found ourselves joining in the chorus of "Jesus Loves
Me." This was not our first church attendance, having been raised in the
Christian faith, nor would it be our last, but it was not what we expected.

The "Seaman's Mission" on the Stockton side of the river where most
of the ships were moored was strategically located to take up the slack
when a sailor's limited funds had been expended in what by no means
could be called riotous living. For the ensuing weeks, the Mission became
our nightly goal. We enjoyed the service, followed by tea and cake and
the program of entertainment featuring local talent under the direction of
the minister, his charming wife, and his beautiful daughter.

CHAPTER 10

LIVERPOOL BUTTONS AND HOMEWARD-BOUND STITCHES

With ballast discharged, a full load of coal on board and hatches battened down, the ship put to sea again. In line with the standard practice developed over the years by navigators, an easterly course was shaped running on the fortieth parallel of south latitude, called the "Roaring Forties," on the stretch between Australia and the west coast of South America, where westerly winds of gale force prevailed. It was known as "Running down the Easting."

Always under reduced canvas, the passage had its dangers. Pushed along by giant combers, a vessel finding herself in a trough between two seas stood in danger of being pooped by a roller breaking over the stern. Helmsmen were secured with a rope around their shoulders, lest the kick of the wheel or a boarding sea toss them into the scuppers.

The composition of the crew had undergone some changes. English and Scandinavian seamen had been signed on to replace those who, having fallen under the spell of local lasses, had been left behind. Throughout the centuries in the mix of commerce between nations, the language on board ship had acquired an international flavor. Among others, English words and phrases were prevalent. In the words of a German author of sea stories, "English is our second mother language." Although none of us spoke English, we managed to communicate with our new shipmates

Wrecked in 1925, I served on the OBOTRITA from 1911-13

From the Gruelund collection.

and started learning a hitherto strange vocabulary.

No work could be performed on deck, constantly awash as the deeply laden ship was, running before a strong gale. One morning, an extraordinarily heavy sea came on board, breaking simultaneously on both sides at the break of the poop, sloshing waist-high as the ship rolled and pitched in a turbulent sea. Ordinarily, it had been my job to fetch the grub from the galley to the petty officers' quarters. In view of the dangerous situation on deck, the three men debated the advisability of having a "kid" like me undertake the perilous mission. I protested, since I had done the job under similar conditions.

After much talk, the carpenter volunteered to go, provided he could borrow the blacksmith's sea boots. The standard sea boot was knee-high, but the blacksmith's boots were expensive hipboots of fine Russian leather. He agreed and the carpenter, thus fitted out with hipboots, oilskins and southwester, sallied forth at an opportune moment, carrying pans and a teakettle.

We waited in silence, hearing only the crash of thunderous seas boarding the ship. Time passed, and our anxiety increased with every minute. In response to a pounding, the sailmaker cautiously opened the door. Through the crack, the carpenter's voice was heard. "Let me in, let me in!" he croaked, his dripping hair plastered over his face.

The author, June 1913. Age 17.

As he lay panting on the deck of the small room, there was no need to ask. He had been caught by a haymaker and had lost pans and teakettle. Groping about in the swirling water for whatever object he could grasp to keep from being washed overboard, he was stripped of his oilskins and southwester, and, worst of all, those beautiful seaboots. To the credit of the blacksmith, his comment was restrained. The carpenter's training had been acquired in the safe surroundings of a boatbuilder's yard. A seaman he was not. None of the lost items was ever recovered, except for the badly dented teakettle, found weeks later wedged under a spar on deck.

Running before a following sea in a strong gale, the yards were squared, the main upper and lower topsails and the fore lower topsail the only sails. I had the early morning wheel watch. Under a leaden sky, the air filled with wind-driven spume off the top of the crested rollers, it took all my attention to keep the wildly yawing ship on course. Out of the corner of my eye, there was a patch of sky visible where a sail should have been. A good-sized piece of the main upper topsail had blown out and was snapping on the outside of the standing leech. Within moments, it had torn away and, borne on the wind, was soon out of sight.

The duty watch was sent aloft to rig a gantline and unbend the damaged sail. The watch below had been called out to haul a replacement out of the sail locker. The task was aggravated by the tons of seawater on deck. Meanwhile, it was well past my time to be relieved at the wheel, but no one came. It took the best part of the day to bend the new sail and stow the old one in the sail locker. It was the longest wheel trick I ever stood, sixteen hours, and relieved only to take care of certain natural functions and to grab a quick bite and a hot cup of coffee.

Finally, an exhausted crew once again "spliced the main brace" with a shot of gin.

Within weeks, the ship left the fortieth parallel for the more favorable southern winds, and in time dropped anchor at the open roadstead of Antofagasta, Chile, ending a run of sixty-three days. For the last time this trip, the portable bonemills were rigged to discharge the cargo of coal and clean the hold for loading the new cargo of saltpeter. I watched with great interest the method of stowing the sacked saltpeter, accomplished by a single stevedore.

From the center of the hatch, a runway of planks to the forward end of the hold was built, shoulder high, at the tweendeck level. As a sling load of the heavy sacks landed on the tweendeck platform, the stevedore, his head, neck and shoulders hooded in an inverted gunny sack, backed to the tweendeck edge. One of our men was detailed to place a sack in the exact position for the stevedore to grasp two opposing ends. With the sack across his shoulders, he carried it at a trot forward and, with a flip of his body, deposited his load into its place with such precision that it was left there, not to be touched again. In the process of loading fore and aft, succeeding tiers would be drawn in until, when finished, the full load had assumed the symmetry of a two-sided pyramid. What manner of man was he, able to stand up under this exhausting task? He was a small, wiry fellow who almost disappeared under his load.

The ship was loaded, the stevedore and tallymen had left. The remainder of the day was spent in taking down cargo gear and battening down the hatches. The cargo winches were dismantled and stowed away. It was the universal custom of the time to celebrate the departure of a ship on the last leg of the voyage, terminating at the home port. It started with the ship's band, composed of accordion, violin, bass drum and other noise-making instruments, parading around the maindeck, followed by all hands. It ended at the break of the poop to serenade the "Old Man." For the last time, he dispensed a shot of firewater to each man.

The second phase of the program included a time-honored custom, peculiar to the saltpeter coast, where it had been developed over the years. Participated in by ships of many nationalities, it was international in character and testimony to the bond of kinship existing among seamen the world over. A large wooden cross with white and red lanterns at each end was hoisted at dusk at the foremast, as a message to the crews of all vessels present that our ship was ready to sail at sunup. The main event of the festivities was the ringing of the ship's bell. The crewman with the loudest voice, through cupped hands, gave "Three Cheers" to the nearest ship by name. The compliment was returned by that crew ringing their bell and answering "Three Cheers for OBOTRITA."

This exercise continued all evening, as all ships within shouting distance sent their bon voyage messages, which became fainter and fainter as ships were farther away. As a dramatic demonstration of international good will, it lasted well into the night, until an exhausted crew lowered and dismantled the cross and turned in for the night.

To ensure a safe departure with the help of the land breeze prevalent in the small hours of the morning, it was "Rise and shine" for all hands at daybreak. The anchor was hove up to short stay by the watch, while others lay aloft to unfurl sails and slack off on buntlines and clewlines. It was an occasion when the skipper himself took the wheel. As the anchor came clear of the bottom, the fore staysail was hoisted and sheeted home to provide steerage way as he skillfully maneuvered the ship to clear others in the anchorage.

Emerging from the chain locker, I was ordered to the wheel. With both watches engaged in making sail, it was only a matter of minutes when, under full canvas, all squaresails, jibs, staysails and spanker drawing in the freshening breeze, OBOTRITA stood out to sea, leaving a straight wake astern, homeward bound at last.

The skipper, having turned the wheel over to me, stood motionless, feet wide apart, thumbs hooked in suspenders as he scanned the lofty spars and sails gilded by the morning sun rising over the mountains. Overcome with emotion, he exclaimed, perhaps to no one in particular, "This is the most marvelous spectacle in the world, a ship under full sail!" Without another word, he turned and slowly made his way to the companion ladder leading to his quarters. Did I detect a tear in his eye? Was it born of an overpowering emotion at the sight seen many times before, a recurring reward to an old-timer who had spent a lifetime at sea?

The ship's bottom was foul, encrusted with barnacles and other marine growth, but she ran before the westerly gales around Cape Horn under narrow stormsails, like the albatross borne on slender wingspan. Fetching the southeast trades and heading north, once more and for the last time, we bent on the older suit of sails, not to be taken down again until we berthed at the homeport, where they would be discarded and exchanged for a new set.

The sails were old, and the canvas would no longer hold stitches at the seams. As the sky appeared through seams rent asunder, the sail would be clewed up, while I laid aloft with palm and needle and sewed on canvas patches with long looping, homeward bound stitches, for neatness was no longer required nor possible under the circumstances.

And what about our clothes? What was left of them was also held together by homeward bound stitches. Missing buttons were replaced by liverpool buttons, a simple device of drawing a piece of sailtwine through both sides of the garment and securing it loosely with a slipknot. Worn out shoes were repaired with pieces of old cowhide which already had done duty in the rigging as chafing gear. A Portuguese shipmate provided canvas slippers with rope soles. But what of it? That wonderful phrase, "homeward bound," made everything nice.

The original allowance of foodstuff had long since been expended and been replaced by the greatly superior fare obtained in Australia. The maggot-infested hardtack had been replaced by biscuits. A better grade of margarine and coffee were welcome additions. Saltbeef and saltpork came in barrels as before, and of much better quality. When opening a porkbarrel, expecting the usual assortment of sow bellies, I was taken aback when I found myself staring into the face of a whole hog sitting on its tail. In the process of transferring the contents to the harness cask, the choice pieces, such as the hams, shoulders, and chops were set aside by the second mate for the cabin mess. We ate what was left, and it was good. Canned mutton was the specialty of the week, served every Thursday.

Weatherwise, there were no surprises this time, as the ship worked her way through the doldrums and picked up the northeast tradewinds. In the North Atlantic, the ship was closehauled against a contrary wind, frequently changing tacks, leaving a zig-zag pattern of courses on the chart. More and more, an odd expression was heard in the daily conversation as

Obotrita wrecked at Ostend.

The end of a noble ship. Although WWI ended in 1918, German sailing ships were not released from their South American ports of refuge until 1921. All ships above a certain tonnage were turned over to the Allies as war reparations. OBOTRITA, below that tonnage, was returned to her owners, Eugene Cellier Co., which operated the ship in the saltpeter trade until she was stranded in a hurricane at Ostend on the Belgium coast in 1925 and then sold to a ship breaker.

From the Gruelund collection.

the men sat around discussing with anticipation the day of arrival at the home port. It sounded like "Daddledoo." No one could fully explain its meaning. In due course, I learned that it was a corruption of the English words, "That will do." As a single phrase, carrying a very special meaning, it traditionally was used only at that precise moment when the last turn of the mooring lines had secured the ship and the voyage had ended, the pay was stopped and the crew released from the bondage of the ship's articles.

One fine morning, a landfall was made at the entrance to the English Channel. I was ordered aloft to furl the fore royal. Upon descending, I was met by the second mate, who looked at me with approval, saying, "Well, you did a slick harborstow in record time." I was elated at this unexpected compliment. It had not been easy to furl that old sail with many patches, some on top of others. I had been aware in these last days of a subtle change in the attitude of the fo'c'sle crowd, where I was regarded with a new respect. I was no longer a child.

Tested in a life of danger, subjected to harsh and unexpected emergencies, I had grown to manhood, lean and muscular. I had been able to hold my own, be it furling a royal single-handed, holding a course in a howling gale, or manning the handle of a bonemill. I had reached the age of seventeen.

Entering the North Sea, we cruised under shortened sail in gale conditions off the Elbe River entrance. During hours of darkness, a blue signal flare was lit to indicate the need for a pilot. We soon made a rendezvous with the pilot schooner Elbe No. 2. A small gig under oars transferred a pilot. He took the conn and, cracking on more sail, headed the ship for the river entrance. Lowland communities of timbered brick houses with thatched roofs, protected by dikes, were on both sides of the river. Cherry orchards in full bloom were visible, the air was filled with the scent of their blossoms. It was the month of June, 1913.

Eventually, the wind slackened and a tugboat, lying in wait, was engaged. It had taken one hundred and twenty-three days from Antofagasta to Hamburg. At the end of a twenty-month voyage, the long awaited hour had come when we all expectantly grouped around the first mate to hear him say those magic words, "That will do." But there were others who had waited for this moment and who now leaped over the bulwarks and landed on deck. Tailors, shoemakers and boardinghouse runners buttonholed Jack to measure him for that new suit, those shining new shoes, or to arrange lodgings while he still had his payday. "The best is not too good, you know," a sentiment shared by others lying in wait ashore, whose motto was, "Strike up the band, here comes the Sailor."

I had a joyful reunion with Mother, aunts, uncles, and cousins. The following day, with Mother's help, I invested my earnings in a double-breasted blue suit, visored cap, shirts, underwear and shoes and an outfit for the next voyage. We took the train home, where I was greeted by my father and sister. I spent a number of pleasant weeks at home, roaming the old familiar trails with my former playmates. A day was dedicated to a visit with former schoolmates and I also paid my respects to former teachers. All listened with interest as I described shipboard life and the foreign ports I had visited.

Days and weeks went by. The time came, though all too soon, when it was time to say good-bye, time to ship out again, hopefully on a shorter voyage.

THE SECOND VOYAGE

In his heyday, Eugene Cellier operated four sailing ships to the West Coast of South America. They were the SCHULAU, built in 1895; BLANKENESE, built in 1898; GLÜCKSTADT, built in 1895; and OBOTRITA, built in 1892. With the exception of OBOTRITA, the vessels bore the names of communities located on the River Elbe, downstream from Hamburg. On the bluffs above the river, the communities, primarily residential in character, afforded a full view of the river traffic and were the favorite retreats of ship owners and ship masters.

With the exception of the barkrigged OBOTRITA, the other three were fullrigged. A fullrigger carries three masts, all fitted out with square sails. Because of my initial employment with Cellier, it was a foregone conclusion that I would continue to serve in his ships for the mandatory term of four years in squarerigged ships. Thus I found myself on board the BLANKENESE* as ordinary seaman (O.S.).

The position of ordinary seaman is "subordinate to an able-bodied seaman (A.B.). After his initial service under sail, he has learned a part of his trade and knows how to reef and furl a sail and to steer." I felt well

---

* BLANKENESE means "SHINY NOSE" in German. Why a community should have that name is beyond my ken.

Author's sketch of BLANKENESE.

qualified to fulfill these requirements.

Both BLANKENESE and SCHULAU, products of the same shipyard in Holland, were originally lofty, with royals above double gallant sails. Their hulls were full-bodied and broad of beam, with bluff bows, designed to carry a good payload at the sacrifice of speed.

As I boarded BLANKENESE, I noted with surprise the absence of all three royals, resulting in a stubby appearance. No one could provide a reason for this reduced rigging. The proverbial Ugly Duckling, she was dubbed a Baldheader. I gave no further thought to the matter until I did some research, in later years, on ships I had sailed in. Then I came up with what I believe to be a reasonable answer.

It so happened that, in 1910, her sister ship, SCHULAU, with a full load of general merchandise, ran into unusually heavy weather at Cape Horn. First, there was a failure of the standing rigging as the ship labored in a heavy seaway, followed by the loss of some masts and sails. It was discovered that the hull had sprung a leak and was making water. This combination of circumstances resulted in the ship's total loss, fortunately without loss of life. It is believed that this experience caused the downrigging in the BLANKENESE to prevent mishaps of a similar nature.[*]

---

[*]   Another unique feature was the main steel deck not covered by the conventional wooden deck. It gave the ship a decidedly unfriendly appearance.

Fully loaded, BLANKENESE cast off her mooring lines and, in tow of a powerful tug, descended the Elbe River, past and beyond the community she was named for. The destination was Talcahuano and Mejillones in Chile, and Callao, the principal port in Peru.

The crew was engaged in clearing the deck of mooring lines and preparing the running gear for sea. The first mate, ascending the ladder to the poopdeck, met the questioning glance of the skipper, who seemed to be asking, "What sort of crew do we have?" I did not hear his reply. Later, in the fo'c'sle, I heard someone say that the mate growled, "The usual gang. Fitted out by the whores and sent to sea by the police!" I did not believe this, inasmuch as the "gang" included the skipper's son and a nephew. I dismissed it as a well-worn hoary fo'c'sle tale.

The cabin crowd consisted of the captain, first mate, second mate, and one of the deckboys as cabin boy. The captain and first mate were two hard-bitten old seamen. Apparently having been together for some time, they had developed a means of communication in which the spoken word was replaced by gestures and eloquent facial expressions. Soon, one became aware that they had the utmost contempt for mankind in general, and for those serving under them in particular. When displeased, the skipper would roll his eyes heavenward, shake his head and mumble under his breath, a procedure fully familiar to the mate.

I recall one occasion when the skipper audibly gave vent to his wrath. The watch was aloft to furl a sail in a wind approaching gale force. The men obviously had difficulty in securing a ballooning canvas. I was at the wheel, both skipper and mate standing in the shelter of a canvas dodger-laced to the weather rigging. Observing the struggle aloft, the skipper was unable to contain himself any longer. He turned to the mate and pointing the stem of his pipe at the scene, shouted, "Look at them, look at them," in a rising voice, "our future admirals!" The mate nodded in agreement. The latter's forte was verbal abuse on deck, directed at the men, more often singling out an individual who had incurred his displeasure.

I was not the only one wondering about an attitude that created a climate of hostility in a life difficult enough as it was. Without a doubt, these two hard cases were seamen par excellence. In the harsh school of experience they had, over the years, attained a degree of expertise and perfection matched only by their intolerance of the perceived inadequacies of others. It was obvious that this would be a voyage full of adversities and never dull.

The men before the mast were, as expected, young men striving for a better future in the developing steamship trade. The voyage ran its course with the customary routine of changing sails and, in good weather, maintenance on deck. A major problem was combating rust on the iron main deck. Wielding hand-held chipping hammers in this most tedious task of scaling the extensive metal surface, progress was slow. The mate, impatiently, one day pounded the deck with a sledgehammer. The concussion of heavy blows caused large flakes of rust to come off the plates. At the time it seemed an efficient method, but a decided disadvantage was that the sledgehammer blows also loosened many rivets, allowing saltwater to enter the cargo hold and damage some of the goods. This disconcerting discovery at the first port of discharge undoubtedly caused some red faces.

The usual stormy Cape Horn weather caused the ship to be driven southward close to the Antarctic Circle, lengthening the voyage by many weeks. The discomfort of bucking adverse winds of gale force in a heavy sea, the cold air filled with spindrift, and the lack of heat in our quarters, took its toll on everyone's disposition. It was a relief when, at the end of a long reach, a course could be shaped to clear the South American land mass and head north.

After what seemed an eternity, the ship made a landfall at the entrance to the Port of Talcahuano, Chile. It was December 1913. A line was passed to a small tug which towed the ship through the narrow channel to a wharf.

Our stay included a Sunday and, with a deckboy and other seamen, I visited the neighboring city, Concepcion, capital of the province. Any memory of our visit to this city was blotted out by the wild ride in the ramshackle conveyance over a roadbed which obviously had seen no maintenance in many years. In the swaying second car, we desperately clung to our seats, hoping the vehicle would not leave the track. Entering the station at a reckless speed, the sudden jolting stop caused the iron towbar between the two carriages to snap. We caught a fleeting glimpse of the operator as he fled the scene.

There being no other transportation available for the return trip, we boarded the tram with trepidation. Another operator was at the controls who, to our relief, proceeded at a moderate speed and deposited us safely at our destination.

Within a few days, the cargo was discharged. On sailing day all hands were on deck to single up lines and unfurl sails, as the skipper impatiently paced the deck, perhaps waiting for the tug that failed to show up.

Fearing to lose the land breeze, he ordered all lines to be taken in at sunrise. The ship drifted away from the wharf. With the first few sails sheeted home, catching the gentle offshore breeze, the ship gathered steerageway and headed for the narrow channel. Following some anxious moments, the ship cleared the short waterway and stood out to sea. It was a daring feat of seamanship.

The next port was Mejillones and then Callao, principal port in Peru, where, across from us, on the other side of the finger pier, lay a French sailing ship. We were engaged in some task on the foredeck when the mate began to pummel Wilhelm, the boy on my watch. It took only moments for the French sailors to line the railing of their ship, shaking their fists and shouting *"Couchon! Couchon!"* ("pig" or "swine"), not knowing that they were lending their support to a Rhineland lad who was equally fluent in French as in German. The mate thought it wise to let up on the boy. That evening, Wilhelm visited with the French crew for several hours. They were glad that their demonstration had had its effect.

Again, it was across the Pacific in ballast to Australia and Newcastle N.S.W. for a load of coal destined for Chile. Nothing had changed: the forest of masts in the Hunter River estuary, the tedious wait for the loading berth. We followed the routine of a few beers in Newcastle as long as the money lasted, then to the Seamen's Mission on the Stockton side. Not unexpectedly, several of the men decided to leave the ship. Had I known what was in store for me, I might have left ship with them.

AMERICA-AMERICA

I awoke with a start. It was mid-morning and the sun was high in the heavens. I surveyed the unfamiliar scene. Where was I? What had happened? I realized the night had been filled with dreams of my youth. This was not a dream. Facing the reality of my displaced situation, I stepped out into the street. In the distance I could hear the screech of a saw. Following the sound I came to a finger pier housing a small saw mill. Moored to the pier was a fourmast schooner. Across the transom stern I could see the name, COLUMBIA, and its homeport, Seattle. She was discharging lumber. I joined her crew that very day.

On a cold and wintry December day, COLUMBIA approached the entrance to Juan de Fuca Straits under reduced sail. Snow flurries alternated with brilliant shafts of sunshine illuminating the densely wooded Olympic Peninsula. A light breeze carried the pungent scent of pine and fir trees down to the water's edge. Climatically, it was a vast change from the balmy air of the Hawaiian Islands to the frosty northern region of the State of Washington on the West Coast of the United States.

Our attempt to enter the waterway was frustrated by unexpected adverse winds and COLUMBIA remained outside for an uncomfortable night, wallowing in a moderate swell. At daybreak, a tug appeared and remained close to windward while both skippers exchanged greetings, the gossip of the day and, following much palaver, agreed upon a price for

Fourmast schooner COLUMBIA.

the tow to Seattle. It was late afternoon when I first set foot on American soil, the land of unlimited possibilities. It was January first, New Year's Day, 1920.

As the sole foreigner in the crew, I was lodged in the Immigration Station for the night. I was cleared the following day for entry and, upon paying a two-dollar head tax, was free to go.

I met my shipmates at a downtown hotel and they suggested that I join the Sailors' Union of the Pacific. We all trooped up to the office and, having given satisfactory evidence of basic seamanship by making a few rope splices and standard knots before a committee of three, I paid an initiation fee and became a member in good standing.

Before being paid off, the Master of the COLUMBIA had suggested that I remain in the ship as caretaker while she was in the shipyard for overhaul. I welcomed the assignment. I stayed on deck during daylight hours and slept in the fo'c'sle at night. I had shelter and a modest income for the duration and time to think things out.

The German economy was in a shambles. Her navy lay at the bottom of Scapa Flow. Her merchant fleet, except for a few ships below a certain tonnage, had been confiscated and divided among the Allies as war reparations. A radical element of Navy and merchant seamen, calling themselves The Red Navy, dominated the waterfront in Hamburg. The onerous conditions of the Treaty of Versailles were designed to keep a productive people in bondage for many years to come.

The prospects for the future were bleak. I stood at the crossroads. Should I return to the land of my birth and face an uncertain future, or should I seek my fortune in America, the land of my dreams? The decision weighed heavily upon my mind. Reports from the vanquished Central Powers were disturbing. Newspaper photos depicted a ragged people in long breadlines. Unemployment and a burgeoning inflation were rampant. Letters from home spoke of hard times and hopelessness, but urged me to come home. It was up to me to come to the rescue, I thought.

Slowly, I became convinced that the best course of action was for me to remain in America, and to assist my parents financially until they were able to fend for themselves. I agonized over this decision during sleepless nights. I was now twenty-four years of age and the urge to make up for lost time dominated my every waking thought. The pursuit of a career at sea, leading to the command of a ship had remained uppermost in my mind throughout the years of stagnation. The drive to reach that goal was like the search for the Holy Grail.

With these considerations in mind, I entered the offices of Immigration and Naturalization and filled out a form declaring my intention to become an American citizen. A lengthy document, with many searching questions, its most salient feature was the requirement that I take this *Oath of Allegiance* to the United States:

> "I hereby declare on oath that I absolutely and entirely renounce and abjure all allegiance and fidelity to any foreign prince, potentate, state of sovereignty of whom or which I have hereto been a subject or citizen, that I will support and defend the Constitution and laws of the United States of America against all enemies, foreign and domestic, that I will bear true faith and allegiance to the same, that I will bear arms on behalf of the United States when required by the law, and that I take this obligation freely without any mental reservation or purpose of evasion, so help me God."

The document further required an uninterrupted residence of five years in the United States. The mere thought of another five years of separation from my family was appalling. It was tempered by the idea that while

The author, age 24 (Seattle, 1920).

serving on American flagships calling at German ports, I might on occasion be able to visit my family. The execution of this awesome document
left me emotionally drained.

There being no immediate prospect of making it to the East Coast and
being short of funds, I signed on as quartermaster in a passenger ship
called ADMIRAL SCHLEY. The ship was operated routinely from Puget
Sound ports to San Francisco, San Pedro, San Diego and return. Of these
ports, I enjoyed the one-night layover in San Diego the most, with its
euphoric climate of balmy air and clear skies. Pollution was not yet a
word in everyone's vocabulary.

It was a year of serenity. A steady income enabled me to send small
sums of money and a monthly food package to my family. From the
University of Washington State, I purchased a correspondence course in
navigation. My watch officer, an elderly gentleman of Norwegian birth
who had once operated his own sailing ship, applauded my decision, but,
shaking his head sadly, he said, "I wish you luck, my boy." He continued,
"The American Merchant Marine has not and will not be able to compete
with foreign flag vessels in international trade. The exception will be the
coastwise and intercoastal commerce, now the exclusive sphere of operation for American flag vessels by an Act of Congress, prohibiting foreign
flag ships trading between two or more American ports."

At the turn of the 19th Century, following the advice of Horace
Greeley, young America engaged in settling and developing the vast territory west of the Mississippi River, abandoning sailing schooners for
lumbering ox drawn prairie schooners. When called upon, they left the
land to man the ships in World War I, at the conclusion of which they
returned to their farms.

As the year ended, I began to cast about for employment with higher
earnings. I had heard about steam schooners carrying lumber products
exclusively and paying high wages. I paid off the ADMIRAL SCHLEY
and within days joined the steam schooner SANTA MONICA. She carried a full load of redwood from Eureka to San Pedro, the latter port
serving the burgeoning Los Angeles area.

Because the work was hard, the ship paid exceedingly well, but higher
earnings were only achieved by working many hours of overtime. At the
end of one round trip, I concluded that this type of back-breaking work
added little to my knowledge of seamanship. I was relieved of the decision to get off when the Sailors' Union called a strike.

It was February 1921. All members were assigned to picket duty. I drew the area of walking the picket line on the San Francisco waterfront between Piers 16 and 18. Pickets in those days carried no colorful scarves or picket signs, but merely walked their assigned beats for the purpose of dissuading prospective strikebreakers from crossing the picket lines. In appearance, we were no different from other pedestrians.

I had taken a room in a small waterfront hotel. The weather was cold and rainy. The days turned into weeks and the dreary rounds at the picket lines took their toll. The Sailors' Union actually had a contract with the steam schooner operators, not with shipowners in the intercoastal and offshore trades, but the union took this opportunity to expand and extend its influence in the industry. It turned out to be a total failure. The Sailors' Union had not had the support of any of the other waterfront unions. The steam schooner operators, knowing what was coming, had stocked their lumber yards to full capacity, tied up their ships on the mudflats of the Oakland estuary and sat back to await the inevitable outcome.

Soon many union members were out of funds and receiving small sums of money from the Union. Some subsisted on sandwiches and coffee served at headquarters; others bedded down on the floor.

Meanwhile, shipowners had no difficulty in manning ships in the intercoastal and offshore trades with the unemployed caught in the wind-down of an economy attempting to adjust from wartime economy to peacetime retrenchment. The process of husbanding the nation's resources was entrusted to Herbert Hoover, a mining engineer who later became President of the United States. "Hooverizing" became the slogan of the day and soon became a word of bitter humor among the desperate jobless. In an atmosphere of disillusionment, "It's everybody for himself and the Devil take the hindmost" was the motto of the day.

A radical element within the Union was beating up strikebreakers wherever they could be found. They'd hired a launch and it was a matter of record that the militants boarded ships at anchor and beat up the crews. With this development, the police department withdrew the old-time, tolerant waterfront cops. With their florid faces, flowing mustaches and long uniform frock coats, they had been a part of the waterfront scene for years. They were replaced by young husky policemen, traveling in squads of six. Came the day when I was confronted on my beat by a young husky of a squad.

"Hey, Bud, what are you doing here?" he asked.

Nonchalantly, I replied, "Just taking in the sights."

He thrust his face forward and snarled, "You've seen enough now; beat it." I did.

Upon returning to Union headquarters I encountered a small group being harangued by a hotheaded member: "I want you to follow me. Wherever we find scabs, it is not enough just to beat them up. Throw them down, stomp them, break their arms and legs, that will teach them."

I listened in silence. To walk a picket line and argue with someone trying to cross the line was one thing, but to engage in acts of mayhem and possible murder was something I was not prepared to do. Others in the group made no comment. The young militant screamed in fury, "You are uninterested! You haven't the guts to defend your jobs!"

The men drifted away from the scene. That evening, the strike was declared lost. The membership was told to return to work. Shipowners now had full control of hiring. They opened a hiring hall presided over by a retired police captain. Every applicant was issued a book recording his name, history of service in named ships, efficiency, sobriety and conduct, over the signatures of shipmasters. It was a system traditionally abhorrent to Union members. But they had no choice.

I took stock of the situation. I had nine dollars left, enough for two more nights of lodging, but nothing for food or Union dues. On board ship, I was certain to encounter the hostility of strikebreakers, nor was I enthused at the idea of becoming shipmate with men who had manned ships while I and others had walked the picket lines.

It was a dreary, drizzly day as I wandered disconsolately up Howard Street. A sign in a storefront window proclaimed it an employment agency. In the open door stood an individual.

"You looking for a job, Bub?" he asked. Without thinking, I said Yes. "Do you have a dollar?"

I exchanged one for a piece of paper directing me to a building on lower Market Street. The logo on the glass pane of the office door read:

George S. Beadle
Lumber and Shipping

At the door, I was met by a portly gentleman. He took my employment slip and instructed me to be at a bus terminal at Fifth and Mission Street the following morning at eight and board a Red Star Stage Lines coach which would take me to a logging camp in the Santa Cruz Mountains. I had been hired to be a swamper.

The destination was Gazos Creek, a deep and narrow canyon, several miles south of Pigeon Point Lighthouse on the California coast. The coach turned out to be a Packard touring car. The five person seat capacity had been increased to seven by collapsible jump seats. As one of the last to board, I drew one of those contraptions. It was not designed for comfort.

Highway One was then a narrow two-lane road, snaking in and out among gullies. The first stop was at Pescadero, a small fishing and agrarian village. Several passengers disembarked, giving me the opportunity to change to a more comfortable seat in the rear. A young man, sitting next to me, introduced himself as the bookkeeper of the logging camp we were bound for.

It was a sunny day in mid March. The clear air was redolent of the aromatic fragrance of the dense chaparral covering the hills. The vast acreage of the flatlands was cultivated and planted in cabbage and artichokes. To the west lay the great expanse of the Pacific Ocean. Viewing this attractive scene, my spirits rose.

In mid-afternoon, the stage deposited us at the entrance of picturesque Gazos Creek canyon where a company vehicle took us to our goal. The camp consisted of a sawmill, skidroad, a millpond, bunkhouse, cook shack and the owner's quarters. I was assigned a one-room shack containing a bed and chair. Ablutions were performed at a pipe extending from a nearby water tank. Another facility was a single outhouse known in the parlance of the day as a "Chick Sales."

In the pecking order of logging camps, the men felling the trees stood at the top. Intermediate jobs were held by others cutting the trees into prescribed lengths. They were called buckers. Choker setters applied a wire to a log hauled by a steam-powered donkey engine to the skidroad where chasers took over until the logs were in the millpond. At the bottom rung of the ladder was the swamper whose duty it was to clear the brush from the base of the trees to provide access for the fallers. It turned out that at the steep hillsides there was no underbrush. The woods boss showed me how to set the wire chokers and follow the logs to the skidroad.

Once a month, the company-owned steam schooner CLEONE would anchor in Pigeon Point Cove to lift sawn lumber, hand-split railroad ties, fence posts and grape stakes, shakes and occasionally products of the Peninsula Farm Company.

With my background, it was inevitable that I should be detailed to the loading operation. On a bluff high above the cove was a platform with a small shack housing a winch surmounted by a high frame accommodating a wire highline and backhaul wire.

Preparatory to the ship's arrival, slingloads of lumber and split stuff had been made up on small narrow-gauge flatcars in the staging area. With the ship secured on station, I would fire a projectile across her maindeck, attached to a line from a linethrowing gun. The ship's crew would send back a rope, called a messenger, which, when bent to the wire highline, was hauled back to the ship. The highline was secured to the top of the ship's mast. The actual loading operation took only the two of us, the woods boss at the winch and myself hooking on the loads to a traveler on the high wire. With the load above the deck, the ship's winch driver took over the load.

With the advent of summer and school vacation, the population of the camp was augmented by the owner's family and a recurrent flow of family friends and their children. All the young folks were of high school age. The boys took over jobs in the camp as they became vacant, to earn some money.

One day, I entered the company store to make a small purchase. I was greeted by a smile that lit up the room like a sunburst. The smile belonged to a young woman behind the counter. Her name was Carolyne. She was seventeen, the owner's daughter. Following an exchange of pleasantries, I stumbled out of the store in a daze, forgetting to take my purchase. It was a fateful encounter for both of us and could only be regarded as love at first sight.

For entertainment, the visitors organized barn dances on Saturday nights, held in the camp's dining room. Along with other young camp workers, I was invited to take part in these festivities. To the music of squeaky phonograph records, we danced the Virginia Reel and others . A Fourth of July hayride and occasional Sunday visits to the beach and boardwalk in Santa Cruz made the summer months go by quickly.

Following the first rain, the roads became impassable and the camp was shut down for the rest of the year. The steamer CLEONE made one last call to pick up a load. Upon request, I agreed to stay at the Pigeon Point establishment, consisting of a bunk house, cook shack and owner's cabin, pending re-opening of the camp the following spring. For company, I was asked to keep the family dog, a mongrel of dubious antecedents, but a faithful companion. I became acquainted with the families of the lighthouse keepers and enjoyed an occasional meal with them. Coastal waters teemed with fish. Fishing off the rocks with a handline and hook baited with limpet or mussel meat always brought in a good catch of sea trout, cabizon, and bullheads. At minus tides, luscious abalone could be pried off the rocks.

In the following year, most of the products were hand-hewn railroad ties, shakes and other split stuff. The mill was operated only part time, as the stand of timber was exhausted and prices for lumber products declined. At the end of the season, the company ceased operations.

Adjustment to life in my new country became an ongoing process. I found the people to have an extraordinarily well developed sense of humor. Trivial as well as serious events of the day were habitually discussed in a droll and frivolous fashion, frequently interspersed with wisecracks. There were times when I was puzzled by a strange or quaint expression. A co-worker would wink and say, "This is the day the ghost walks." A walking ghost? I wondered what he meant by that. I soon learned it referred to payday. Silver dollars became "iron men," lower denominations of paper money because of their color became "greenbacks" or "lettuce."

Another peculiarity was the universal usage of calling people by their first names immediately following introduction. Total strangers became "first name friends" at once. It was not easy for me to accept this custom, coming from a country where daily contact even with close associates was governed by a formality that had reached the stage of a fine art. In certain middle-class circles it had attained the ultimate level of freakishness, as wives were addressed by their husband's titles of office: Mrs. Teacher, Mrs. Postmaster, Mrs. Stationmaster, etc.

Visiting with newly made friends, I was impressed by the opulence of the daily dinner table even in the most modest of homes. Following the main dish of meat, potato and gravy there was always dessert of fruit and cake, *every day*. I came to understand the meaning of "The great American dream." By contrast, at home a full dinner was served only on Sundays at noon—perhaps a goose or a rack of venison when in season, a gift from the local game warden, a close relative. The venison would be prepared by my mother with infinite care. Employing a larding needle she would lard the lean venison with narrow strips of bacon and liberally baste it with sour cream while it was roasting. A side dish of potato dumplings stuffed with croutons was a great Bavarian specialty. Rounding out the meal was a fruit compote *or* cake, *never both at the same time.*

When we were newcomers to the region, the family was invited to my aunt's house for Sunday dinner. It was my first encounter with potato dumplings and a negative experience. I didn't like them and pushed them aside. An irate cook berated my mother. "This kid (she actually called me 'lausbub,' which, in this case, was not exactly a term of endearment) "doesn't like my dumplings? I know how to cook," she declared heatedly. Mother, ever the diplomat, succeeded in casting oil on the troubled waters. In the end it did not take long to become accustomed to the local cuisine; in fact, I developed a decided preference for this Bavarian specialty. Thinking about potato dumplings made me realize how much I missed my family and how long it had been since I'd seen my parents.

FAMILY REUNION

I presided over the shutting down and dismantling of the Pigeon Point establishment. At our last meeting, Carolyne and I agreed to correspond. I returned to San Francisco and registered at the shipowners' hiring hall. Shipping was slow. I paid daily visits to the hiring hall and within weeks signed on as quartermaster aboard the steamer LURLINE of the Matson Navigation Company. As the manager of the hiring hall handed me the seaman's book, he lectured me on the evils of striking and the consequences of disobedience to civil authority. I made no comment. The LURLINE was a single-ender, meaning her engine was aft. She operated on the triangle run from San Francisco, Seattle, Honolulu and return carrying passengers and freight.

I enjoyed the run until midyear and then paid off to join the steamer SEQUOIA as quartermaster. The ship was operated by the Lighthouse Service under the Department of Commerce and was berthed at the east side of Yerba Buena Island in the Bay of San Francisco. As a lighthouse tender the ship was at sea for periods of twenty-one days at a time, doing maintenance work on navigational aids on the California coast ranging from Northwest Seal Rock in the north, to San Diego in the south.

SEQUOIA, a twin-screw ship, was a honey to steer and handled well in a seaway. Of all the jobs on the maintenance run, one of the most difficult was coaling and watering the Blunts Reef lightship stationed at Blunts Reef south of Eureka. A mooring line was passed to the stern of the lightship, along with a water hose. The SEQUOIA's workboat was loaded with sacked coal, each sack weighing a hundred pounds. Along a messenger rope between the two ships, the workboat was hauled alongside to an open sideport in the lightship.

A rough-running sea had built up under a strong northwesterly wind. The lightship rode head to sea and could not provide a lee. Two crewmen held the workboat in position. Whenever an oncoming whitecap lifted the boat high enough, two of us would grab a sack of coal and toss it into the open sideport. It was a backbreaking day's work.

Supplying Northwest Seal Rock Light was a more dangerous undertaking. Located on a rock, seaward of St. George's Reef off the Northern California coast, the lighthouse sat high above sea level, exposed to weather from all around the compass. From a high platform, a cargo boom with a single whip, powered by a one-lung motor, extended well clear of the submerged rock.

On windless days, provisions were hoisted aboard in net slings from our workboat. The heaviest parcels were 55-gallon drums filled with kerosene. Although the sea was calm, there was always a swell. The second mate in charge of the boat had warned us to be prepared to roll overboard. He explained that the hoisting engine had a tendency to stall just when the load was suspended above the boat which, when lifted by an oncoming swell, would crush us under the hanging load. In anticipation of having to take to the water, we wore lifebelts. As predicted, the engine stalled at the first lift, but our alert oarsmen moved us clear in time.

En route south, we picked up buoys to scrape off their barnacles, gave them a coat of quick-drying paint and, having examined their anchor chains, returned them to the water at their charted positions, which were verified by the captain's taking crossbearings on charted objects on land before leaving the scene.

Approaching the channel islands, we stopped at Anacapa Island to refuel the automated light in a skeleton tower at the southern end of the island, then on to San Diego and return to the home base at Yerba Buena Island. Between trips, there were generally thirty days' layover, interrupted at times to tend the buoys and other navigational aids in Bay Area waters, or to inspect and overhaul anchor chains ranged on the pier.

Throughout the year, Carolyne and I corresponded. When I was in port, we spoke on the telephone and took Sunday outings. One outing took us to the top of Mount Tamalpais, then served by a unique narrow-gauge railroad. The descent was by gravity car to Muir Woods. It was an exhilarating day.

Occasionally, I was invited to dinner. The family observed with tolerance and with a certain degree of amusement that their older daughter had a boy friend, but they were not fully aware of the strong attachment we had for each other. We both thought of marriage but believed a formal engagement was premature. We agreed to keep company, awaiting the day when I made my way and was in possession of a competence sufficient to support a family. Going to sea was the best way to save money.

In December 1924, SEQUOIA went to a shipyard for inspection and overhaul. Leaving the yard one evening, I was hailed by a fellow whom I recognized as a former shipmate, a fireman from the ADMIRAL SCHLEY. He pointed to a white-hulled ship in drydock, GUIDE, a converted mine sweeper operated by the U.S. Coast and Geodetic Survey. "There's a vacancy on deck," he said. "We need a boatswain's mate, and you are just the man to fill the job."

The billet paid fifteen dollars more than I was getting and, following an interview with the executive officer, I signed on. Following overhaul, GUIDE sailed south to operate out of San Pedro. Her mission was to survey the waters west of San Clemente Island, the southernmost of the Channel Islands off the California coast. Included was Tanner Bank with a depth of ten fathoms.

The first job was to establish two radio stations on the west coast of the island, one on the northern and one on the southern end. The stations were manned by radio operators and their wives. Operators lived in tents and were provided with kerosene cook stoves. It was my job to put the operators, their equipment and provisions ashore by running a whaleboat under oars through the surf pounding the beach. It became a weekly operation. I found the work interesting and challenging.

Connected to each radio station were hydrophones attached to concrete blocks sunk well off shore. When out of sight of the island, a gunner's mate on board would drop small bombs overboard at scheduled intervals. The time the sound took traveling underwater to the beach was recorded at the radio stations and relayed to the ship to plot her position, additionally verified by soundings of the depths of water. The operation was conducted from sunrise to sunset. At night, the ship anchored on Tanner

U.S. Coast & Geodetic Survey Steamer GUIDE. Picture taken at Hanlon Dry Dock, Oakland, Nov. 1924., by E.C. Forner, 2nd engineer.

Bank. Each Saturday morning, the ship returned to San Pedro for fuel and provisions and went to sea again on Monday.

Prohibition was still the law of the land. One night, when at anchor, a powerful speedboat came within hailing distance, mistaking GUIDE in the darkness for a rumrunner. Using a megaphone, the operator attempted to place an order for various liquors identified by numbers. When informed that he was talking to a government vessel, the launch quickly disappeared in the darkness.

There was evidence that the island had been used to cache illegal alcohol. A number of five-gallon glass demijohns were found buried in the sand. Some crew members siphoned some alcohol into small bottles, and the deck crew got gloriously drunk that night. There were no future landings unless an officer was present.

During the months I was operating out of San Pedro, I received several notices to appear in naturalization court. Unfortunately, I was always at sea at the scheduled dates, which came at ninety-day intervals. In midsummer, GUIDE was ordered to Alaska via San Francisco, and I left the ship at that port to be available to appear when next summoned.

Going to sea was now out of the question. In order not to deplete my

The author, 1925. Bos'n's mate in U.S. Coast and
Geodetic survey ship GUIDE.

savings, I took a job in a lumberyard fronting on the Alameda side of the
Oakland Estuary. The wages were three dollars and seventy-five cents a
day. I paid forty-five dollars a month for room and board in a boarding
house that had once been an elegant old mansion. In past years, I had
acquired a rudimentary knowledge in lumber grading from my former
employer, George S. Beadle. Because of this and my background of
service with the steam schooner SANTA MONICA, I was placed in
charge when the steam schooner F.S. LOOP came alongside the yard's
pier to discharge lumber. Throughout the years, I had not neglected my
study of navigation, cargo and shiphandling. I had learned that evening
summer classes in navigation were to be held by a unit of the Humboldt
High School in San Francisco. I enrolled, and attended classes in the San
Francisco Ferry Building five nights a week during June, July and early
August.

From one of my classmates, I learned of a ship named MONTPELIER,
operated by the United American Line, a subsidiary of the Harriman
railroad interests. Running intercoastal and offshore, there was a strong

possibility of a call at Hamburg, Germany. I felt I could not miss this opportunity, citizen or no citizen, and immediately quit the lumber yard. My shipping card at the hiring hall was at the top and, within days, I was on board the MONTPELIER as an able seaman.

The first week in August 1925, the ship sailed north to load lumber and returned to San Francisco to complete loading. In my mail, I found a summons to be in court and, along with others, I became a U.S. citizen on August 31, 1925. Immediately following, it had been my intention to sit for a license in San Francisco. The imminent departure of MONTPELIER to New York and Hamburg frustrated that idea. I decided to sit for that coveted ticket in New York.

En route to the East Coast, I continued my studies, spreading my charts and books at night on the messroom table. I was observed by the chief mate, who offered his help, which I gratefully accepted. Some of my ship mates scoffed at my idea of sitting for my license in New York. One of them said, "When that old crank of an examiner finds out you are from the West Coast, you won't have a ghost of a chance."

He would not elaborate. I dismissed the thought from my mind, and pursued my studies, believing that solving all the problems in the examination room would have to result in the issuance of a license. Arriving in New York, I was granted a leave of absence. I rented a room at the Seamen's Friends Society, a place of barebone austerity but scrupulously clean. The following day, I went to the U.S. Customhouse at The Battery, where the Steamboat Inspection Service was located.

Entering the hallway, I observed a sign reading, "Get license application here." Most applicants filed for a third mate's license. As provided by the regulations, I was able to file for an original second mate's license, because of my many years of service before the mast. I filled out the form and presented it to the examiner in the examination room. He asked, "Are you ready to sit?"

I was. Three days later, I walked out of the building with an original, unlimited second mate's license in my hand. It was the 13th day of October 1925. Regarding the term, "unlimited," I quote in part:

> "That he is a skillful navigator and can be entrusted to perform the duties of second mate on steam vessels of any gross tons, upon the waters of any ocean."

I rejoined the MONTPELIER the same day and soon was at sea, bound for Hamburg. It was an overcast and chilly day in mid-November when

Family reunion, 1925.
The author with father, mother and sister.

MONTPELIER arrived in Hamburg. Parents, sister and other relatives were at the pier to welcome me amidst laughter and tears. After a separation of fifteen years, it was a moment of high drama.

Although I had not intended to do so, the family insisted that I leave the ship for a prolonged visit at home. I tried to explain that it would not be easy to break the articles. The captain was reluctant, fearing that the action would set a precedent, but he finally consented to pay me off.

The next hurdle was at the American Consulate, where the consular agent first violently objected, but finally authorized my severance from the ship's articles. His parting shot was, "When you are broke, don't come around here looking for sympathy; you won't get any." I assured him I would not trouble him.

Erika.

During my absence, the family had left Bavaria and settled in Bad Pyrmont, a well-known spa in northern Germany. In the ensuing months, I
visited relatives in various parts of the country, including a nostalgic call at
the scene of my school years, and a reunion with my former playmates who
had survived the war. As time went on, I became acutely aware of the
severe impact the Versailles Treaty had had upon the German economy.
Unemployment was rampant throughout the land. A day laborer could
find an occasional job, but for the youth of the middle class, the pickings
were slim. I made the acquaintance of young men who had no prospects
and existed precariously, along with their war-widowed mothers, on
modest pensions provided by the government. It was most discouraging.

Any hope that my family entertained that I might stay on diminished with each passing day. Carolyne and I corresponded frequently. Realizing that my heart and hopes lay in America, my parents reluctantly agreed to let me return to the land of which I had become a citizen. Staying with relatives in Hamburg, I visited the harbor daily in hopes of finding a vacancy on an American flag vessel.

Because of the widespread political unrest, security was tight in the harbor area and access was by daypass only, which I obtained from the American Consulate. A new member of the consular staff had taken over and, when he learned of the purpose of my daily harbor visits, he issued me a weekly pass. I thanked him and said, "If I can't get a job soon, I will pay my fare back to the United States."

He replied, "Better hold off on that until you hear from me."

The day the weekly pass expired, he informed me that he had arranged for my passage in the German passenger ship ALBERT BALLIN of the Hamburg-American Line as a consular passenger, a euphemism for "workaway." I thanked him and was at sea a day later, bound for New York. Upon arrival, the ship swarmed with Prohibition agents, a mean-looking bunch of cutthroats spawned by the Prohibition law. I sat in the fo'c'sle with my bag packed, awaiting debarkation, when a burly individual clad in overalls and armed with a flashlight and small wrecking bar burst into the room. He bellowed, "Who are you and where in the hell is the crew, and what's in that suitcase?"

I explained to him that I was a temporary crewman ready to leave the ship. He ordered me to open up my bag and rummaged through it. Not finding anything, he barked, "Better get that crew in here fast, before I start tearing things apart."

I sought out the boatswain and gave him the word. Moments later, the boatswain entered the fo'c'sle. A redheaded six-footer of bone and muscle, he said with a deceptive calm, "We are still tying up the ship. Do you want the crew in here right now?"

The agent, no doubt reading the storm signals, visibly wilted and became almost obsequious, as he said, "No, no, boatswain, just any time you are ready."

I stepped ashore, and again took quarters at the Seamen's Friend Society. I intended to get a firm footing on the East Coast, sailing in ships calling at German ports. I registered at the hiring-hall and also joined an association of Masters and Mates. I was prepared to take any job on deck and remain in the ship in expectation that in time a third officer vacancy would occur, which I was qualified to fulfill.

Within a week, I signed on as Able Seaman in the passenger ship PRESIDENT ROOSEVELT, operated by the United States Line between New York and Bremerhaven, Germany. It appeared to be a real stroke of luck. The chief mate appointed me gearman in charge of cargo-gear maintenance. Instead of a watch-stander, I was a day-worker. It was a good arrangement, with Saturdays and Sundays off when in port.

En route, the ship called at one Irish and one French port to disembark passengers and mail. These calls were always at night. As gearman, I drove winches to offload the mail. No overtime was paid, but compensatory time of one day was given in each such case.

As scheduled, the ship arrived in Bremerhaven on Thursday. Friday was my compensatory day off, followed by the free days of Saturday and Sunday. I left Thursday night for a two-hour train ride to enjoy a three-day visit with my family, and rejoined the ship on Monday. It was a beautiful arrangement I ardently desired to continue in this fashion in anticipation of a vacancy in the third mate's billet, for which I hoped to be considered.

Following several months, a new third mate was hired. When I asked the chief mate why I had not been given a chance, he said, "Sorry about that, fella. It is company policy that every watch-standing deck officer must have a Master's license." It was a crushing blow. I decided it was time to quit the fo'c'sle and sail on my license.

Again, I took up quarters at the Seamen's Friends Society. In my daily rounds of the steamship offices, I soon found out that shipping was in the doldrums. My funds were low and with no licensed berth in sight, I took a job as A.B. in an American flag vessel. When I presented my papers to the mate he said after a pause, "You don't really want this job, do you?"

I realized later that it was a statement rather than a question. "I need the job," I replied.

It didn't take me long to puzzle out the reason for his remark. In the years immediately following the end of WWI, the ship regularly operated from New York to London. All the men in the deck department had married English women and established homes in the London area. With American wages and a favorable rate of exchange it was a good life. The men would go to any lengths to keep it so.

Throughout the years I had acquired the habit of doing a full day's work. What I saw here was pathetic. The men worked feverishly and kept glancing furtively in the direction of the bos'n or the mate. There was an aura of fear in the men's quarters. Near the end of the voyage, I was doing a paint job on the superstructure. The bos'n came along and stood by for a few moments before saying, "You are a bit slow on the job, aren't you?"

I knew what was coming, so I replied, "Don't worry bos'n, my bags are packed. I am going to sign off when we get in."

One morning, as I entered the hall of the deck officers' association where I was registered, a face appeared at a sliding office window and sang out, "We need a third mate for the steamer CASTLE TOWN."

Being the only one present, I said, "I am it." I finally had it made. The ship was owned and operated by the Nelson Steamship Company of San Francisco. Because of the 1926 coal-miners' strike in England, the ship had been chartered for a full cargo of coal in bulk, destined for Glasgow, Scotland.

On a wintry day in November, we left Norfolk, Virginia, deeply laden and decks awash in a rough crossing of the North Atlantic. It took twenty-one days to discharge the coal. It rained every day and every rain drop carried a bit of coal. It was a dreary mess.

Our next destination was Fowey, a small community in the duchy of Cornwall, situated on the south coast of England. As we entered the narrow channel leading to the small port, the pilot pointed out ancient iron fittings embedded in the rocks on both sides of the entrance. He explained that, in ancient times, a chain was stretched across the entrance at night to keep out French smugglers. I recalled later that the romantic environment of the port and the surrounding countryside formed the locale of the novel, "Frenchman's Creek," by Daphne de Maurier.

The task before us was far from romantic. The cargo to be lifted was China clay in bulk. Considering that black coal and white clay were total opposites in color and composition, the job of cleaning the cargo holds in preparation for the return cargo proved to be a difficult and extensive undertaking. The entire deck crew was in the holds with brooms, shovels, and brushes to remove chunks of coal and coal dust from behind transverse frames, overhead cross members, and out from every nook and cranny, of which there were many.

At the end of every day, when it was thought the holds were clean,

First license. Third Officer. S.S. CASTLE TOWN.

inspectors ran their hands over the surfaces to show more coal dust. Finally, in desperation, the chief mate ordered the holds to be washed down, employing fire hoses and bilge pumps to get rid of the water. All in all, it took a week before the ship was certified by the inspectors to be clean, and loading began.

Again, it was a messy affair. Instead of black coal dust, the ship was now covered with a white clay dust. With hatches battened down, CASTLE TOWN again braved a turbulent North Atlantic, bound for Portland, Maine, U.S.A.

Following the discharge of cargo at Portland, the ship called at a number of East Coast ports to load general merchandise destined for Los Angeles and San Francisco.

Like many other shipping firms, Nelson Steamship Company, initially a coastwise operator, entered the intercoastal trade with six warbuilt freighters of varying design that had been acquired from the Shipping Board for the proverbial song. CASTLE TOWN was one of them and the largest, capable of lifting more than a million feet of lumber.

With the ship's arrival, I had a joyous reunion with Carolyne and her family. I continued to sail in the CASTLE TOWN until 1928, when I paid off to sit for my chief mate's license. It appeared I was back in the West Coast for good.

In my years serving in freighters I became aware and grew appalled at the low standing of the merchant ship's officer in American society. He was at the bottom rung of the social ladder. Obviously there were compelling and practical reasons for this. In the three decades following WWI, conditions in the American Merchant Marine could at best be called chaotic. In a wartime economy, American shipowners had acquired and operated ships worldwide with profits guaranteed. With the end of the war and no longer subsidized by the government, they were unable to compete in a peacetime economy. With the exception of well-established passenger services, shipping concerns operating dry cargo ships folded up overnight. A few held on to protected domestic routes, but even their service was sporadic in the face of fluctuating and uncertain freight rates.

In a declining economy men took extraordinary steps to hang on to their jobs. It was not unusual to find one or more men with licenses, including masters, sailing in the fo'c'sle. Reporting on board as third mate I asked a bystander, "Where can I find the mate?"

"Down there." he said, pointing to an open hatch. I found the mate in the lower hold pushing a broom. There were other occurrences of that nature. It was the custom in the trade to bring a ship into the home port cleaned, painted and washed down.

Coming off watch on a Sunday morning I was met by the mate at the foot of the bridge ladder. "When you have had your lunch," he said to me, "I want you to come out and give me a hand painting the deckhouse."

I hesitated. "Mister Mate, it has taken me fifteen years to get out of the fo'c'sle. I don't think I should be required to do sailors' work."

"You won't help me then?"

"No, sorry about that."

Turning away, I said, "I know you may think of getting me fired, but I am way ahead of you. I have asked the skipper to pay me off. I am due to sit for my chief mate's license."

Clinging to the work ethic of the fo'c'sle and with a disdain for the uniform as "Putting on the Dog," freighter mates were recognized mostly by their visored cap with gold braid chin strap. Unlike their colleagues in other maritime nations who were always in uniform, they preferred casual dress as more practical. A story making the rounds on the waterfronts indicated not everyone felt that way.

For years the "Blue Ribbon" given to the fastest ship in the trans-Atlantic run had been held by British and, occasionally, by a French or German liner. As a matter of national pride it was decided to have an American flag vessel enter the competition. The senior shipmaster of a prestigious company took command as Commodore of the newly built ship. Included in the appointment was the advice to acquire membership in a ship's officers association. Allegedly he exploded, "In a British ship of this class they would give me a title. Here you want to give me a Union book."

Actually Masters and Mates Associations were not considered unions in the fullest sense of the term. It was known that many were subsidized by shipowners' associations.

THE SAN FRANCISCO
WATERFRONT

Carolyne had not been idle during the years of our courtship, She took a three-year course at San Francisco State Teachers' College, graduating with a degree in General Education. She taught kindergarten for two years in Scotia, a lumber company town in Northern California, and then taught at a private school in Oakland.

With my new chief mate's license, I shipped out again in the CASTLE TOWN as second mate in the intercoastal run. Then came the 1929 stock market crash, and steamship operators reduced their schedules to a minimum. Between runs, ships remained idle for long periods, their crews out of work. I was more fortunate than many. I filed an application at the Marine Department of an oil company. Although I had no tanker experience, I was hired immediately as third mate. With the prospect of steady employment at good wages and two weeks' paid vacation a year, the future looked bright.

With the assurance of a steady income, I proposed marriage to Carolyne. This was not done on impulse, so it might have lacked the customary flowery language and fervor. We had decided long ago that some day we would share a life together. She said quietly, "Will you speak to Father tonight?

It was late in the evening with most members upstairs preparing to

Father in law, George S. Beadle, c. 1930.

retire. Perhaps not exactly by chance I met her father in the living room. Inwardly quaking I said, "Sir, I wish to take this opportunity to ask for the hand of your daughter Carolyne in marriage." Having delivered myself of this formal speech, I swallowed hard awaiting his reply.

"We welcome you into the family, my boy. Her mother and I know you both will be very happy," he said as we shook hands. The ensuing months were filled with plans as the women went into high gear. The society editor of the local paper was notified, floral pieces for the wedding dinner were ordered. Bridal gown and gowns for the bridesmaids were selected. Arrangement was made with a minister with whom we had a preliminary meeting to be instructed in ceremonial procedures. Carolyne's brother Howard was to be my best man. It was my function to procure a ring and the bridal bouquet. I chose a diamond set in platinum and gold. The bouquet featured a large centerpiece of white sweetpeas

Carolyne the bride.

and bright blue bachelor buttons. A wedding guest commented on the floral arrangement, asking, "Why only white and blue? And bachelor buttons in a bridal bouquet?"

"I think the arrangement is quite appropriate." I explained, "White for innocence and blue for fidelity. Besides that, bachelor buttons were the only blue flowers available. Furthermore white and blue happen to be the colors of my home state, Bavaria."

"Well, I never! Seems like you still have one foot in the 'Old Country.'"

Pondering her last remark I concluded that this native-born American had never known the trauma experienced by an alien filing for citizenship, a step involving unconditional abjuration of former loyalties and associations while at the same time pledging total allegiance to his new country. I recalled the words: "Taking this obligation freely, without mental reservations, or purpose of evasion, So help me God."

I was about to suggest to her that a reading of this awesome document might clarify a few things, but I thought better of it. Throughout the years there has always been a soft spot in my heart for the land of my birth. To feel otherwise would be unnatural. I knew Uncle Sam would understand and think no less of his adopted nephew.

Friz' crest.

The marriage, a black tie affair, was performed at the family home in Oakland. We had the loan of a Chevrolet coupe for our wedding trip to Lake Tahoe. When my bride confided in me that she had never been out of the State of California, I drove her across the Nevada state line. We spent the day in Reno, which was still somewhat of a cowtown. We were now a twosome, and subsequent decisions were made accordingly.

Beadle's crest.

Back at work, I studied the company's operating manual and, by observation, learned the loading and discharging of crude oil and other more volatile products. Within two years, I was promoted to chief mate. Hitherto, I had served in ships with a single pipeline, carrying a single product. Following a vacation, I was assigned to a larger ship with a double

Father, 1929

Mother, 1929

pipeline arrangement and departed for Honolulu with seven different products on board. Upon our arrival in Honolulu and with pumps started, the pumpman requested an hour's leave to get a haircut. I never saw him again. Perhaps he became the victim of a powerful home brew that was sold locally in quart bottles.

I single-handedly tackled the job of discharging the various products and, in spite of my limited experience, succeeded without mixing up any of the cargo. It was an exhausting experience.

At sea on the return trip, I received a message of my father's death. The second mate, noting my distress, volunteered to stand part of my watch while I went below to regain my composure. Later, back at the home port, the Captain mentioned a letter he had received from the company, complimenting him upon the untainted delivery of the various products. There was no word of praise for me.

In time, I was assigned to another ship, carrying crude on a short coastal run. In a twenty-four-hour period in port, I was lucky to be able to spend four or five hours at home. We both chafed under this situation, but I stuck it out for a few more months.

During my two weeks' vacation, I sat for my Master's license in San Francisco. I also studied for the examination for Pilot of San Francisco Bay and San Pedro, should I have the opportunity in later years to serve in that capacity. It was the proverbial anchor out to windward. When I received my Master's license on the 13th day of September 1931, it read, in part:

> "That he can be entrusted with the Duties and Responsibilities of Master of Steam and Motor vessels of any gross tons upon the waters of any ocean, and Pilot, Bay of San Francisco to Martinez via main channel routes, to Sea and Return and authorized as First Class Pilot on Los Angeles Harbor to Wilmington."

On this proud day, we celebrated with the family in one of the finest restaurants in San Francisco. Carolyne and I had mutually agreed that I should not continue in the tanker trade. In the ensuing year, I served as third and second mate in various ships of the Nelson Steamship Co. As before, employment in their ships was sporadic and dependent upon offerings of freight in the intercoastal service, which had become highly competitive. Between ships, I remained on the company's payroll as a dockworker. It was an interesting experience to observe events and meet some of the characters for which the San Francisco waterfront was famous.

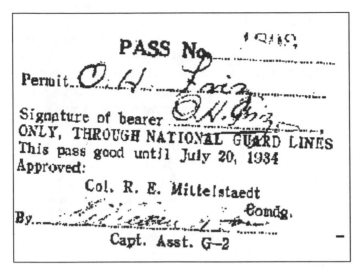

Pass No. 1808

The daily hiring of longshoremen took place in an open area near the Ferry Building. Stevedore bosses circulated through the crowd to pick the men for their gangs, a process known as the "Shape-up." Wages were eighty-five cents an hour. The most prominent among the bosses were three individuals well known on the waterfront by their nicknames. They were referred to as Gloomy Gus, Hungry Gus, and Sunset Gus. I never found out their real names.

Gloomy Gus was a large man. Everything about him was large, his face, his hands, his feet. He habitually wore a doleful expression and moved about ponderously, seldom raising his voice.

In contrast, Hungry Gus, herding his gangs through the portals of the pier sheds, was heard to scream at the top of his voice, "I want to see those hooks traveling with full sling loads. I want to see the plunder out first." Plunder referred to small units of cargo of less than carload lots (LCL) and carried at a higher freight rate than full cargo lots of a single commodity. During the operation, he would exhort his men to speed up the process. This earned him the name of Hungry Gus, as he was always hungry for more.

The third member of this distinguished triumvirate was Sunset Gus. A quiet man, his specialty was the handling of lumber cargoes at the Sunset Lumber Co., situated at the Oakland Estuary and owned by the Nelson

S.S. Co. I worked for him most of the time.

The hauling of cargo along the San Francisco waterfront was still largely by horse-drawn vehicles. Most noteworthy was a fleet of low-bed trucks owned by a large drayage firm. These trucks of special construction were used to transport heavy items, especially large rolls of newsprint paper. They were drawn by massive dappled grays of the Belgian Percheron breed.

The Embarcadero was covered daily by the droppings of many draft horses. Flattened by the traffic, rarely cleaned up and dried out by sun and wind, the stuff was whirled aloft during the summer months' prevailing northwesterly winds sweeping the area. To the locals it was known as the Horseshit Typhoon.

Earlier, following the 1929 financial debacle, my father-in-law, George S. Beadle ("George S.") informed me that he had acquired the steam schooner FORT BRAGG, and with a partner had formed his own company, Beadle and Antz. When I asked him what he meant by entering a business most others were getting out of because of the dismal economic climate, ever the optimist, he calmly replied: "When others are getting out, they leave a vacuum. I intend to fill it."

The backbone of this new enterprise was a contract he had negotiated with the Royal Dutch Shell Oil Company to carry their gasoline and other petroleum products to ports in Northern California and Oregon. The oil company's refinery was located in Martinez in the San Francisco Bay area, and since the company was foreign owned, they could not, under the law, operate ships in the coastal trade.

On the foredeck of the FORT BRAGG, a large square tank, holding several thousand gallons of gasoline, was installed. The business prospered from the beginning. Aside from petroleum products, which provided the principal income, the company, as a common carrier, also freighted dry cargo to the ports of Eureka and Crescent City, California and Coos Bay in Oregon and returned with a full load of lumber and its byproducts. Webster defines common carrier as an "individual or corporation carrying other peoples' goods for compensation."

In time and with the retirement of Mr. Antz, the company was reorganized as Beadle Steamship Company Ltd., with George S. as president and his son, Howard, as operating manager. A treasurer, bookkeeper and typist completed the organization. Nelson S.S. Company acted as agents. Within two years, the business had expanded to a fleet of ten ships of the steam schooner type, some owned, others under charter. All had tanks installed on deck to carry gasoline. To cope with the increased workload, it was proposed that I join the company.

I accepted the offer as a timely opportunity to enjoy a better family life, for a daughter had been born to us in September 1932. We named her Georgia Luise after her maternal grandfather and paternal grandmother.

To the men in the ship I was known as the Port Captain, but I simply regarded myself as the "outside legman." I would meet a ship upon arrival and stay with it until departure. My day began at six in the morning and often ended at one o'clock the following morning. It was a routine operation. Arriving at the San Francisco Ferry Building at seven a.m., I would call the longshoremen's hall and order a gang for eight a.m. With the lumber cargo discharged, I would follow the ship across the Bay to various terminals to be present at the loading of general merchandise.

At the end of the day, the ship would depart for Martinez to load Shell Oil products and return the following day in the late afternoon, when I would pick her up at Pier 7 in San Francisco to complete loading. As a last act, I let go her lines around midnight and sprinted to catch the last trans-bay ferry at one a.m. In ensuing years, I came to regard it as a rich experience from the management side.

Meanwhile, the waterfront labor force had become increasingly restive. Negotiations by the International Longshoremen's Union (ILA) with the Pacific Steamship Owners Association (PSA) for higher wages, better working conditions, and improved hiring practices had led nowhere. Embittered by the hard-nosed opposition of the ship operators, the longshoremen, led by Harry Bridges, called for a strike.

It was a bitter battle, with no holds barred. Although the longshoremen had the full support of all the maritime unions as well as the teamsters, negotiations dragged on. The meetings were acrimonious and laced with invectives on both sides. Stake trucks, filled with strikers brandishing pick handles and baseball bats, roamed the waterfront unhindered. Police used tear gas against groups of demonstrators, some of whom picked up canisters and threw them back at the police.

We spent hours daily on the roof of our office building at No. 1 Drumm Street and, from there, witnessed the death of two strikers by police gun fire. It was an ugly scene. The day became known as Bloody Thursday and was observed each year for many years, when union members stood guard on the flower-covered sidewalk where their comrades had fallen. It was the incident that led, in 1935, to the General Strike that brought a vibrant city to her knees. It was also the year when a second daughter joined us. We named her Janet Erica.

As I joined the daily throng of commuters leaving the trans-bay ferries, I was struck by the absence of hustle and bustle along the waterfront. The bellow of steamer whistles and the pounding noise of heavy streetcars on four tracks on lower Market Street had given way to a deadly silence. Only the resounding click-clack of heels on the sidewalk pavement was audible as office workers made their way up Market and California Streets. In the very heart of maritime commerce, a once thriving business now lay prostrate. It was an unforgettable, eerie spectacle.

From the beginning, I had paid daily visits to two ships, UNIMAK and HELEN P. DREW, tied up at the San Francisco waterfront. Their former crews manned the picket lines. I knew all of them by name and was never denied access to the ships. Both were woodenhulled single-enders.

Noting the trim of the UNIMAK, I knew she had made water astern. I manned the long handle of a pump located on deck, forward of the pilot house. The single leather-lined plunger was dried out. Priming the pump with a few buckets of water, I obtained suction and pumped her dry. The HELEN P. DREW was well down by the stern, her engine room half full of water. Following several hours at the pump, I was able to enter the engine room and, finding a wrench, managed to tighten up the stern gland to reduce the entry of seawater through the stern tube. Manning the pumps became a daily chore for the duration.

Following the city's shutdown by the general strike, the National Guard had been called out to patrol the waterfront. To continue my daily inspection of the ships, I was issued a pass over the signature of the Commanding General of the National Guard. It enabled me to pass through their lines but boarding the ships became more difficult. The regular crews had been transferred and the picket line was now manned by militant union members, none of whom I knew. Somehow, I talked myself through the line to board the ships and keep them afloat.

Although the strike was settled following weeks of tumultuous nego-tiations, peace by no means returned to the waterfront. A hiring hall had been established to be shared by the ship owners and the union. It was a short-lived arrangement. Within days the employers' representatives were ejected and the union took full control of hiring.

Among the many conditions agreed upon were the composition and size of gangs, working hours, straight time pay, overtime pay, penalty pay for hazardous cargo, the size of sling loads and a multitude of other functions. Noteworthy was the establishment of a standard six-hour work-day. It was based on the idea of four shifts within a 24-hour period. The intention was to provide work for as many gangs as possible and to relieve the congestion of cargo in warehouses and pier sheds. The regulation also provided for the overtime payrate to begin for all hours worked after three p.m. It was a scheme whose time had come and gone at the first attempt of implementation.

It was the first day of return-to-work and the UNIMAK was on berth to load. A gang of longshoremen had started at eight a.m., worked till noon, took one hour for lunch and returned at one p.m. to finish their six-hour work day. I was present to observe the loading and became a witness to a development that sounded the death knell of the six-hour workday. At three p.m., a gang of longshoremen appeared and the following exchange took place: "What are you doing here?"

"We have come to relieve you."

"Like hell you have. You guys think we are going to work at straight-time pay and then you come in at overtime rate?"

"Yes, but we were sent down here."

"Ya gotta be crazy if you think we're gonna stand for this. You go back to the hall and tell those guys we're gonna get in on some of that overtime, and don't come back until six p.m." That took care of the six-hour work day. I did not hear of any incident of this nature taking place anywhere else.

I had the impression that the new union leadership had acquired a power it was not quite ready to handle effectively. Militant members in the leadership, as well as individuals in gangs, would call for a work stoppage at the slightest pretext. Another factor contributing to the chaotic conditions in the industry was the uncontrolled internecine warfare among some of the maritime unions. The pendulum had swung the other way.

My brother-in-law, Howard Beadle, boarded one of our ships with me to inquire into a stoppage that threatened to prevent the ship's sailing at the scheduled time. In the ship's salon, we found three men engaged in an argument. It involved the ship's cook-steward, a member of the Marine Cooks and Stewards Union (MCSU), a representative of his union, and a representative of the Oilers, Watertenders and Firemens Union (OWFU).

We gathered that the cook, a prominent member of MCSU, had incurred displeasure by expressing allegedly moderate views when attending caucuses held by the various unions. It was the OWFU leadership that demanded his removal from the ship and any future employment, as well as his exclusion from future caucuses. In the ensuing discussion, the MCSU representative said to the OWFU functionary, "We have gone along with you on other such occasions. This time we take a stand. Our man stays on the ship."

We noted that these two men were not the proverbial heavyhanded sons of toil. They wore business suits, ties, and expensive wristwatches. Their words were well chosen and contained none of the usual waterfront jargon. As the discussion continued, one of them turned to us and said, "You fellows leave now. We are going to hold a caucus and settle this matter."

We were stunned by the bizarre development in which union representatives conducted business of a parochial nature on an owner's property without regard for the consequences to the latter. The ship sailed late, with the cook still on board.

There were numerous other incidents throughout the year. Frequent stoppages were called by anyone in gangs on the work scene under the pretext that this or that part of the agreement had been violated. Not only were such disruptions caused by actions of longshoremen, but also by radical, irresponsible members of ships' crews.

A ship had completed loading and, with a pilot on board and tugs standing by, was prevented from sailing. Her berth, when vacated, was to be available for one of our ships approaching in the stream. No one seemed to know the cause of the delay. As I arranged for another berth for our ship with the terminal manager, he said, "You'll never believe this. The crew found out there was only vanilla ice cream among the provisions delivered to the ship. The men refused to sail unless some chocolate ice cream was provided."

As I left the manager's office, I met the pilot on the pier. He said, "I am going home. No one knows when this ship is going to sail. The owners can call for a pilot when the dispute is settled."

The ship departed the following day. Whether the chocolate ice cream had been delivered or some other cause had delayed the ship's departure, I could not find out. This and similar incidents rendered sailing schedules meaningless.

I recall the case of a chain store at a port of call which had announced a one-day sale of a popular item. The timely delivery of the goods was frustrated by some union action, delaying our ship's departure for a day, causing the cancellation of the sale. We received a strong letter of protest from the store's manager, announcing his withdrawal of any future business. A protest to the union leadership elicited the reply: "If you can't hack it, get out of the business."[*]

The corporations weathered the storm and fought back via extensive mechanization of cargo handling, but no privately funded concern could continue to function through the disorder then prevailing on the waterfront. Beadle Steamship Company Ltd. struggled along under these adverse conditions until 1937, when the company sold its remaining assets to satisfy creditors and ceased operations for good.

Many people who were close to the scene believed that a militant, uncompromising group in the union leadership, as well as in the membership at large, exerted a disproportionate influence in the maritime labor movement. Having achieved the initial basic aims of the strike—higher wages and improved working conditions—this vengeful element, for purposes of their own, appeared to be bent upon wrecking the corporate structure whose money and expertise was the lifeblood of the industry. They succeeded only in destroying small enterprises. With continuing interference in their legitimate business and with limited resources at their disposal, they could not survive.

---

[*]   The era became known as "The three bridges"; that is, the Golden Gate Bridge, The Oakland-San Francisco Bay Bridge, and Harry Bridges.

IN SEARCH OF A JOB

In 1937, I was in search of employment. I registered with the Masters, Mates and Pilots, Local 90 organization, but there was no call for licensed deck personnel. I made frequent calls at waterfront steamship offices. The answer was always, "No."

One day the regular employee of a certain company was relieved at the window. His place was taken by a young fellow who listened politely to my spiel. I felt encouraged. Finally, he said, "How old are you?"

"I am forty-two."

He said, "I am sorry, our insurance policy does not permit hiring anyone past the age of thirty-nine."

There I stood, in the prime of life, my hat in one hand, an unlimited Master's license in the other, and a thousand years of experience handed down to me by those who had followed the seas since the days of antiquity. As I turned away, I felt a tap at my shoulder. The man who stood in line behind me said, "I heard what the fellow said. You should take this up with the newspapers. The American Civil Liberties Union (ACLU) would be delighted to take on this case of discrimination."

I did not give the idea a second thought. Notoriety I did not need; what I needed was a job. Besides that, I considered the trouble the young man might be in for disclosing something not intended for the public ear. The wounds of the recent labor upheaval were beginning to heal slowly, and any further disturbance of the fragile peace in the waterfront community would not serve my cause. I continued to make the rounds until my hopes were shattered.

I had talked myself into a port captain's office. He looked at me grimly. "What the hell do you expect me to do?" he exploded. "I have no job for you!" I ventured the opinion that, here and there, men seemed to go to work.

"Yes, I know, cadets at seventy-five dollars a month. You wouldn't want to take that, would you?"

I got the pitch. I was overqualified!

During my years ashore, I had made friends on both sides of the fence. Waterfront labor was tightly organized. The mere fact that I had been a management employee during the recent conflict had made me persona non grata in certain union circles.

With no foreseeable prospects in employment afloat and with a wife and two children to house and feed, I cast about for work, any kind of work. Through a former associate and member of the dock clerks' union with whom I had frequently worked loading and discharging ships' cargos, I succeeded in getting a temporary permit in his union. A dock clerk's function was to check cargo delivered to the docks by truckers or railroad cars to assigned spaces in the shed, to make note of damaged or missing items and to check such goods in or out of ships.

As a permit man, I was expected to fill in when a regular member was not available. I was also informed that I could be relieved any time in the midst of an assignment, should a regular show up for work.

I worked out of the hall in Oakland. Terminal owners and managers everywhere told me that if and when I could show them a union book, I could have a permanent job with them. But the books were, and remained, closed. The pickings were slim. Most of the assignments were at odd hours at night in the cold and drafty pier sheds that no one else wanted. Nevertheless, it put bread on the table.

Occasionally, I would be called upon by a motor transportation company to deliver new cars to local dealers. Whenever I felt certain that none of these activities were in the offing, I would stand at the gate of an Oakland shipyard at the beginning of the workday, hoping to be hired as a rigger in the event a regular failed to show up. To be able to obtain such employment, I took out a card in the Boilermakers' Union, Local 39, rigging division. More often than not, there were no openings. But eventually, luck was with me one day. When I called in one morning, the rigging boss pointed to a ship in drydock. "This ship is completing annual inspection. You take this young fellow with you and stow the anchor chain in her chain locker."

As I boarded the ship, I immediately recognized her as my former ship, the CASTLE TOWN. The chains were ranged on the floor of the drydock. We hauled the bitter end of the chain up through the hawsepipe across a slotted wheel, known as the wildcat, on the windlass and down through the spillpipe to the bottom of the chain locker, to be shackled to an eyebolt. While formerly the chainlockers had extended the full depth of the hull, they had now been rebuilt and reduced in depth, for reasons unknown to me.

I explained to my helper that stowing the chains into these smaller lockers would require extra care. I casually mentioned the fact that I had served in this ship some ten years ago as a deck officer. Little did I know that I was talking to the boss rigger's son. From then on out, whenever I was at the gate, I would be the first to be called in to fill a vacancy. The San Francisco Bay Area was humming with activities. The Golden Gate Bridge and the Oakland-San Francisco Bay Bridge were under construction. In preparation for the International Golden Gate Exposition scheduled for 1939, an artificial island was created, adjacent to and north of Yerba Buena Island, to house exhibits from all over the world. Still, there was no employment for anyone in my line of work. My earnings and the things of value we pawned, plus the indulgence of a sympathetic landlord, kept us a cut above starvation level.

Political upheavals in Europe in 1938 and the competition by the New York World's Fair, also scheduled for 1939, cast a pall upon the local scene. But commitments had been made and activities proceeded as planned. I had learned that the Oakland-based Key System Ferry Company, in addition to the regular transbay commuter service, was to provide a ferry service to the exposition grounds, called Treasure Island, from Oakland as well as San Francisco. This called for the acquisition of more ferries and the hiring of qualified personnel—an estimated sixteen crews—to man these ships. Key Systems also intended to run excursions in San Francisco Bay during the Exposition. This operation required officer personnel with pilot license endorsements covering the navigable channels of the Bay Area well beyond the limited routes of the regular transbay commuter service.

Master, First Mate, Second Mate aboard the ferry boat SAN LEANDRO, 1939.

Holding an unlimited Master's license with an endorsement of first-class pilot in waters of San Francisco Bay and tributaries, I filed an application with Key System in early 1938. Although the opening of the Fair was still a year away, it was proposed that I join the service immediately as a deckhand to acquire seniority and go into training to learn the skills necessary in this highly specialized service. As I came home that afternoon, my wife met me at the door.

"Any luck today?" she asked. "Why do you look so glum?"

"Yeah, I have a job."

Her face lit up. "Wonderful, tell me about it."

"I have just been promoted from chief mate in deepwater ships to deckhand on a ferry boat."

She caught her breath. "Did you take it?"

"I sure did, honey. It was an offer I could not refuse."

The following morning, I joined the day shift crew of the ferry SAN LEANDRO, a complement consisting of a Master, First Officer, Second Officer, and the requisite number of deckhands to handle the lines. When crossing the Bay, I was frequently in the wheelhouse at the Master's invitation to observe the docking of the ferry. During these periods, I had

First officer, ferry boat SAN LEANDRO

the privilege of being coached by superb shiphandlers, men with nerves of steel and skills acquired over the years of operating ferries under highly adverse tidal conditions.

The entrance openings of the ferry slips on both sides of the Bay were at right angles to the tidal currents. Initially, I was given the opportunity to land the ferry at slack water, that brief period between tide changes when no current exists. In time, I learned to land the ferry at maximum ebb or flood currents. It was always a tricky maneuver, for the heading of the ferry's bow had no relation to its final course. When close to the coneshaped slip, the engine would be stopped and the ship allowed to drift with the current until abreast of the slip entrance, then entered under a full-ahead bell. When halfway in, the engines were under a full-astern bell until the apron had been reached. It was a maneuver that had been practiced routinely for many years by the ferryboat captains and first officers under whom I had served my apprenticeship.

There was little difference between the two positions, except that the Master was in full command at all times and drew a higher salary.

Actual shiphandling was at the same level. It was the accepted practice for the First Officer to take the ferry out of the Oakland Terminal. When halfway across the Bay, he would be relieved by the Captain, who landed the boat at the San Francisco Terminal. Conversely, the Captain would take the boat out of the San Francisco slip, to be relieved when halfway across the Bay by the First Officer, who docked the vessel at the Oakland Terminal.

At the docking phase at either terminal, the Captain and First Officer were together in the wheelhouse at all times, the Second Officer was at the maindeck to supervise the passenger disembarcation.

It was a well-established routine, where everyone knew where to be and what to do: "Shipshape and Bristol fashion," a term indicating duty performance in a seamanlike manner.

A week before the opening of the Fair, I left the ranks of deckhand and stood a watch as Second Officer, thus becoming eligible for promotion to First Officer. I was assigned to the ferry PIEDMONT, leased from the Southern Pacific Railroad. She was a handsome old lady, a real queen. I met the Captain, a middle-aged man. Something in his walk as he strode across the deck seemed familiar. I stopped short, and said, "Sir, were you by any chance a third officer in the steamer ADMIRAL SCHLEY, back in 1920?"

He eyed me. "Yes, I was, and now I remember you being there as a quartermaster." It was a good start in a relationship that we both enjoyed while we were together.

We made several practice runs (no passengers) to get the feel of the ship. A sidewheeler, she handled beautifully.

Contrary to the old transbay ferry slips, at right angles to the currents, the new slips on the east and west sides of Treasure Island had their entrances facing south and thus in line with the tidal currents, a very unfavorable situation.

The PIEDMONT operated from the Oakland mole to the island's east-side slip. Entering the slip on the ebb tide, constant backing was required to overcome the momentum of the current. Conversely, against the flood current it was necessary to maintain engine speed ahead to the last moment until mooring lines held the boat in place.

It was a different ballgame. There were times when the old lady shuddered under some hard landings. Eventually, this service was discontinued as the Oakland-San Francisco Bay Bridge, with on and off ramps to the island, was opened to auto and bus travel. At times, I was assigned to the ferry YERBA BUENA, when chartered to service clubs and other organizations for excursions in Bay Area waters covered by my pilot license. Wednesday was my day off and I took the family to the Exposition. The Golden Gate Exposition was a huge success, and plans were afoot for a re-opening in 1940, at the end of which all ferry services were to be discontinued, both bridges then being able to handle all the traffic.

I remained in the employ of Key System in the commuter service to be available for the Fair re-opening the following year. Beyond that, the specter of unemployment again loomed large on the horizon. I continued to work in the Treasure Island run in the ferries SAN LEANDRO, SIERRA NEVADA, YERBA BUENA, and others. At the close of the Exposition, these ships were laid up or sold and the crews disbanded, leaving a feeling of regret as good shipmates parted company. It was the end of an exciting time and, in retrospect, a highlight in a varied career in deepwater which now included inland waters where the rules of the road and navigation were different.

So, back to the gate at the shipyard every morning to pick up a day's work.

For the second time in the century, Europe was at war. As a neutral, the United States continued trade relations with both warring parties. Nevertheless, notably in the English speaking world, there was widespread opposition to the Hitler regime in Germany. Incidents involving the tearing down of the Swastika flag from embassies and consulates became more frequent. In view of the portent of things to come, a long dormant shipbuilding industry came to life again. Activities at the Moore Shipyard and Drydock Company located at the Oakland Estuary now included new ship construction at an accelerating pace. From the end of the company pier I had a full and unobstructed view of the estuary. I observed a large vessel heading downstream. There was something peculiar in her movements. Instead of appearing larger as she approached, the hull began to look smaller and less visible. Ostensibly, the ship was dead in the water. With a start I realized she had sunk and was aground in mid-channel. At her bows appeared her name: VANCOUVER. Black, white and red bands on the buff-colored funnel indicated German registry. The Hamburg American Line (HAPAG) were her owners.

Rumors were floating around and newspapers and radio stations had a field day speculating about the cause of the sinking. Most leaned toward an engine-room explosion causing a rupture in the hull. This was not quite true. Investigation disclosed that the force of the explosion had bent the edges of the ruptured plates inward. It indicated that an exterior force had been responsible for the implosion and sinking. It was a widely accepted assumption that an underwater demolition expert had, under cover of night, attached a limpet mine to the hull below the waterline. To my knowledge it was never fully determined whether this had been the act of an individual or instigated by a local dissident group. The incident caused an uproar nationwide.

The German Counsel General in San Francisco was furious and in a scathing interview accused the United States government of a violation of neutrality. In a rapidly developing wartime situation, the incident was lost in a sea of other events.

Another development had caught my attention. It was the completion of the Stockton deepwater channel, which cut across the San Joaquin River Delta and made the Port of Stockton accessible to seagoing vessels.

With the idea in mind that there would be employment for river pilots, I visited the office of the River Lines and secured permission to ride one of their river crafts at weekly intervals for the required ten round trips necessary to have my pilot's endorsement extended to the Port of Stockton. When I informed my wife that I would study for the river pilot's license, she said calmly, "You'll be a student all your life."

I took it as a compliment. I had no difficulty in passing the examination and felt that I now had another anchor out to windward.

Earlier in the year, the Lighthouse Service had invited applications from qualified personnel to the position of second mate in lighthouse tenders. No examination was required. Applicants were selected solely on the basis of experience and possession of the requisite license. I applied, time passed, and I had almost forgotten about the application when the mail brought a list of names, including mine, of accepted applicants.

A notice attached to the document stated that the Lighthouse Service had been transferred from the Department of Commerce to the United States Coast Guard. Because the latter, as a military organization, did not recruit personnel from the Civil Service list, the roster of eligibles had been transferred to the Army Transport Service and the U.S. Army Engineers, which operated transports and dredges respectively. I laid the notice aside. Just another chance gone down the drain.

The two years' service in Key System ferries provided us with an income that covered our basic needs and enabled us to start paying off the landlord. Again, as I returned to shipyard work and clerking on the docks,

I faced an uncertain future. Then, toward the end of 1940, the phone rang. It was the Army Transport Service. A voice said, "Would you accept a Third Officer's position, for which we have an opening?"

Gladly. I reported to the office at Fort Mason in San Francisco the following morning and became an employee of the United States Government. It was the sixth of December, 1940.

I was assigned as a deck officer to a passenger steamer moored at a pier in San Francisco. The ship was undergoing repairs and conversion to military transport. A Master and skeleton crew of unlicensed personnel had been assigned to cover port watches.

Ominous war clouds in Europe were visible only in the headlines of American magazines and newspapers as they rolled off the presses with the ubiquitous comic strips in daily and Sunday editions. One of the most popular comic characters was Popeye, who, besides rescuing his girl, Olive Oyl, from various daily dangers, performed other feats of derring-do while sustaining himself by consuming phenomenal amounts of spinach, sometimes without bothering to open the cans.

Arriving at the foot of the gangway of my newly assigned vessel, my ears picked up the familiar tune of "I'm Popeye the Sailorman," intoned by a gravelly voice. As I stepped off the plank on deck, there arose from a bench an apparition—none other than Popeye himself—coarse red hair, rolling eye, jutting jaw, tatoos on both arms and a visored cap at a rakish angle. He introduced himself as quartermaster on gangway watch. I forgot his name promptly as he assured me that he was known to everyone as Popeye, a role which had become to him a permanent routine, and Popeye it was from then on out. He was a lonely man and loved conversation, providing he could do all the talking. In the ensuing minutes, I learned Popeye's colorful history, which allegedly included a hitch in the French Foreign Legion.

Before I could break away to my quarters, Popeye assured me that any help I needed he would gladly provide. Little did I know at the time that henceforth I was to be chaplain, advisor, solver of daily problems and sounding board whenever I hove into sight. Luckily, I immediately and firmly declined to take care of his money and to act as his treasurer.

This was the beginning of a relationship, sometimes irksome but never dull, which was to govern our daily routine for months to come. One of the first things I noted was a limp in one of Popeye's legs, which seemed to become more pronounced each day. I questioned him about it and accepted his explanation that there was nothing to it, just the result of the rough life he had led, etc. But, eventually, I got him off to the Marine Hospital for an examination. He returned with a cast, a sheepish grin on his face, and the news that a hairline fracture had been responsible for his limp.

He resumed his duties at the gangway, his gravelly voice always humming that familiar Popeye tune, and, for a while, things were fairly calm, just as long as everyone stayed out of Popeye's earshot. There came a day when Popeye informed me that he desired to visit his sister "down south somewhere."

For the ensuing week, this became an engrossing topic of conversation, during which time I essayed the role of travel agent, ship's purser to assist him in preparing leave papers and in securing a relief quartermaster, and ultimately acted as valet to see that he was properly dressed to face the outside world.

Popeye had no civilian clothes. He presented himself in the standard double-breasted uniform with brass buttons and quartermaster insignia on visored cap with white cover. So far so good, but khaki shirt and brown shoes with blues? Absolutely not. "With that combination, the shore patrol or M.P.'s will haul you in," I told him.

"Oh no, they won't," he growled.

"Oh yes, they will," I growled back.

"But my only white shirt came back from the laundry today with the collar half torn off."

He fetched the shirt and we tried to pin the collar together, but it was a failure. All this on the day he was to leave. I gave him one of my white shirts, two sizes too large, but we hauled it around his neck with a tightly knotted black tie. Meanwhile, I had an ordinary seaman bring a can of black shoe polish and they fell to work on his brown shoes. The result was not perfect but somehow would pass if not too closely scrutinized.

I kept urging Popeye to get going, lest he miss his bus. I pressed the ticket into his hand and told him to make his way to the bus depot at Fifth and Mission by 2 P.M. Halfway down the gangway, he stopped short. "I don't know how to get there," he grumbled. "I don't know where it is."

"My Gawd, you don't know?"

"No, I ain't never seen the damned place."

What to do? We made the dock gate at a trot and, luckily, found a cab. I gave the driver the destination and an extra buck, asking him to be sure his fare got into the building and on the bus. As the cab roared away, I got a last glimpse of Popeye, the great adventurer. His face bore an expression of bewilderment and I had the sudden feeling that he never really wanted to make this trip, perhaps didn't even have a sister "down south." But the die was cast. Popeye was about to cross the Rubicon, or Market Street if you will, into the wilds, south of the Slot. I returned on board and quietly collapsed on my bunk.

Peace had settled upon the ship as she rode quietly at her moorings, but not for long. Less than a week had gone by when, on a late afternoon while making a final round of inspection, I stopped short at the gangway area, trying not to believe what I saw. There was a dishevelled and bedraggled Popeye hauling himself up the gangway, his hat askew, his shirt open with tie hanging outside of his coat, and his blues in a condition indicating that, somewhere on his journey, he had encountered the vicissitudes which are historically the lot of the sailorman who forsakes the security of his shipboard environment and, in a hostile world, finds that the customary three meals a day, a bunk to sleep in undisturbed, and other amenities cannot be taken for granted.

Popeye eased himself with a groan onto his familiar bench. His demeanor was unusually subdued and he mumbled something about being broke. Could he have a cigarette and a cup of coffee? Following a good night's sleep, Popeye requested cancellation of his unused leave and was restored to duty status, probably the best medicine for him.

Understandably, my curiosity prompted me to seek some explanation from Popeye regarding the events leading to his premature return to duty, but the attempt was frustrated by his rambling conversation, which touched on many subjects except that having to do with where he'd been and what had happened, a method of discourse in which Popeye was a consummate master. I had to content myself with the conjecture that he failed to make connections at the bus depot and, while waiting for the next departure, had drifted into the nearest gin mill and temporary oblivion. How he made his way back to the ship without being picked up by the military police, considering his condition and appearance, merely added to the mystery.

In time, the ship was readied for sea, crewed and provisioned, and we headed out through the Golden Gate. With his usual adroitness, Popeye managed to be assigned to my watch.

In anticipation of a possible hostile encounter or other emergency that might arise during the voyage, use of the automatic steering device was discontinued in favor of hand steering. This was fine, as long as Popeye was not at the wheel. Inasmuch as either my junior watch partner, a seaman engaged in some task, or I were always in the wheelhouse, Popeye could not control his compulsive urge to talk.

Admonishing him to keep quiet, or ignoring him altogether, had no effect, except when the captain made his daily visit to the bridge. Popeye then clammed up immediately, devoting his whole attention to the business of maintaining a course. Thus the skipper remained unaware of the dilemma we were in and no official report was made to him. We kept hoping against hope that some solution could be found to a problem which became more intolerable as time went on.

In desperation, we finally hatched a plan we believed would bring home to Popeye that we were tired of his act. We would deprive him of any listener within earshot. Since we were now in fairly clement weather, upon relieving the watch, all watch personnel immediately went to the flying bridge above the wheelhouse, leaving Popeye alone below. Like the interior of the wheelhouse, the flying bridge was fully equipped with compass, peloruses, engine room telegraph and secondary steering station. A brass speaking tube behind the standard compass binnacle ensured immediate communication with the wheelhouse.

So now Popeye had no one to talk to, and we congratulated ourselves upon this nifty scheme, which seemed to hold great promise. Alas and alack, our elation was premature. The skipper came to the flying bridge and inquired about the presence of the entire watch. The time had come to tell him, and I explained the problem and the remedy we thought would bring about a solution. We were standing next to the compass and the skipper, bending his ear to the speaking tube, said, "I can see the entire watch up here, but there must be someone in the wheelhouse, because your helmsman is down there, talking away a mile a minute."

Incredulously, I lowered my ear to the speaking tube and, sure enough, there was Popeye holding forth, but with whom? Followed by the Captain and the watch, I entered the wheelhouse. There was no one there but Popeye. "What's the idea, Popeye? Are you talking to yourself?"

"Yeah, I am talking to myself. You guys left me alone down here and I am lonesome, ain't got nobody to talk to," he squawked, close to tears.

The voyage continued. Somehow, Popeye got the message. He was never entirely cured but, when it was necessary, I would point upward to the flying bridge, without saying a word. He understood the meaning of the gesture and would grumble, "Yeah, I know what you mean." Then he'd stop talking. Poor Popeye. Except for the obvious physical characteristics, he did not resemble the roistering, brawling character in the comic strip, but he had retreated into a fantasyland without relinquishing his need for the attention and support of those around him.

The military on board were an anti-aircraft battalion. Our destination was Kodiak Island. As a portent of coming events, we were accompanied by the cruiser USS CHESTER.

THE ARMY
TRANSPORT SERVICE

In 1941, the Army took possession of the passenger liner PRESIDENT CLEVELAND from the Dollar Line. As Third Officer, I made a lengthy transpacific voyage, calling at Honolulu, Manila, and the Chinese ports of Taku Bar in the Gulf of Pohai, Shanghai, and Hong Kong. In Europe, Poland and France had fallen and Great Britain was under siege. Along with others, I had been offered a commission as Lieutenant j.g., in the U.S. Naval Reserve. The recruiting officer said, "In your current position as Third Officer, I can't offer you a higher rank."

I consulted with the Army Transport Service Port Captain. His advice was, "Take it, we might all end up in that service, anyway." It was a prophecy that was to come to pass in later years. I joined the Naval Reserve.

America had not yet entered the war against Germany. Neither was the United States neutral in the strictest sense of the word. The Roosevelt Administration had transferred a fleet of World War I destroyers to Great Britain to deal with the U-Boat menace.

I had been promoted to Second Officer in the United States Army Transport (USAT) PRESIDENT CLEVELAND. The ship was on berth loading for Honolulu as a first port of call. The day of departure was December 6, 1941, exactly one year to the day since I had joined the

Army Transport Service. It was late afternoon when we passed through the Golden Gate, discharged the bar pilot and, having cleared the Farallon Islands, shaped a course for Honolulu. The following day at sunset, I had just turned on the running lights when the Captain entered the wheelhouse. He seemed agitated. "Turn out all lights and reverse course," he said, "we are going back to San Francisco."

He left the bridge without explanation, but I heard him giving orders to black out the entire ship. There was a flurry of activity as deadlights were closed over portholes that had them, with others receiving a coat of lampblack.

We were 450 miles at sea. It was late afternoon when we picked up the pilot. It was only then that most of us learned of the Japanese attack on Pearl Harbor. It was December 7, 1941, the Day of Infamy. Within 24 hours, the hull and white-and-buff superstructure was under a complete coat of battleship gray. The ship put to sea again, with a full load of military personnel. Joining the ship's complement, a detachment of Naval Signal Corpsmen headed by a Lieutenant, Chief Petty Officer and enlisted men, were on board.

Berthed in Honolulu, I was at the embarcation deck when I spotted the CPO ascending the gangway. He had been to Pearl Harbor. He looked stricken; his face was ashen. As he stepped off the gangway, I asked him, "Chief, what happened, what did you see?"

Without a glance in my direction, his voice barely audible, he said, "I can't talk about it," and turned away.

The dismal employment picture of the Twenties and Thirties changed radically when the United States entered the war. Merchant Marine officers, beached for years in the backwaters of a stagnant industry, suddenly found their services once more in demand. Any marine license was an Open Sesame for employment with steamship companies as well as branches of the armed services competing for men with these qualifications.

Merchant Marine officers holding commissions in the Naval Reserve were called to active duty. This included deck and engineer officers serving in the Army Transport Service. The Army, aware of the fact that the Navy was raiding their ships of personnel for which there was no replacement from a depleted manpower pool, protested vigorously in Washington, and won. Following several trans-Pacific voyages with Melbourne, Australia a last port of call, USAT PRESIDENT CLEVELAND, now

U.S.A.T. PRESIDENT CLEVELAND. Seward, Alaska, July 29, 1941

renamed USAT TASKER H. BLISS, departed for Norfolk, Virginia, carrying a full load of baled wool and 90 aviation cadets, destined for training in Canada. Following passage through the Panama Canal, BLISS joined a 20-ship convoy and, on a cold and rainy day in September 1942, arrived at Norfolk, Virginia. I put a long-distance call through to my wife. Before I had a chance to exchange greetings, she blurted out, "I bought a house!"

It was a fine surprise to add to the joy of my homecoming, and welcome news. During the twelve years of our marriage, we had paid rent and moved four times. At last, we had a home we could call our own. I recall my younger one asking me, "Daddy, will we have to move again some day?" I assured her that this time we had come to stay, and she seemed relieved. I realized that in the mind of even a young child, a secure future was an important ingredient of life.

Word had come down that TASKER H. BLISS would remain on the east coast to become part of a Naval task force. The Captain, First Officer, and licensed engineers remained with the ship. I drew the task of herding the remaining civilian crew back to San Francisco by special train. I then took annual leave, most of which was spent moving into our new home in lower Piedmont. Built in 1923, it sat on a gentle slope on a large lot. With four spacious bedrooms, living room, dining room and

We lived 45 years in this house on Rose Avenue, Piedmont, California

kitchen, it was a homemaker's dream. The future had never looked brighter.

I learned later that TASKER H. BLISS had been lost at the invasion of Casablanca.

The Army Transport Service had a ship under construction in the Puget Sound area named USAT FUNSTON. I joined the Captain, First Officer and others assigned to the ship as Second Officer. With compass adjustment and sea trials completed, FUNSTON went to sea with a full load of war material, including an artillery battalion and their howitzers.

Our destination was the island of Guadalcanal. The Marines had secured a landing field, but Japanese forces still held out in the hills. Contrary to expectations, the voyage was uneventful. We were daily in the shadowy presence of what seemed to be large naval vessels of a type and construction hitherto not seen. Their large superstructures barely visible above the distant horizon, they were part of the New Navy, the nemesis of the Japanese, who were to regret the day they attacked Pearl Harbor.

FUNSTON anchored close to a sandy beach at Guadalcanal and began discharging her cargo to flat barges. Every day at sunset, the ship crossed a narrow channel to Tulagi Harbor on a neighboring island to lay there overnight. Work was resumed daily at daybreak, after we crossed the waterway known as Torpedo Junction, named after the naval engagement to secure Henderson Field. In ensuing days, we observed white puffs of smoke in the hills as the Marines fired their howitzers into Japanese positions.

Upon returning to San Francisco, I was detached and assigned as First Officer to USAT BARBARA C., a woodenhulled steamschooner with three sets of cargo gear. She was a double-ender and, like others of her kind, was still considered seaworthy at a time when anything that could remain afloat was pressed into service.

Her destination was Australia, with frequent fuel stops enroute. At an average speed of eight knots, it would be a long voyage. It was my task to prepare a list of spare cargo gear, topping lifts, cargo falls, a set of mooring lines and small stuff. Having been employed exclusively in short coastal runs, the ship lacked charts, sailing directions, a nautical almanac, azimuth tables and, most important, a set of chronometers. Her two life-boats were equipped with oars, masts, and sails, nothing else. I ordered water casks, provisions, sea anchors, lifejackets and bails.

In the midst of all these activities, I was transferred as First Officer to USAT CHARLES P. STEINMETZ, so named after an electrical engineer famed for his many inventions and innovations in the field of electricity. In the media, he was known as the Wizard of Schenectady, where he was employed. STEINMETZ, a liberty ship, was on berth, loading for Australia. Her cargo gear had been modified. The standard three-ton booms and single cargo falls had been replaced with booms rated at ten tons with three-and two-sheave topping lifts and purchases. Standard equipment included a 50-ton boom at Number Two hatch and a 20-ton boom at Number Four hatch.

In March 1943, a gun at her stern manned by a naval armed guard detachment, the ship took departure for Melbourne, Australia. She carried a full load of asphalt in drums below deck and 125 creosoted poles as deck load. Whether it was just a rumor or a fact, the story got about that the asphalt was to pave a road in the Australian outback to a community known as Alice Springs. The poles were to be used to build wharves.

In anticipation of having to carry troops in the course of the voyage, the ship's tween decks had been provided with fittings to erect bunks for a thousand men. With cargo discharged, word was received that the ship was to transport elements of the First Cavalry Division to the forward area. Shipyard workers came aboard to set up bunks, but sanitary facilities for a thousand men? There were none, neither could the ship's galley feed a crowd of that size.

At whatever level the problem was discussed, it finally landed in my lap. In consultation with shipyard engineers, it was decided to install a latrine on the after-deck abreast of Number Four hatch. I had designed a 20-foot long metal trough with a varnished length of a two-by-four as seat, a roof, a back and two side panels completed the structure. A saltwater line for flushing was installed. Two wooden cook shacks were built on the fore deck to house mobile field kitchens.

The Commanding General of the First Cavalry Division Brigade, his staff, and a thousand enlisted men came on board. Their destination was Goodenough Island in one of the many archipelagos dotting the Southwest Pacific. It was a pleasant voyage. The regimental band on board gave morning concerts, boxing matches provided entertainment in the afternoon.

With our mission accomplished, the next port of call was Port Moresby to lift detachments of Australian and New Zealand troops who had cleared the area of Japanese troops. The ship next called at Brisbane for fuel and provisions and proceeded to Cairns, a small port on the Australian east coast. Here we learned the purpose of ten-ton gear. Under contract, a local firm had mass-produced, on an assembly line, landing crafts for vehicles and personnel (LCVP) weighing nine tons each. With range fuel in drums in the lower holds and tween deck wings, LCVPs in the hatch centers, and combat-loaded trucks on deck, we made several runs to small outposts in New Guinea.

From Port Townsend, a small port behind the Great Barrier Reef, we lifted an assortment of war material. The heavyset piece was landing craft machinery (LCM) weighing 26 tons. Using the 50-ton boom, we loaded it on top of Number Two hatch, the only place to accommodate an item of that size. Rumbling down the pier came a power shovel on caterpillar tracks. There was no place left on deck, but the officer in charge insisted on loading it. The equipment weighed 15 tons. It was picked up and loaded inside the LCM.

But we had not yet seen the end. A jeep came to a screeching halt at the gangway. An officer jumped out and, pointing to a pile of creosoted poles, declared, "They must go." The Captain was furious. I wondered if

The author, First Mate.
U.S.A.T. CHARLES P. STEINMETZ, a liberty ship, 1943.

these were the same poles we had landed at Melbourne. How had they found their way up here? In any event, they had to go. In a three-way conversation between the Captain, the stevedore officer and myself, it was decided to load them athwartships across Number One hatch. We snaked them aboard and secured them with chains and turnbuckles as I had done years ago with deckloads of lumber.

It was a strange sight as the ship went to sea, with the poles extending some 20 feet across the hull on either side. It was contrary to all accepted practices of cargo handling, but the exigencies of war demanded strange solutions.

Our first port of call was Oro Bay on the east coast of New Guinea, nothing more than an open roadstead. The first item to go over the side was the LCM with the power shovel inside. The piece weighed more than 40 tons. As a precautionary measure, I had reinforced the straps that came with the LCM with some wire straps of our own. The 50-ton boom lowered the LCM into the water. From a waiting boat an Army sergeant clambered in, started the motor and shoved off.

Through field glasses, I observed him as he beached the LCM, dropped the gate, cranked up the power shovel and drove it ashore. The entire operation had taken less than half an hour. It was all in the day's work.

The Port of Finchhafen was next up the coast. Alongside the pier, we offloaded the poles, the rolling stock, and other war material. Our next voyage took us from Brisbane to Darwin in northern Australia. On the evening of our arrival, the Captain, Chief Engineer, the two Navy officers on board and I were invited ashore to the officers' club. Following introductions, all remained standing, drinks in hand, until the regimental commander entered the room. All stood at attention as he raised his glass and intoned: "Gentlemen: The Queen."

Chorus: "The Queen."

I was about to say, "Down the main hatch," but caught myself in time. When seated, the officer next to me leaned over, "I say, old man, you were about to say something?" Before I could reply, the red alert signal came on. The party broke up, and everyone left the building. We headed for the ship on the double. In accordance with local regulations, the stevedore battalion streamed ashore and away from the pier area.

The officer in charge said, "Take the ship away, we don't want to see it sunk alongside the wharf."

With mooring lines trailing in the water, we headed out into the stream.

The hum of aircraft was audible as Japanese bombers returning from some inland mission, appeared high overhead. Against a cloudless azure sky, their broad wings gilded by the the last rays of the setting sun, every detail of the fuselages stood out clearly. Below them, puffs of black smoke hung in the air as the armed guard on board fired their guns. The squadron, probably having dropped all the bombs at an inland objective, droned on serenely. In disdainful disregard of the antiaircraft fire that kept the formation high, they disappeared in the distant haze. It was the only time during the voyage that our gun was fired in anger.

We sailed empty from Darwin and stopped at several Australian ports to load return cargo, mostly junked war material. At last we were homeward bound. It had been a good trip, but not without some difficulties. When joining the ship, I had been told that the captain had a reputation of being a hard taskmaster. It hadn't bothered me one bit. We were both cast in the same mold, having served our time in Cape Horn windjammers. At times he was moody and hypercritical of everything and everybody to the point of eccentricity, but I had stood my ground.

The deck crew was entirely composed of young men with a 90-day training course in seamanship at some mockup establishment. They were good youngsters. I enjoyed working with them and teaching them elements of marlinspike seamanship that had not been part of their initial training. At times I found it necessary to intervene on their behalf when the skipper bore down hard in a fit of explosive anger. In early March 1944, the ship tied up at the Fort Mason docks. I had been away from home a full year.

THE FIRST COMMAND

The armed forces of nations on both sides of the world continued to be engaged in a bitter struggle. Ships, whether in convoy or singly, maintained radio silence. Communication between ships, or ships and shore stations were by visual means only, either by flaghoists, signal lights or handheld flags.

Due to an acute shortage of qualified personnel, deck officers, including Masters, were required to take courses in the international signal code as well as the handheld flag code. Instruction was provided by chief petty officers of the U.S. Coast Guard. Upon completion of annual leave and while still at large, I passed both courses and was so duly certified.

In response to a telephone message, I reported to headquarters at Fort Mason. In his office, the port captain handed me my new assignment papers, saying, "You have been promoted to Master and will report tomorrow morning to your ship USAT WILL. H. POINT. Let me be the first to congratulate you," he said, as we shook hands. I thanked him and headed for the nearest telephone to pass on the good tidings to a jubilant family. Like many of my contemporaries, I had begun my career before the mast in merchant ships. The hawsepipe route from the fo'c'sle to the bridge had been beset by frustrations arising from the rapid decline of U.S. shipping during the decades following World War I and the chaotic conditions prevailing in the maritime industry prior to the outbreak of World War II.

Those long, bitter years of struggle and financial hardship in a turbulent and insecure shipping world weighed heavily on my mind as I summed up the past. I was forty-eight years old. It had taken me thirty-three years of unceasing effort to reach that dreamed-of pinnacle.

USAT WILL. H. POINT, ex WEST CAMARGO, was one of many freighters built during World War I to carry war material for the Allies. Following a brief time in commercial service, she was retired, like many others in the reserve fleet, only to be hauled out again to serve in World War II. A low-powered vessel, she could develop a speed of ten knots under favorable weather conditions.

I boarded the ship at an Oakland shipyard where she was in the process of undergoing voyage repairs and annual inspection. I did not meet the captain I was supposed to relieve. He had already left.

My quarters, consisting of a bedroom and adjacent office, were immediately below the bridge. Aside from the conventional furniture in my office, because no other compartment was available, there was a master gyro compass. I welcomed the fact that this equipment was under my immediate, sole control. Having attended earlier a course provided by the Sperry Gyro System and what with my more than fifteen years of experience in using and maintaining this equipment, I had the qualifications that no one else in the ship's company had.

In addition to a civilian crew of fifty-eight, the ship had on board a second lieutenant and four enlisted men representing the Army, a Navy armed guard detachment of twenty-six, headed by an Ensign to man the gun, for a total of eighty-eight souls on board. A newly installed automatic towing winch was at the stern, its purpose not known to me until I received my sailing orders on the morning of departure.

The ship was fully loaded with war material below deck and an enormous deckload of crated goods which turned out to be landing craft machinery (LCM) crated in three sections. In addition to this, the mission included the towing of a wooden six-hatch barge with a full load of range fuel in drums for Army field kitchens and manned by a crew of six watchstanders and a cook.

It was the evening before sailing. The ship was quiet as most on board had gone ashore for a last farewell. Having made a final round of inspection, I stood on the bridge for a last look across the foredeck. There was a brief moment when I felt my knees turning to water as I contemplated the enormity of the task before me.

U.S.A.T. WILL H. POINT, my first command (sketch by author).

On my first command, I was taking a 25-year-old ship, towing a deeply laden vessel across close to eleven thousand miles to a port far off the usual trade routes. I certainly had been handed a mission out of the ordinary. But I recovered quickly, knowing myself to be equal to the assignment.

Our destination was Milne Bay, a little-known harbor in New Guinea, with a fueling stop enroute at Pago Pago in American Samoa. On sailing day, the ship moved out into the stream. Pausing briefly abreast the Fort Mason docks, the barge named REDWOOD received our towing cable shackled onto a triangular plate at the end of a heavy chain-towing bridle. The barge was towed on short scope through the Golden Gate and the buoyed main ship channel across the bar. When past the Farallon Islands, the towing cable was paid out until the barge rode about a shiplength astern. The great adventure had begun.

From time immemorial, the Master, or Captain so-called, as a matter of courtesy had virtually unlimited responsibilities and powers, within the framework of maritime law, when at sea. Traditionally, he was the only person on board who was theoretically on duty twenty-four hours a day. He was the fountainhead of expertise and wisdom in all matters pertaining to the conduct and successful prosecution of a voyage. Consulting with department heads about problems of a general nature, he was, in the end, the sole arbiter dealing with all matters germane to the safety of the ship, her crew and cargo. In time, I was to discover that not everyone on board shared my belief in that lofty concept.

Master U.S.A.T. WILL. H. POINT, 1944.

Following replenishment of fuel and water at Pago Pago, the voyage continued. So far, we had been favored by fair winds and moderate seas, a condition which miraculously stayed with us until we arrived at our destination. During the weeks at sea, the barge had ridden slightly to windward. Because of the good weather, she had never activated the automatic towing mechanisms, the weight and the deep bight of the heavy towing cable being sufficient to keep her in position. From time to time, I had let out the cable a few inches beyond the roller chocks to prevent chafing in the same spot. This also provided an opportunity for me to exchange brief messages by hand signals with the cook on the barge, regarding the state of affairs on the barge.

Milne Bay turned out to be a narrow and very deep inlet. The depth of water precluded the possibility of anchoring in midstream. In fact, the place had become known as a graveyard to anchors and chains lost by ships in the great depths.

We let go of the barge to a tug and tied up to a small wharf. The following morning, an Army officer came to sign for the cargo. He eyed the deckload and said, "Why did you bring this stuff here?"

I countered with the question, "Now that it is here, what are you going to do with it?"

"You really want to see?"

"Yes, I would!"

A wild jeep ride on rutted roads through a partially destroyed coconut palm plantation ended up on a sand spit. From a small building, a slowly moving assembly line emanated carrying three tightly fitted sections of an LCM. A soldier with a welding torch connected the forward section with the midship unit by welding a heavy bead all around. A second soldier armed with a power steel brush removed the slag from the weld while others spray-painted the sections with a fast-drying green paint. Using the same procedure to connect the after end, the LCM was fully assembled and operational as the assembly line reached the water's edge.

Even before the craft was waterborne, sections of another LCM were on the assembly line to be similarly put together. This whole astonishing operation had taken little more than an hour.

Following discharge at Milne Bay, the ship was ordered to Sydney, Australia. Here it was learned that the WILL. H. POINT was to remain in the area for an indefinite length of time in the service of the U.S. armed forces under the command of General Douglas MacArthur.

The crew was in an uproar, having been under the impression that they had embarked for a six-to eight-week voyage. I pointed out to them that they had signed articles for a year and expressed doubt that the local Army command would agree to an earlier repatriation. In retrospect and in the light of coming events, I would have been better off with a new crew hired locally. The reason for the ship's retention soon became apparent. Aside from dry cargo spaces, there were forty thousand cubic feet of reefer space, available to carry refrigerated meats and vegetables to the camps and field hospitals in the forward area.

The initial leg of the voyage across the Pacific had provided me an opportunity to size up the men I had with me. The department heads were longtime employees of ATS, and seemed competent, or so I thought. As deck officers, I had an odd assortment. The First Officer, although holding the requisite license, apparently had no practical experience in seamanship. The Second and Third Officers were retired enlisted men, the former a storekeeper, the latter a pharmacist's mate. Both had been appointed on the basis of some general shipboard experience while serving afloat. Neither of them knew one end of a sextant from the other, let alone being able to obtain a navigational fix. In the parlance of the day, "Neither would have been able to navigate himself out of a chamberpot." Another Third Officer had a license backed up by some experience on deck.

With this disturbing assessment in mind, I accepted the fact that I was on my own and that full responsibility for anything and everything ultimately rested squarely on my shoulders. I expected that everyone not only would follow my orders, but would also fall in line with the tone of personal and professional conduct I intended to set. Nevertheless, leaving nothing to chance, I prepared a set of standing orders, outlining in detail the duties and responsibilities of watch-standing personnel. Every deck officer was required to sign these orders, attesting to the fact that he had read and understood that document. Additionally, each night before retiring, I issued night orders regarding course and speed and actions to be taken in case of emergencies. Each watch officer was required to acknowledge these orders by affixing his signature.

Navigation is divided into two phases. Celestial navigation (celonavigation, for short) involves determining a ship's position at sea by daily observations of celestial bodies such as the Sun, planets, and stars. The other phase is known as piloting, the art of conducting a vessel from place to place by soundings or taking bearings on charted landmarks, such as lighthouses, beacons and well-defined promontories and cliffs, illustrated and described in sailing directions. In some circles, piloting is also known as conning. The person in charge directs the helmsman and is said to be "at the conn."

Most landsmen are of the opinion that a ship is in greatest peril when on the high seas and out of sight of land. Nothing could be further from the truth. Experienced seamen know that the heavy traffic near land, fog, adverse tidal conditions, reefs, and shallows present hazards that require the utmost in caution and an expertise that can come only with years of experience. There were some good men on board, but the majority turned out to be individuals picked off the street with no background in seamanship and totally ignorant of shipboard life and the customs of the sea. In gathering this crowd, the service had truly scraped the bottom of the barrel. I foresaw troublesome days ahead.

In time, WILL. H. POINT was on the loading berth taking on war material and fresh meats and produce in the reefer spaces. Water and provisions for ship's use had been routinely provided, but getting bunkers was a more formal affair. Being in short supply, fuel was tightly controlled and issued only for the length of a voyage. The Master was required to pay a call on the naval officer in charge of the fuel depot, who held the rank of Commander in the Australian Naval Force.

Following a cup of tea and an exchange of pleasantries, I was asked how much fuel I needed. Knowing beforehand that the ship's tanks would not be topped off as was the peacetime custom, I was prepared to state the exact quantity needed for the coming voyage. Having signed for the fuel, I took my departure and headed for the hydrographic office to draw the necessary set of charts to cover this and future trips.

The routes led along the east coast of Australia, inside the Great Barrier Reef and across the Coral Sea to New Guinea ports such as Oro Bay, Buna, Draeger Harbor, Finchhafen and the island of Biak. I received two charts, one covering the Australian east cost, the inside of the Great Barrier Reef and the Coral Sea. The other covered the waters of eastern New Guinea. As I spread out the charts on the chartroom table to plot courses and distances, I was aware of the legend: "Surveyed by Matthew Flinders in 1802. Resurveyed by HMS DART in 1860."

I was not unfamiliar with the name of Flinders, having noticed it often on visits to Australia in previous years. There was Flinders Island, Flinders Street, Flinders Station, Flinders Range and a host of others. There was also Flinders Bar, a bar of soft iron encased in a brass tube attached vertically to the binnacle stand housing the magnetic compass. Its purpose was to compensate for certain compass errors. No one ashore seemed to know much about Flinders. When I asked someone at a social gathering, he scratched his head and said, "I've never met the bloke."

It was not until months later, when browsing through a bookstore in Sydney that I came across a tome with a colorful cover depicting a 17th Century ship of the line under full sail. In answer to my question, the seller said, "That's the story of Captain Flinders." At Last! I parted with seven shillings and sixpence and in the ensuing weeks delved into the life story of this remarkable man, a sailor, scientist, navigator and cartographer.

A contemporary of Captain Cook, Lieutenant Bligh and Sir Joseph Banks, a socialite with large private means, Flinders had been given a ship and commissioned by Banks and his associates to survey the lands down under and return with specimens of plant life from the unknown continent. Here was a story of high achievement, of despair and tragedy.

In the months to come, I was thrilled to sail along the coasts and travel the sea lanes charted with incomparable accuracy by this great navigator 142 years earlier, the man who had presented to the world Australia, the Fifth Continent.

CHAPTER 18

SAILING THE WATERS OF
AUSTRALIA AND NEW GUINEA

Sydney, as the seat of the U.S. Army Transport Service responsible for seaborne transportation in the Southwest Pacific, became our base of operations in the ensuing year. During all succeeding voyages, the ship was never out of sight of land, except when crossing the Coral Sea.

Piloting, conducting the ship from point to point to her final destination, was the primary means of navigation. Radar equipment, that great innovation responsible for major changes in navigational procedures, had not yet been made available to civilian-manned vessels. The equipment had been issued only to commissioned ships in the naval establishment.

Because of my years of experience in piloting ships in coastal and intercoastal waters, this was no problem to me. I soon discovered that none of the watchstanding deck officers had had any experience whatsoever in piloting. They had never heard of that old reliable, the bow and beam bearing, that simple and time-honored method of determining a ship's position relative to a safe distance from any charted point of land. It involved taking a forty-five degree bearing on a known object on land and a second bearing when the object was abeam. The distance traveled between bearings, as read from the taffrail log, was equal to the distance between ship and shore.

There were other methods, routinely used when operating in restricted waters. I instructed the watch officers in these proceedings, but always remained conscious of the fact that constant, close supervision on my part was the price to pay for the safety of the ship.

Along the coast and inside the Great Barrier Reef, I took the conn, taking short naps between positions. Exit or entry at the northern end of the reef was by way of the Grafton Passage, the only channel in the reef not mined. It led into the Coral Sea, the crossing of which had afforded as close to a night's sleep as I would ever get in these waters.

Approaching the southeastern tip of New Guinea, one entered China Straits, a body of water characterized by swift and treacherous currents and sudden rain squalls. Exit from the Straits was through the Raven Channel, a narrow opening in a coral reef, allowing a clearance of only inches on either side of the ship. I remained at the conn daily between the various ports and landings on the coasts of New Guinea and Papua, catching a nap here and there.

USAT WILL. H. POINT was a well-built and comfortable ship and should have been a happy ship. Any attempt on my part to foster a climate of amity was frustrated by an unruly and rowdy element in the motley crew. I was further aggravated by the department heads' failure to exercise any degree of control over their subordinates. In retrospect, it was simply a case of a hastily-thrown-together group of men from greatly divergent levels of society, most of them unable to make the adjustments necessary to cope with the limitations inherent in shipboard life.

Sydney, our temporary home port, was a freewheeling and hospitable city offering the many entertainments beloved by seafarers. Because of wartime conditions, pubs, the poor man's clubs, were opened only a few hours at the end of the workday, when masses of the thirsty bellied up to the bar in lines five deep to quaff as many beakers of the local, potent brew as they could handle within that short period of time. Bottled goods were available to those who knew how to get them. Alcoholism became a severe problem.

On a run along the coast, the ship developed steering gear trouble. My request for adjustment was met by the engineer with, "Hell, there is nothing wrong with the steering gear. You have no wheelmen worthy of the name, nothing but a bunch of cabdrivers."

This issued from a man who had been dismissed before and was allegedly reinstated only as the result of intercession by a highranking church-man, as I learned later. When I told him that I would signal the nearest port for permission to enter for steering-gear repairs, he said, "No, no, don't do that. If you can lay to for half an hour, I can fix it."

As time went on, there were other incidents that soured the relationship between departments. A troublesome development was what seemed to be a design failure in the anchor windlass. A newly cast slotted wheel, called the wildcat, had been installed. Anchoring at the various open roadsteads at the New Guinea Coast had become a nightmarish experi-ence. Once the anchor was let go, the chain would jump the slots and could not be controlled by the brake. Chunks of metal of the new casting flew through the air, causing the men on the fo'c'sle deck to run for cover. The cause of this malfunction was anybody's guess.

It took letter writing and many personal calls to convince the authori-ties that the equipment was unsafe and a change was mandatory. Over the objection that no replacement was available, I pointed to a half-sub-merged wreck of a liberty ship on a nearby beach and succeeded in having that windlass, complete with anchors and chains, transferred to the POINT.

In dealing with these problems, I did not have the support of the engineer. At times, I thought I felt his opposition and was puzzled as to his motives. I laid it to the fact that, in accordance with official policy, he had been required to sign off on this equipment at the completion of voyage repairs at the home port and now felt responsible for these fail-ures.

From the Hydrographic Office, I had received a new chart with the explanation that a new and shorter route had been cleared of mines, eliminating the hazardous narrows formerly used. It involved long stretches of open water leading through one single wide channel between two islands with newly installed navigational aids. It was called the Jomard Passage, and would I be willing to pioneer this new route? I welcomed the opportunity.

Following a sleepless night crossing a stormy Coral Sea, the ship en-tered the calmer waters leading to the Jomard Passage. I laid out a new course and distance to a point at which a course change was to be made in the direction of the new channel. I marked the point and time of course change on the chart. In my night orders, I entered the time of the course change to be made by the watch officer, in this case the second mate. I also entered the time I was to be called when the new navigational light on one of the islands was sighted, and I would take the conn. I believed that these simple procedures could be followed without difficulties. I was wrong.

Fully clothed, I stretched out on my bunk for some much-needed sleep. Perhaps it was a sixth sense that awakened me from a troubled sleep. My clock told me it was not yet time for me to be called, but I decided to get up anyway and go to the bridge.

Entering the wheelhouse, I saw in the distance, dead ahead, a large island that should not have been there, and realized immediately that the watch officer had not made the course change at time and point directed. He remained standing in the bridge wing, oblivious of my presence and apparently unaware of the fact that I had changed the ship's course. I took the wheel and sent the helmsman down to call the chief mate to come to the bridge and be a witness.

I called the second mate into the chartroom and pointed to his signature on the night orders and asked him. "Is this your signature?"

"Yes, sir."

"Had you read the night orders before you signed them?"

"Yes, sir."

I had him read the night orders out loud. When he read the part ordering the course change, I stopped him and asked, "Why did you not change course, as directed?"

He looked puzzled. "I guess I forgot."

Right then and there, I took a solemn vow: No one, but no one, would ever have the chance to wreck my career! I relieved him of his duties, turning the remainder of the watch over to the chief mate. I ordered the second mate to his quarters, to remain there until called. I later found him in his bunk in a drunken stupor, clutching an empty wine bottle. In the presence of another officer, I searched his room and confiscated his cache of bottles of wine. Upon the ship's return to Sydney, he disappeared, abandoning his belongings and pay, never to be seen again. For the record, I reported the incident to the local authorities.

Weeding out the incompetent, the unfit and the incorrigibles became an ongoing, difficult process. The Army dealt with their offenders in accordance with military justice, but was reluctant to handle cases involving civilian personnel in their employ. There was no shipping commissioner I could turn to, to prefer charges. In one of the outports, a fight among crew members resulted in injuries, vandalism, and destruction of ship's property. I turned the offenders over to the military police, to be held in the stockade pending investigation and possible trial.

DAY 1: At the request of a law officer, I filled out a charge sheet. He left, promising swift action.

DAY 2: Two Army officers boarded the ship. They identified themselves as prosecutor and defender, respectively, and requested more information and evidence to support my case. I showed them the broken furniture, slit mattresses and broken mirrors in the crew's quarters, and filled out more forms.

DAY 3: An Army officer came and identified himself as a deputy provost marshal. He said, "Captain, upon advice of counsel, it is the opinion of this command that there is insufficient evidence to justify keeping your men in the stockade any longer. It is recommended that you fine each man an appropriate sum of money, to be deducted on payday."

"Fine, hell!" I exploded. "These fellows will laugh at the idea, and will tell you and me that they will do this 'standing on their heads.' To be sure, I can invoke the logging process," I said. "According to maritime law, this involves logbook entries, stating in detail the nature of the offense and the fine, known as logging, to be assessed. None of this will become effective until the final payday at the home port. There it is subject to review by a shipping commissioner, who may reduce the fine or even cancel it. The remedy I need now is the permanent removal of the hoodlum element from this otherwise fairly decent crew."

The officer said, "Well, I see your point, and I will see what I can do, but I promise nothing."

DAY 4: He returned, saying, "Your men are very restless and are getting worried about what is going to happen to them. They request release from the stockade and promise that nothing like this will ever happen again. They want to return to the ship."

In a fit of sarcasm, I was about to say, "Well, send these poor, innocent boys back, fine me a hundred bucks, and call it a day." Fortunately, I thought better of it, and said, "Send them back today, but keep the ringleaders until we have sailed."

I identified three of them. A subdued crowd boarded the ship in time to enjoy a good lunch instead of the field rations that had been their daily fare in the stockade. The men were put to work to clean up their quarters. The engineers made temporary repairs to the plumbing and wash basins.

> DAY 5: Sailing day. As we were about to take in the gangway, the troublemakers were brought on board under guard. "It is the decision of the command to return these men to your custody," the Provost Marshall explained. "They cannot be held here any longer. Neither is transportation available for their return to Sydney. Sorry about this, and good luck," were his parting words.

With this failure to get rid of the bad apples, the days to come were far from trouble-free.

It had come to my attention that, from time to time, the Navy gun crew had taunted the civilian crew, calling them draft dodgers and overpaid by comparison with their pay as enlisted men. It became a sore spot with our men, who felt themselves to be on the defensive. They countered with the opinion that the gun crew was not exactly the cream of the crop, either. It was the sort of trouble we did not need, I explained to the young officer in charge of the Navy detachment. He promised to put a stop to it.

As time went on, the character and composition of the cargo we carried had undergone some significant changes. No longer was it all war material, but now included large quantities of comfort items donated by patriotic citizens to be distributed in the field by Special Services, attached to the various military branches. To name a few, there were such items as towels, wash cloths, bathing trunks, socks, hard candy, peanut brittle, and cigarettes.

At the first New Guinea port of call, a military stevedore battalion composed of close to a hundred men took over the discharge of cargo. Almost immediately, they ripped open all the boxes and cartons they could lay their hands on, stuffing their pockets with cigarettes and candy, also socks and bathing trunks. Anything they could not use, they dumped, much of it behind the sweat battens to wind up in the bilges. Very soon there seemed to be nothing but empty boxes laying about as the result of this frenzy of destruction.

Having been brought up with the idea that cargo on board ship was inviolate, I looked on with horror at these proceedings. There seemed to be no one in charge. I finally located an officer and showed him what was going on. He shrugged his shoulders. "They are entitled to it, they will eventually get it, anyway," was his comment.

The people on the pier finally woke up to the fact that there was plenty of activity in the holds, but not much was coming out to be landed ashore. A ranking officer came aboard to investigate and, seeing the picture, immediately ordered a halt to all activities and ordered everyone out of the hold. The ensuing spectacle was something to behold.

Everyone began to divest himself in a panic of the goods in his bulging pockets, throwing away cigarettes, candy and other things, here, there, and everywhere. The situation was not without its humor. Exit from the cargo holds was by means of steep, narrow iron ladders leading on deck through manholes just large enough to accommodate an average-size person. One tall, skinny lad made it halfway through, but got stuck in the middle. He was forced to descend again to get rid of six or eight bathing trunks, believing all the while that his silly performance was unobserved.

Operations ceased for the day and the hatches were battened down for the night to protect the goods against the nightly torrential rain squalls. The stevedore battalion returned the following day, but another and, for the ship's company, more severe problem arose.

Sanitary facilities on board had been constructed for an initial standard crew complement of thirty-seven. With an increased wartime manning scale and the addition of military personnel, the setup was strained to its very limits. With no facilities in the pier area, increasing numbers of stevedores began to use the crew's heads, with the result that, within hours, the place was a mess, the toilets plugged, the deck covered with excrement, and washbasins and fittings vandalized.

I called in the Army lieutenant attached to the ship to view the scene and requested that a stop be put to this intolerable situation. He protested hotly. "These men are out here fighting for their country and are entitled to anything the ship can provide."

I said, "Lieutenant, with all due respect to the military, these men are not combat soldiers, probably have never been exposed to enemy fire, or been out of the rear echelon."

He sputtered. "They are still soldiers and doing their duty by their country. That's more than your people are doing here in the safety of their ship."

Somehow I held my temper in check. "Mister, you stop right there. Just remember, you are also privileged to be on board this ship and I don't see you armed to the teeth, attacking the enemy. What's more, if the sanitary facilities of the battalion's compound ashore were to be found in this condition, the regimental commander would not tolerate it for one moment."

He stalked ashore in a huff. An hour later, he returned, saying, "I have a message for you. The Colonel says that if you don't like this situation, send your crew ashore to dig a latrine."

I felt that, in this highly charged atmosphere, any further contact with the local authorities would be useless, might even make matters worse. Yet something had to be done. With tempers cooled down, it was mutually agreed that the ship's force would build something on deck. I instructed the ship's carpenter to fabricate, out of lumber, a temporary structure to serve as a latrine. It was mounted on the ship's offshore bulwark, overhanging the bay water.

It was not a total solution. At least it demonstrated a willingness on the part of the ship to deal with a problem that should not have been ours in the first place. Sailing day came, and as the ship moved away from the pier, the crew dumped overboard the structure, which had become known as "the lieutenant's folly."

THE MAKING OF
A SHIPMASTER

Outwardly, peace had been restored to the ship, but old quarrels soon surfaced again. Most of them occurred among the unlicensed crew. In the traditional lore of the sea, a tough skipper would have called a miscreant out on deck and flattened him into pulp, as an example and warning to all hands as to who was boss. As a solution to disciplinary problems, it had its place in popular romantic tales of the sea, but in modern times it was not permissible and would have only created more problems.

Under the pressure of necessity, a civilian organization, operating out of Sydney, had come into being. It was called the "Southwest Pacific Patrol." It was composed of retired New York cops who, in a lifetime of law enforcement, had dealt with everything from juvenile delinquents to hardened criminals. Their mission was to deal with matters affecting the civilian components attached to the military.

Back in port, I called upon the Patrol for advice and assistance, and with their help succeeded in disposing of the undesirables. Next to fall by the wayside was the Chief Steward. A confirmed alcoholic, he was rarely sober when in port. During a lengthy layover in Sydney, he was picked up at various times for being drunk in public. The climax came when he was ejected from one of the best hotels, having urinated on one of their valuable Persian rugs in the foyer. He was taken into custody at other times for his disgraceful conduct in public, bringing disgrace upon the uniform of the Army Transport Service.

A local replacement reported for duty. An Australian, I liked him at once. Aside from being a professional in his field, he was also a seaman and conducted himself accordingly. But the end was not yet in sight. I had spent a great deal of time trying to figure out the reason for the engineroom crew's bitter antipathy towards the men on deck.

Some of it was known to be traditional. Because of the early days of coalburning engines in ships still carrying sails, the men in the engine room were often referred to as "the black gang." But here was a degree of hostility pointing to an underlying cause more severe than mere name-calling. I knew that the former master was an alcoholic, a very amiable person when in his cups. He probably had a good drinking companion in the engineer and allowed him considerable latitude in running things his way. Since I had other ideas on that subject, it was inevitable that we should clash at times.

When in port, he drank heavily and at times engaged in drinking bouts in his quarters with his subordinates. When I remonstrated with him, I encountered a sneering contempt, an attitude with which his whole department had been indoctrinated and whose motto now was, "The Skipper? Who the hell is he?"

It was time to clear the decks. I called on the Commanding Officer of the Army Transport Service and laid the case before him, concluding, "There is going to be only one skipper in this ship, and I intend to be it."

Obviously, he had not been unaware of the situation. His only comment was a terse, "Check."

I returned to the ship in late afternoon. One of the engineers confronted me, saying, "How come you fired the Chief?"

My reply was, "What do you mean, I fired him? Don't you know he was transferred to another ship for the good of the service?"

The following day, a new Chief Engineer came on board. He was a Hollander. He lasted three days. When he left, he said, "Good luck to you, Captain, I don't want any part of that gang down below."

Another Chief Engineer was assigned who seemed capable of taking matters in hand. I had filled the second mate's billet by temporarily promoting one of the third mates. That vacancy was filled by a young fellow from the local vessel-manning cadre. He was dressed in a black, metal-studded leather jacket, black pants, black boots, and he wore a visored cap at a jaunty angle. When I questioned him about his background, he said, "I have been a deckhand on some of the Army's small craft. In my peacetime employment, I am a test driver for a motorcycle manufacturer."

Under the circumstances, I felt I could do no better. I assigned him to the 8 to 12 watch where I could keep an eye on him. I told him, "Just do what I tell you and you'll be all right."

The ship was quiet now, and resumed her regular runs to New Guinea ports. On one of the voyages, in addition to war material we carried a large consignment of canned beer and soft drinks. At the port of discharge, the goods were stowed in a large open compound protected by a cyclone fence topped with rolls of barbed wire. At two opposite corners, watchtowers had been erected and manned by rifle-toting guards to prevent pillage. Bright lights illuminated the area at night.

The ship had now been in the water for nine months. In the warm tropical waters, the underwater hull had become encrusted with barnacles and other marine growth. To my delight, the ship was ordered to Newcastle, New South Wales for drydocking and an anti-fouling paint job. It was for me a nostalgic return to the past. I had last been in Newcastle in 1914, thirty years ago, as an ordinary seaman in a German sailing ship.

But times had changed. No more forest of masts of dozens of Cape Horn windjammers of many nationalities awaiting loading berths in the Hunter River estuary. A lone rustbucket, her sides stained red from iron ore, was the only ship present. No more visits to the old Seaman's Mission for a bit of religion rewarded by tea and cake. No more roaming the beach on warm moonlit nights and a forbidden dip in the breakers, taking flight upon approach of the constable. "Have you been swimming? Have you now?" And, knowing very well we had, he let us off with a warning.

Now there was no more clambering over the old wreck of a French fourmast bark on the breakwater at the harbor entrance. Our pleasures then had been few and easily satisfied, for we were teenage boys and on the lowest rung of the professional ladder.

Times had indeed changed and, with this return to Newcastle in 1944, as a shipmaster, one of the most respected callings in the nations of the British Commonwealth with a place second to none in her social structure, all doors were open to me. With the ship cold and the galley closed while in drydock, the crew was housed ashore. With a room in the best hotel in town, I enjoyed the status and concomitant prestige but not without an occasional whimsical contemplation of carefree, bygone days. What price nostalgia?

With repairs completed and hull shining with a new paint job, the ship was again waterborne and taking on fuel and water. On the embarkation deck I was met by a man I had seen about at times. "Compliments of the paint company for using their products," he said, as he handed me a check.

"I had nothing to do with choosing your paint. It was entirely in the hands of the shore-based authorities," I protested.

"Take it. It is customary to do this in the interest of good will."

I had known for years that the spreading of gratuities was an accepted practice in the European shipping communities. For shipmasters and other functionaries it was a welcome source of income to augment their modest salaries. It was condoned by employers who thus saw no need to raise anyone's salary. Gratuities were always handed out after services had been performed; therefore, they were not seen as bribes. I knew the visitor was familiar with this universal custom, but I was unwilling to accept it. "I don't think it would be wise for me to accept this gift," I said, as I returned the check to him. "If word leaks out, I might be subject to criticism. What's acceptable in Europe might not go over big in the States. In the USA, even people in semi-public positions must be Simon-pure, don't you know?" "As you wish, Captain. By the way, you still have a full day in port. I am making the rounds of my customers tomorrow. How about coming along for the ride. We'll stop for dinner somewhere at the end of the day. What do you say?"

In all my calls at Australian ports, I had only seen the port cities. To see something of the hinterland had a strong appeal. "My friend," I said, "I shall be delighted. I am looking forward to it."

A bright morning sun illuminated a treeless landscape. Through low brush an unpaved country road, often no more than tracks with a grassy center hump, wound its way. Stopping at isolated communities I took a short walk while my friend negotiated sales with his customers. There were no filling stations anywhere; none were needed. From time to time the driver would stop, haul a small bag of charcoal pellets out of the trunk and dump its contents into a container under the hood. As the ancient Chevrolet sedan, in the heat of the day, wheezed along over rutted roads through a featureless landscape, I began to long for a cold beer. It was late afternoon as we stopped at a combination country store and restaurant for dinner. Eying the enormous slab of well-done beef on my plate I said to my companion, "This looks like half the side of a cow. Is this customary?"

"Yes, there are a lot of wild cattle running around here and beef is cheap." We washed it down with copious drafts of the local potent brew.

I awoke in the morning, stiff and sore from the ride. As the ship passed through the breakwater, Newcastle once again lay astern. I was never to see it again. The pleasant interlude had come to an end, and the ship resumed her runs to New Guinea ports, which now included Biak Island. Christmas and New Year found us in Sydney, climatically the hottest days in the Southern Hemisphere.

One day, I received a visit from the Southwest Pacific Patrol. They had with them my former Chief Steward, flanked by two men. "Captain," they said, "he is dried out now and would like to rejoin your ship. He is really a very nice fellow."

I knew he had sold the patrol a bill of goods. I said, "Gentlemen, I know him to be what you say, but I don't need nice fellows that can't stay sober, so please keep him or ship him out elsewhere. I am satisfied with the man I have."

We were now in the year 1945, and the shipping articles would be up in March. I made arrangements to have the men paid off and repatriated.

They were replaced by locals, including a chief mate. All of them were professional seamen, and for the first time I felt that I was in full and undisputed command, and for a while I entertained the idea of staying with the ship. But I thought of my family and decided it was time to go home. I wrote a letter to the home office, requesting that I be relieved. It took about six weeks before a new man showed up. I was given a railroad ticket to Brisbane for repatriation.

It was a memorable ride in rickety old railroad equipment retired years ago and recalled into service. There were many stops enroute, and every time the train started up, I sometimes had the feeling that the part of the coach I was in might not follow. The hard wooden benches had not been designed for comfort and I was exhausted when I disembarked early in the morning in Brisbane.

I had been directed to report to Camp Ascot and hired a cab to take me there. A racetrack by that name had been converted to a camp where military and civilian personnel awaiting repatriation were housed in tents and fed out of field kitchens. To my shock and surprise, I found my crew still there. When I questioned the young lieutenant in charge, he shrugged his shoulders. "We have not been able to get transportation and I don't know when we will."

He gave me the number of a tent. "You will be housed there, with three others of your crew. You can draw a blanket and pillow from the sergeant." Noting my expression of disbelief, he said, "Sorry, that's the best I can do for you."

I had the impression that he savored my discomfiture. I called for a cab and returned to town for lunch at a local hotel dining room. Sitting at a table with several Army officers, I told them of the Camp Ascot situation. One of them pointed to an officer. "Talk to him, he is the billeting officer."

The billeting officer said, "I can get you a room here, but the charge will exceed your food and lodging allowance."

"No problem," I said. "I'll make up the difference.

I returned to camp to pick up my gear. The lieutenant said, "You will have to report here every day at 9 a.m. In person."

"Can't I do it by phone?"

"No, sorry, we have to have a daily head count, with everyone present." I went away, vowing to have my revenge if the day ever came.

Having settled in, I had my well-tailored suntan uniform cleaned and pressed and paid a courtesy call on the local U.S. Army Commanding Officer at his office in Victoria Park, a prestigious suburb of Brisbane. In the course of the conversation, I mentioned that my crew had been sitting here for nearly two months with uncertain prospects for repatriation, while in the States they were crying for men to man the many new ships that had been built. From the expression on his face, I could tell that he had been unaware of the situation.

When I reported at Camp Ascot the following morning, I was met by the Lieutenant, his face dark with anger. "So, you have been talking at headquarters, eh? You sure have done a job on me. The Colonel has been on my back, giving me hell by the hour on the hour."

I smiled sweetly at him. "Now, why would the Colonel do a thing like that to a nice fellow like you?" I'd had my revenge.

That week, Germany surrendered. On. V.E. Day, U.S. personnel had been advised to stay in their quarters. From my hotel room window, I

Master U.S.A.T. WILL. H. POINT, 1945

watched the milling, cheering and dancing crowd in the streets, giving
vent to their feeling of relief in a noisy demonstration.

A few days later, I embarked with the rest of the crowd in the transport
WEST POINT, a converted passenger ship. With an overflowing throng,
the ship's facilities were strained to the limit. Berths designed for one
person now held three. All washing and bathing facilities had been converted to saltwater. The only fresh water available to passengers was in
drinking-water fountains, guarded by marines. The exception was a daily

allowance of one bucket of hot freshwater to the men and their warbrides and babies, of which the ship seemed to carry a full load. An all-pervading smell of diapers hung in the air. Meals were served in three sittings.

I made full use of the ship's good library. Between reading and hour-long walks on whatever deck space was available, I managed to stave off boredom.

It was a sunny day in late May 1945, when I stepped ashore at the San Francisco waterfront for a jubilant reunion with wife and children. For the second time, I had been away for more than a year. We both had chafed under the strain of these long absences. We also knew that, with the realization of my fondest dream and the security of a permanent status in Federal service, I would follow the sea for the rest of my working days.

Carolyne came from a California shipowner's family and a New England ancestry dating back to 1656. We were both proud of the fact that her forefathers, through three centuries, had included eleven mariners, seven of whom had been master mariners in sail, trading in the West Indies and as far away as the Spice Islands. She understood and accepted the fact that being married to a sailor would involve periods of separation. She understood a man's love of the sea and his ship, and would say at parting, "Go back to your second wife now."

USAT WILL. H. POINT, my first command, had been a learning experience in the course of which I had passed through the crucible of baptismal fire. The difficulties experienced faded into the background, when compared to the success of a mission that included operating without benefit of convoy in waters not yet entirely cleared of enemy submarines. Piloting a ship successfully through many dangerous waters had never been a chore, but rather a thrilling challenge to be met as a matter of course.

The experience had conditioned me to be a shipmaster, capable of dealing with any and all problems the future would hold for me. The world was my oyster.

Upon my return I found a notice in the mail promoting me to Lieutenant in the Naval Reserve. My brother-in-law, Howard Beadle, like myself and many others, had been commissioned as a Lieutenant·j.g. in the Naval Reserve. Following the closing down of the family business, he had joined the staff of the Interocean Steamship Co, an agency handling U.S. and many foreign vessels. A hard worker, he had been well schooled by his father in the steamship business. A handsome lad, endowed with extraordinary good looks, a heritage from his grandmother, Sarah Stetson, his charismatic personality and professionalism in the field of shiphusbandry had earned him the friendship and esteem of his co-workers, his employers and the many shipmasters who had benefitted by his services.

After Pearl Harbor, his employers released him to serve in the Navy. Attached to the 12th Naval District in San Francisco, he almost immediately came to the attention of ranking Naval officers, who recognized his expertise in the field of ship operation. The Navy had taken over Encinal Terminals in Alameda, California, as a major shipping point for the distribution of war material. Howard, now definitely on the way up, assembled and trained a large staff of naval and civilian personnel to conduct the affairs of the fledgling establishment of considerable magnitude. Some of his associates from Interocean became members of his staff.

Advancement in rank was speedy and partly necessary to enable him to deal on an even footing with commanding officers of naval transports and supply ships. Thus, within the space of three years he advanced to Lieutenant, Lieutenant Commander and Commander, a process which in peacetime would have taken at least fifteen years. The war ended, and Howard was discharged from the service, receiving a letter of commendation and appreciation from Secretary of the Navy Forrestal.

Upon his return to Interocean, he was immediately promoted to Man-

Encinal terminal group photo. Second row, center, CDR Howard Beadle, USNR.
Photo by Moses Calhoun, Commercial Photo Co.
Moses Cohen photo collection housed at the Bancroft Library and Oakland Museum, Oakland, CA .

Howard G. Beadle

ager of Operations with full power and responsibility for all phases of operation of the entire establishment. His star was on the rise.

The president of Interocean and his associate had acquired the steam schooners WAPAMA and CELILO to be operated between San Francisco and Los Angeles, replacing the steamers HARVARD and YALE, and their predecessor, the White Flyer Line. It was only natural that the handling of these ships would become a part of Howard's duties. With characteristic energy, he plunged into the business of managing these two relics of a past era, devoting full time and much more to the multitude of assignments. In time, it proved to be his undoing.

On a cold gray morning in July 1946, we led his father, George Beadle, who was living with us, into the kitchen. We sat him down and told him that his son had succumbed to a cardiac arrest. Howard and his wife, the former Elizabeth Hutcheson, and their young daughter Brooks, returning from a business trip in Washington State, had retired for the night in a small country hotel in the Redwoods. Near midnight he stirred, sighed, and was gone. No medical help was near, and in any case would have come too late. At age 40, a meteoric career had come to an end. Why? Overwork? Definitely. The anguish of his father was indescribable. Bursting into tears, he cried out, "Why could it not have been me!"

He never fully recovered, and followed his son a year later. Elizabeth returned to Washington State, where she was born, to rejoin her large family, taking Brooks with her. Grief and the difficulties inherent in early widowhood took its toll. Within four years, Brooks became an orphan. At a family council, it was decided that she should live with us under the guardianship of her Aunt Carolyne, her mother's family being blessed with many children, but not with an abundance of worldly goods. In late 1950, we welcomed Brooks, age eight, to our family as another daughter.

TRANSPACIFIC VOYAGES

The Army Transport Service, now called the Army Transportation Corps, controlled all transportation, afloat and ashore. Ships were operated by the Water Division. Returning from leave, I was assigned to various ships to relieve shipmasters for their vacations. In August 1945, I took command of USAT YARMOUTH, chartered from the Eastern Steamship Company in Boston, Massachusetts. A twin-screw vessel, she could develop seventeen knots. For the remainder of the year, she carried troops to various Pacific islands.

One of the more notable voyages was when, in addition to troops, the ship carried close to one hundred young women, volunteer employees of the American Red Cross, bound for Manila. The group, headed by a tall woman with a commanding presence, was to provide Red Cross services to military and civilian personnel stationed in the Philippines.

Waystations enroute were two Pacific Islands, Ulithi and Eniwetok. Arriving at the former in the early morning hours, the island's Commander invited all the women and the Commanding Officer of the military department and his staff ashore for lunch. None of the several hundred troops were granted shore leave, and they did not hesitate to voice their displeasure by shouting "discrimination!" None of the civilian ship's officers had been included in the invitation, which was just as well. When I was approached by some of the crew asking why they had not been granted shore leave, I read them the regulation which prohibited shore leave when the layover in port was eight hours or less. We sailed in late afternoon when the visitors had returned to the ship to the resounding boos of the troops on board.

In Eniwetok, no shore leave was granted to anyone. My military counterpart and I were ordered ashore to attend a briefing by the resident naval officer regarding the last leg of the voyage, ending in Manila. YARMOUTH was to join, along with other ships, a convoy of naval transports through the island-dotted waters where enemy forces were believed to be still active, not having received the message about the end of the war.

In civilian-manned transports, military as well as civilian passengers were under the administrative control of the military department aboard. To a degree, I shared that responsibility and had let it be known to the crew that fraternization with female passengers aboard would not be permitted. Nevertheless, there were some Romeos, civilian as well as military, who believed that the entertainment of female passengers was part of their duties. It had not been easy to exercise full control in the situation, and it was with relief that I saw this consignment of pulchritude go ashore in Manila.

The ship had a week's layover, at the end of which I was invited by the Red Cross supervisor to have lunch with the group. With characteristic efficiency, they had erected a compound to house the company. It included an open-air dining area, complete with tables, chairs, red-and-white checkered tablecloths, napkins, and shiny eating utensils. Table service was provided by employees recruited from the local population. Overall, there was an aura of competency, and I complimented the supervisor upon her leadership.

Back in San Francisco, I was informed that YARMOUTH was to be returned to her owners. Enroute to the East Coast, we stopped at San Pedro to pick up six hundred German POWs, to be returned to Camp Shanks in New York State for repatriation to their homeland. At the Panama Canal, representatives of Eastern Steamship Company came aboard to survey the ship along the way, with respect to her return to commercial service. With the exception of myself, most of the crew were former employees of Eastern and expected to return to that service. I was asked to stay with the ship and the company, but with my wits sharpened by earlier experience in the uncertainties of a chaotic industry, I wisely declined the offer.

Following the return of the ship at Boston, I herded the crew back to the West Coast by train. It was a long trip by circuitous routes, with many stops to allow more important trains to go by. The rolling stock of ancient Pullman cars was drawn by a coal-burning engine, depositing layers of cinders throughout the train.

Traveling mostly along southern routes and away from congested centers of population, the weather was hot. The men were getting restless and bored. I was approached by a delegation. "Captain, would you get us some cold beer? We will hold a tarpaulin muster to pay for it."

I counted noses and agreed to provide two cans of beer per man per day for the rest of the trip. Following consultation with the conductor, a number of cases of beer was brought on board. I charged the bo's'n with the daily issue. This was a mistake. Within a day, the supply was exhausted. Some of the men had gotten drunk and smashed some windows. When I contacted the conductor, he laughed. "Don't worry about it, Captain, this equipment is ready for the scrap heap, anyway." Needless to say, there was no more beer.

In time, I discovered a stowaway on board and had him ejected when we stopped at a siding. But, no doubt with the connivance of some crew members, he was still on board when we disembarked at San Francisco. Joining the crowd, he swiftly disappeared, not to be seen again. Fortunately, no one questioned me at headquarters as to why there had been one more person than the travel document had allowed.

In the early months of 1946, I was assigned to USAT CHATEAU THIERRY. Built during WWI as a passenger ship, then converted to a troop carrier, her last service had been as a hospital ship. She was scheduled for lay-up in the Puget Sound area in Washington State.

U.S. Hospital ship CHATEAU THIERRY, Port Madison, Washington, April 1946.

Her engines were designed to develop a speed of eighteen knots. Following a long period of idleness, her propulsion machinery had failed at several attempts to put her to sea. With a skeleton crew on board, we took to sea for one more try. A tug had been assigned to follow and take the ship in tow in case of a breakdown. By the end of the first day, the tug was out of sight, a black plume of smoke the only sign of its presence. With the ship now cruising at fourteen knots, it was deemed safe to dismiss the tug. Two days later, the ship dropped anchor at Port Madison, in Puget Sound.

Within days, the crew and I were ordered to Seattle, where I took command of USAT GENERAL A.W. GREELY. The ship had been manned by a Coast Guard crew and attached to U.S. Naval forces during the war. Now acquired by the Army Transportation Corps, the ship departed for San Franciso for the removal of armament, overhaul and refurbishing.

The vessel was a C4 type, meaning a cargo ship with four hatches. Like many others of her type, she had originally been laid down as a cargo carrier. All or most of them had been converted to troop carriers by

U.S.A.T. GENERAL A.W. GREELY, O.H. Friz, Master, Spring, 1947.

adding on a superstructure, nearly the full length of the hull. In fair weather, the ship could cruise at fifteen knots or better, still well below the design speed, and it had poor seakeeping qualities in rough weather.

A few days before sailing, I was called to the Port Captain's office for some instructions. His secretary said, "The Captain is out right now, but will be back shortly; why not take a seat and wait for him?" She added, casually, "On this voyage you will have with you Mr. B. as third mate. We know you can straighten him out."

I was immediately on guard, seeing trouble headed my way. I had never met Mr. B., but knew of him by his reputation as an alcoholic. A veteran employee of the service of close to thirty years' standing, he had never risen above third mate. With my WILL. H. POINT experience still fresh in my mind, I felt it was time to speak up. I said, "For years, Mr. B. has been employed here and is, like many others, an oldtimer. You are asking me, a newcomer, to do within a few months what the Service has not been able or willing to do in years. I don't wish to become known as the fleet disciplinarian. It is not my style of operation. So, please lady, don't do this to me."

I went home when the Port Captain phoned, saying he would not return to his office that day. A few days later, GREELY put to sea. Mr. B. was not on board. I had spoken my piece in the right place at the right time!

Many years later, while in port, I received a visitor. He was well dressed and the picture of glowing health. It was Mr. B. "I came aboard to pay my respect to you, Captain," he said. "I am retired now and have been clean for a number of years. When you declined to take me with you on the GREELY, it was a jolt to me. I resolved to quit drinking, and I made it stick." I did not know what to say. I did not ask him whether he'd had help in his cure, and he did not volunteer the information. Over a cup of coffee, I congratulated him, and we parted as friends.

The year-end holidays found the ship at sea. Dining rooms, crew messes and troop messes were decorated with Christmas trees and tinsel. I joined the ship's company in the officers' mess for the traditional holiday fare. There was an air of expectancy as the waiters moved about serving individual portions of white and dark turkey with all the trimmings, ignoring my presence. Looking around I saw expressions of amusement on some faces; others remained serious. The mystery was solved when a waiter approached carrying aloft a large platter.

"Compliments of the Chef," he said as he placed it in front of me,

Master O.H. Friz
aboard U.S.A.T. Army Transport ship A.W. GREELY, April, 1948.

along with a set of carving tools. I knew at first glance this was not the traditional turkey but a goose. In the course of the voyage I had learned that the cook had worked on transatlantic liners, many of which carried German cooks. In this manner, he had learned about the Christmas goose. As a member of the party conducting daily inspections of galley and mess rooms I had stopped and chatted with him briefly. On the ship's articles he was listed as Chief Cook, but I always called him Chef. Of all the black crewmen I'd had with me he stood out. He was blacker than anyone I had ever seen. His features were regular with an aquiline nose and a strong chin. Tall and erect, he carried himself with innate dignity. His overall appearance bespoke a noble lineage.

Following dinner I went to the galley to express my appreciation. "Chef, how did you happen to find a goose among all the turkeys?"

"I think it just came aboard by mistake," he said, trying to look innocent and make deprecatory gestures with his hands. I thanked him, but I thought I knew better. In the course of time I lost sight of him but I never forgot his act of regard and kindness.

Ports of call for GREELY were Guam, Manila, Yokosuka, Japan and Pusan and Inchon in Korea. Aside from troops, the passenger list now included dependents, wives and children. Arrivals and departures at these ports were mostly routine.

Yokohama, at the southern end of Tokyo Bay, was reached via a headland called Kanon Sake on the port side. Then we passed through a channel guarded by three small fortified islands, known as Forts 1, 2, and 3, a waterway often congested by small craft.

Approaches to Inchon, Korea, presented more of a challenge. The entrance to the main ship channel was marked by a sea buoy, often out of place because of strong tidal currents. A twisting, narrow channel, flanked by forbidding rock formations on both sides, led into a wider bay.

The channel was used by most ships when a pilot was available. Scoured clear of sediment by currents, the rocky bottom provided no holding ground in which to anchor in an emergency. Entering or leaving port was only during daylight hours and always against the current, running from eight to ten knots an hour. A second channel was available, called the Western or Flying Fish channel. I was to use it often in later days, following a near disaster.

GREELY was outbound on a clear and sunny morning, stemming the flood current. Preceding us was a converted landing craft (LST). Upon

Open House on Maritime Day, 1948 at SFPE aboard U.S.A.T. GENERAL GREELY.
Captain O.H. Friz explains navigation aides to visitors, from left: daughter Georgia,
sister-in-law Doris Bruce (holding Carol), wife Carolyne, and others.

entering the channel, the landing craft and rock walls had suddenly disappeared in an unexpected, dense fogbank. It was too late to turn back. I
could hear and follow the fog signal of the LST. Using the depth-sound-
ing machine and echoes from the rock walls, the ship was kept in mid-
channel. Eventually, according to the chart, the ship entered an open body
of water surrounded by islands on all sides. In the dense fog, the depth-
sounding machine was the only means of navigation. Having steamed
slowly in circles for nearly an hour, the fog lifted and we gained the open
sea. It had been a harrowing experience.

Later, I chose the Western Channel. Flanked on both sides by extensive mud flats, a safe anchorage could be found in an emergency. The
drawback was the absence of navigational aids, such as channel buoys,
but there were charted points of land on which bearings could be taken.

Pusan, the principal port on the southern tip of the Korean peninsula,

Captain and wife, 1948.

presented no special problems, except for the fact that the harbor was crowded with ships at anchor, and there were many submerged wrecks. Winding our way past these many obstacles toward the pier, someone facetiously remarked, "With another coat of paint on the hull, we wouldn't have made it!"

I had been on this run now for more than a year, and it was time to take annual leave. I took the family up to Richardson Grove in the Redwoods, where we spent an enjoyable two weeks, hiking, horseback riding, and swimming in the Eel River.

Captain and children, 1948.

One morning, having bought a San Francisco newspaper at the local store, I observed a photo on the front page. It showed the bow of a large vessel surrounded by rocks and concrete slabs. A bulldozer, operated by a U.S. soldier, attempted to push the slabs away from the ship's bow. The name of the vessel read USAT ADMIRAL W.S. SIMS. The location of the stranding was Fort No. 2, at the entrance to Tokyo Bay.

I read the short article under the picture. It provided no information as to the cause of the mishap or the name of the Master. I laid the paper aside, and promptly forgot about it.

With our vacation ended, we chose to drive home by way of coastal Highway One. Passing Point Arena Lighthouse, some ninety miles north of San Francisco, we entered a fog bank. A still air carried the fog signal of a ship offshore. I turned to my wife, and said, "By the sound of that signal, that ship is much too close to shore, I hope she doesn't wind up on the rocks."

I had the car radio on for music. Less than half an hour later, the program was interrupted by an announcer who said, "Word has just been received that a British steamer has been stranded on a rocky ledge off Point Arena Lighthouse."

I listened for more information. It was not long in coming, and I stopped the car to get a full account. It was a tragic story. The Master was on his last trip before retirement. The employees of the San Francisco branch office had been waiting for him, to present him with the traditional gold watch in recognition of his many years of faithful and loyal service to his company. Subsequent newspaper reports did not elaborate whether the Master was on the bridge or a watch officer had the conn. The ship was declared a total loss. The tragedy of an experienced shipmaster losing his ship on his last voyage and facing ruin at the end of an honorable career made a deep impression on me. Maritime history was full of events of that nature, and I made a solemn vow never to burden a watch officer with the responsibility that, in the end, would be mine and mine alone.

I still had a few days' leave left, at the end of which I reported to the office to learn when my services might be required. It was late afternoon

U.S.A.T. ADMIRAL W.A. SIMS.

when the secretary said, "You may as well go home, Captain. It doesn't look like there is anything doing today, anymore."

Arriving at the house, Carolyne stood on the front porch, "Where have you been? The phone has been ringing constantly this last hour."

I phoned the office to learn that there had been an unexpected change. I was to be at headquarters in the morning at eight thirty. I was met by the Port Captain who said, "The Chief of Transportation in Washington, D.C. has ordered the immediate relief and retirement of the Master of the SIMS and has ordered this command to fly out a replacement without delay." He continued, "The ship has been repaired and will be ready to sail. You are to bring her home."

I was startled, but before I could say anything, he handed me my travel orders and plane-ticket on a commercial flight to Honolulu. "From there, you will proceed by Flying Tiger Line to Tokyo. A car from the motor pool will take you home to pack what you need and take you to the airport. Your family can see you off there."

"But," I stammered, "there must be others more senior."

"There are," he said, "but the decision has been made to send you, so go now."

In Honolulu, I boarded the aircraft that was to take me to Tokyo. It was a cargo plane with freight lashed down in the center. Benches on the sides were the only seats. I took off my blues and changed into khakis. I stretched out on a bench and was asleep instantly. I awoke at daybreak.

As the only passenger on board, I was invited to the cockpit to meet the flight crew and have breakfast. It was a smooth flight, with the aircraft on automatic pilot. We cruised above a scattering of cumulus clouds tinted pink by the rising sun. Below was an incredibly blue ocean, flecked with whitecaps. Following several stops enroute, I stepped ashore at the Tokyo airport after a flight of fifty-one hours.

At the bottom of the stairs, I was met by an Army Major. Noting the look of disbelief on his face, I could read his mind like an open book. "My Gawd, they must have robbed the cradle to send this fellow out here."

I was fifty-one but looked a young thirty-five. I was also a veteran of thirty-five years of sea service, but he couldn't know that, could he? We rode to the ship in uncomfortable silence. I invited the Major to join me in my quarters. "Give me a chance to shave and wash up before I meet the department heads," I said.

Top Brass inspection party on board U.S.A.T. ADMIRAL SIMS upon return. Left to right: First Officer Hilton, Capt. Albert Berry (Marine Superintendant ATS), General McKay (Commander SFPE), Capt. O.H. Friz (Master of U.S.A.T. ADMIRAL SIMS), Major General Leavitt (Chief of Transportation—Army).

With all assembled in my office, the Major introduced me as the new Master. His manner was perfunctory, and he evinced a noticeable lack of enthusiasm. I took over.

"Gentlemen, I did not seek this assignment, regretfully built upon another man's misfortune. I was told to come, and here I am. I ask for your help and cooperation in the fulfillment of my duties."

I turned to the Major. "I would like to pay a courtesy call on the former Master later this evening. Will you now join me and the department heads on a brief tour of inspection?"

He declined, but said, "There will be a car and driver from the motor pool at the gangway this evening to take you to the Grand Hotel, where the Captain is staying." I thought I detected a note of regard as he was leaving.

I found the Captain on the hotel roof garden, overlooking Tokyo Bay.

It was the same Master I had relieved three years ago in the WILL. H. POINT. I introduced myself and ordered a drink for me, as he was well supplied.

It was a dark and clear night. The air was mild. In the distance, one could see the riding lights of many ships at anchor. Our conversation was desultory. I studiously avoided any reference to the ship and the mishap that had put her ashore. In time, I took my leave. W.S.SIMS departed the following morning. Upon arrival at the home port, I turned the ship over to another Master.

The Port Captain said, "Sorry you can't keep her, but your relief has more seniority."

He seemed apologetic. I assured him I understood. I had not expected to stay in her anyway. I returned to the GREELY in the Transpacific run for another two years until she was transferred to the East Coast. Following several runs to Puerto Rico and Panama, I left her in New Orleans and turned her over to the International Refugee Organization (IRO).

Shipmasters of the U.S..A. Transport Service Water Division.
O.H. Friz fifth from left.

REUNION
WITH AN OLD SHIPMATE

In June 1949, I was appointed Master of USAT D.E. AULTMAN, a C4-type cargo vessel and troop carrier. One morning, a person presented himself at my office, saying, "I have been assigned second mate to your ship, Captain." As he handed me his papers, I knew him at once. It was the kid I had stowed away in the brigantine GENEVA, more than thirty years ago in Taltal, Chile.

His blond hair had turned white, his once rosy face was pale and lined, but his blue eyes carried that same guileless look of years ago. We both had been part of that erstwhile group of enemy aliens at the Maui sugar plantation in 1917, during WWI. He had been employed in the blacksmith shop, and had become an accomplished farrier, shoeing the horses and packmules of the plantation. I handed him back his papers.

"Go and see the mate, he will show you to your quarters." As he was about to turn, I called out, "Henry, can you still shoe a mule?"

A grin split his face from ear to ear. "By Gawd, I knew it was you all the time, Captain!" he hollered. "I'll make you the best second mate and navigator you have ever had."

We met that evening ashore over a beer to share our experiences of the years. Like myself, as a youngster, he had embarked upon a career in sail with the expectation of becoming a shipmaster, an ambition to be delayed

Master of U.S.A.T. GENERAL D.E. AULTMAN, 1947.

for many years by the outbreak of WWI. I had last seen him in Long Beach, California, working in a yacht harbor as a sailmaker. At times he had skippered pleasure craft for Hollywood personages. His last had been the yacht of John Barrymore on a cruise to Alaska. Later, he had entered commercial service and had gained mate's and Master's papers.

AULTMAN put to sea on Transpacific runs to Hawaii, the Philippines, Japan, and Korea. No ocean voyage is ever routine. Old problems appear in a new light; new problems come up, awaiting solution. And so it was to be in the ensuing months.

In the early years of our association, I had known Henry as a loner, one who never mingled with our group. I knew nothing of his background. He never spoke of his parents whom, I suspected, he had never known. As an orphan, he had been sent to sea. In his adolescent years, he had always sought the companionship of older people. In retrospect, I realized his old chief mate in the GENEVA had been to him a father figure.

Throughout the years, I had always required every deck officer to take

Master and deck officers of USNS AULTMAN.

sights and turn in a noon-position. So it was this day when, on the bridge, Henry showed me his new sextant. "Captain," he said, "with this 'perambulating Lick Observatory,' I can get you the best of observations at any time."

He had named his sextant after an observatory in the mountains of Central California. I examined it, and found it to be a foreign imitation of a well known instrument of German manufacture. Aside from the index and horizon glasses and the usual different-colored shade glasses, the sextant featured the most powerful prism telescope I had ever seen, and of a weight almost unbalancing the handheld instrument.

Alas, poor Henry, it turned out to be a lemon. Morning and evening twilights, he would take sights of stars and planets. In daylight hours, he would be out on the bridgewing, making adjustments to the index and horizon glasses. Taking the daily noon sight became an ordeal. Long after I had determined my noon position and had accepted the positions of his fellow officers, Henry would still be bending over the chart, muttering under his breath while trying to plot his position.

In time, he became the butt of jokes. Being thin-skinned and not endowed with any notable sense of humor, he became more and more irritable as the days went by. I never doubted his ability as a navigator. That damned sextant of his was the cause of his troubles. The need for frequent adjustments, especially at the critical moment when the heavenly body observed was briefly in transit, clearly indicated a faulty instrument requiring the manufacturer's attention. Henry had turned a deaf ear to my advice in this matter, and it took a drastic step on my part to put an end to this nonsense. I said, "If I see you once more on the bridge with that sextant of yours, I am going to take it away from you and throw it overboard. Henceforth you will use the ship's sextant you will find in the chartroom."

It was a solution to the problem, but there were days when I observed him on the deck below the bridge, fiddling in dogged persistence with his sextant. In time, our association came to an end, and over the years I lost sight of him. He had held one job as chief mate, but not for long. His skipper told me, "Good man, but can't get along with people."

Years later, I received a letter from him after he had retired. It started on a friendly note, reminiscing about the old days, but it ended in a bitter tirade, accusing me of never recommending him for promotion to Master. What he didn't know was that his name had never come up for consideration. Later, I received a letter from his wife. He had been terminally ill. She said, "I had him before the 'Throne of God' every day before he was called Home." In a way, Henry was my last link to a distant past we had shared.

The weather was fair and, as was my custom, I walked the length of the boat deck for my daily exercise. A civilian passenger stopped me and introduced himself. "My name is McVeigh. I am going to be stationed with the Army in Japan as boxing instructor. In my day I have fought Bennie Leonard and other title holders," he said. I vaguely remembered him. He handed me a small pamphlet he had authored. It was illustrated with various positions and maneuvers in the ring and photos of luminaries of the boxing world he had known and fought. He continued, "Everyone needs exercise and if you like I would give you and any of your officers some lessons in self defense. My mind went back more than twenty years ago and I thought silently, "Where the hell was he when I needed him?" While in port one day I had come out on the short end of a bareknuckle fight. A shipmate examining the cuts on my face said, "He really did a job on you. Did you know this guy was a 'Ham n' Egger'?"

" 'Ham n' Egger'; what's that?"

"Young fellows who go four rounds in a boxing club for the price of a meal, not necessarily ham and eggs. Even so they're called 'Ham n' Eggers.' By the way what was this all about?"

"I have no idea. He was drunk and spoiling for a fight. He entered my cabin and, while I was in the process of getting up, he landed a couple of blows that drew considerable blood. I was so surprised I forgot to get mad. I simply bearhugged him and threw him out on deck. Some of the fellows intervened and broke it up."

Coming out of my reverie I heard McVeigh say, "How about starting tomorrow morning, Captain?"

"Very well, tomorrow morning."

A small group—the Commander, military department; his executive officer; the doctor and I—followed McVeigh's demonstrations of hooks, jabs, punches, and shifting. We were middle aged and a bit on the flabby side. To bystanders it would have been a hilarious performance in slow motion. In any case it was fun.

Throughout the war years, it had been a standing joke that the Army had more ships than the Navy. This came to an end in 1949, when President Eisenhower ordered the combination of all civilian-manned transports of the Army Transportation Corps and commissioned Naval transports into one organization under the name of the Military Sea Transportation Service (MSTS), to become part of the Naval Establishment.

Under Presidential order, the Secretary of Defense directed the Chief of Naval Operations to organize and assume direction and control of the Military Sea Transportation Service to provide, under one authority and control, sea transportation for personnel and military cargoes of all the armed services of the Defense Department. Cognizant Naval personnel and their civilian counterparts were detailed to the offices of the Water Division of the Army Transportation Corps at Fort Mason, California, to become familiar with the requirements of the new service in the allotted one year's transition time, at the end of which control on the West Coast would pass to the Military Sea Transportation Service, Pacific (MSTSPAC).

The organization of MSTS involved the acquisition of government-owned transports formerly assigned to the Department of the Army and the Department of the Navy, respectively. Ships controlled by the Army and operated by the Water Division of the Army Transportation Corps as public vessels of the United States, had been manned by civilian officers

Presentation of Port Efficiency Plaque to U.S.A.T. GENERAL D. E. AULTMAN, November 30, 1949. Major General James A. Lester, Port Commander and Captain O.H. Friz, Ships Master, holding plaque.

and men, recruited through the Civil Service Commission from the Merchant Marine.

They had been non-military in character, except for temporary defensive armament in time of war. Ships controlled and operated by the Naval Transportation Service were commissioned ships and military in character. Among other things, the charter of the Military Sea Transportation Service provided for "the protection of the rights and privileges of Civil Service personnel, now employed by the Army and who may be transferred to the Navy," and further provided that "consistent with the orderly and efficient conduct of its business, MSTS will utilize to the maximum practicable the existing services and facilities of the bureaus, offices and agencies of the Department of the Navy."

For commissioned officers serving in Naval transports, no significant changes, administrative or operational, were expected, since they remained with the parent organization to carry on in the familiar traditions of that service. However, for civilian shipmasters of the former Army transports, significant changes were to be expected in administrative and operational procedures, because the Navy, with a vast experience in ship operation along military lines, could be expected to apply methods geared to military standards to all ships under their control, regardless of how manned.

Needless to say, as this panorama unfolded, civilian transport masters and officers regarded their future with misgivings, wondering how they would fare under this new regime. Some were convinced their careers would come to a speedy end, in spite of assurances to the contrary, while others hoped to continue and serve until retirement age. On the other hand, it was not amiss to speculate on the mixed feelings of high-ranking Naval officers charged with the responsibility of implementing in all its details the official directives creating the Military Sea Transportation Service. This involved, perhaps for the first time in the history of the modern U.S. Navy, the control, operation and administration of Naval vessels manned by civilian crews.

In 1950, a Navy Vice Admiral with offices in Washington, D.C. was appointed Commander, Military Sea Transportation Service (COMSTS), in full charge of the new organization. Branch offices on the East and West coasts were headed by Rear Admirals. The earlier prefix of USAT was replaced by USNS, United States Naval Ship. The Army stack insignia were replaced by blue and gold bands under a black smokestack top. MSTS was off and running.

In March 1950, I was detached from the AULTMAN and transferred to USNS GENERAL NELSON M. WALKER, to relieve the Master for his vacation. The early months had not been without its difficulties for the new establishment.

The principal problem was the disparity in compensation between Naval and seagoing civilian personnel. According to the MSTS charter, "Pay scales and working conditions for civilian employees transferring to the Navy will follow the practices prevailing in private industry, as far as it is in the public interest." Wartime union payscales in merchant ships were above that of commissioned officers and enlisted men, leading to complaints on the part of the latter that their civilian counterparts were greatly overpaid by comparison. On the other hand, the civilians countered with the idea that they did not enjoy the privileges of post exchanges and the many perquisites available to Navy personnel. With this introduction of a discordant note, heads of the establishment pondered the problems of operating ships on two levels. With the end of the war, a solution was found in the gradual phasing out of commissioned transports. Some were decommissioned and turned over to MSTS, others went to the reserve fleets.

To meet the needs of peacetime operation, USNS GENERAL NELSON M. WALKER had undergone a Safety at Sea conversion, and a partial conversion as a dependent carrier. On March 27, 1950, the ship departed on Voyage One, her first under the exclusive management of the Military Sea Transportation Service, Pacific (MSTSPAC). Serving Okinawa, WALKER became a familiar sight to every man, woman and child. Affectionately known as the "Okinawa Express," she was the last link between their new domicile and the continental United States.

What had been expected to be a routine operation was rudely interrupted by the invasion of South Korea by North Korean forces, who had taken the capital of Seoul. Inadequate forces defended a small area in the extreme south known as the Pusan Perimeter, so named after the Port of Pusan.

This unexpected development posed a severe test of the capabilities of the Military Sea Transportation Service, still a fledgling organization. At sea on her second voyage to Okinawa with Army and Air Force personnel and dependents on board, we learned of the outbreak of the Korean War and its ominous trend. Having crossed the International Date Line, weather reports indicated the presence of two developing typhoons, Flossie and Grace.

Steaming at twenty knots, the vessel cleared the Bonin Chain, approximately seven hundred miles east of Okinawa. Sangley Point weather station in the Philippines reported that Flossie and Grace had merged, their combined force now posing a serious threat to Okinawa and shipping in the vicinity. Wallowing in a heavy swell, with rising wind and sea and a falling barometer, the ship had come under the influence of the disturbance. There was no longer any doubt that Grace and the WALKER were on a head-on collision course. Accordingly, the ship was hove-to, head to the sea, and snugged down for the night to allow the storm to draw ahead.

The following twenty-four hours were a communication nightmare, the radio shack being bombarded with requests for information regarding a firm arrival time. It appeared that among the passengers was a group of

B-29 personnel urgently needed for service in Korea. The WALKER, pressing on under reduced speed, was within half a day's steaming time of Buckner Bay, one day late. In a sixty-mile gale, heavy rain and zero visibility, the surrounding waters were dotted with ships which had left their anchorages to ride it out in the comparative safety of the open sea.

At daybreak the following morning, the WALKER entered Buckner Bay, whose turquoise green waters were still ruffled by a strong breeze. Following several unsuccessful passes, the ship was finally moored to the pier, which only a few hours ago had been awash under the battering of a lady named Grace.

The B-29 personnel were off the ship in record time and on their way to Korea. Debarkation and embarkation, although hampered by storm damage to the pier, went on as scheduled, the ship sailing the next day for San Francisco where, upon arrival, I turned her over to her former Master.

TYPHOONS ARE HELL

My next assignment was to the USNS GENERAL WILLIAM WEIGEL, a P2 class (passenger) ship, two stacks (or two engine rooms). Powered by steam turbines, she was one of the largest vessels in the MSTS fleet.

The ship was in a shipyard for overhaul and conversion to carry double the number of troops, employing the system of "hot bunking," meaning that when one man left his bunk, another immediately took his place. In a time of fast-moving events, the system was never fully implemented.

The ship was ordered to San Diego to load elements of a Marine division with its armament. In the ensuing week, the tween decks were stripped of bunks to make room for trucks and tracked howitzers. In anticipation of rough weather, the rolling stock was secured with chains and turnbuckles to eyebolts welded on the steel deck.

On sailing day, the Marines embarked while a Marine band played martial music. Family members and friends thronged the pier, waving a last farewell as the ship moved out in the stream. The destination was Kobe, Japan. The ship made a record passage from the United States to Kobe. The twin cities Kobe-Osaka had become the staging area for American troops, arriving in such numbers that they overtaxed all available shore billets. To alleviate this plight, the WEIGEL was held over to provide barrack service for the troops, rotating the clock around for meals, bunks and sanitary facilities.

From the bridge, I observed the steady two-way procession of troops over the gangway. The hull and decks were hot to the touch under the oppressive heat. Portholes, sideports and doors were open, inviting any errant breeze which might waft by. It was a forlorn hope, in the face of the overpowering effluvium emanating out of the ship's interior: a malodorous mixture of human sweat and cooking odors commingling with the fetid smell of troop washrooms and the pervading reek of fuel oil and bilgewater.

I was joined by the chief mate, his shirt streaked with perspiration. "This is not exactly my idea of going to sea. I wonder when we are going to be released from this chore, " he speculated idly.

I handed him a radio message I had been reading. It warned of a tropical disturbance to the south, heading in our direction. The harbor was choked with shipping. Attack transports, supply ships and troop carriers crowded the piers. Anchored inside the double breakwaters were miscellaneous amphibious craft being loaded by stevedore battalions with combat equipment to accompany the troops destined to relieve the beleaguered garrison in the Pusan perimeter. The radio operator appeared with a second message. "Here is more on the typhoon," he said.

"Looks like she is coming this way. Just what we need to make a helluva mess around here," the mate growled. "Captain, I think we should get out of here while we still have a chance."

Both of us had witnessed the destructive effects of typhoons on shipping caught in port. "It would be safer to ride it out outside," I agreed. A sortie to clear the approaches to Kobe and the outlying landmasses, waiting in the open water for the disturbance to pass, and subsequent return, would take several days. "Meanwhile, what about the thousands of troops we are housing and feeding. We can't just leave them on the beach to shift for themselves," I explained. "For the sake of the troops we must stay, much as I dislike the idea. By the way, how are we fixed for extra mooring gear"?

"It's a tough decision to make," the chief mate agreed, "but you are the doctor. Most of our mooring lines are made of sisal—poor stuff, you know. Luckily, we still have some genuine manila lines, still in coils and never used."

Messages from the radio shack indicated that the disturbance now had reached the force of a fullblown typhoon, named 'Jane.' Subsequent plottings of the storm's progress left no doubt that Kobe was in direct line of

U.S.N.S. GENERAL WM. WEIGEL.

Jane's path. There was no time to lose. I cancelled all shore leave and directed the chief mate to bring out every spare line on board. I sent out a call for all deck officers to report to the bridge. I also contacted the Commander of the military department on board and invited him to join us. I rang the Chief Engineer's office and asked him to come to the bridge.

"Gentlemen," I addressed the crowd, "you will take your customary mooring stations, fore and aft. The entire deck crew will be standing by. Haul in any lines that part, put a bowline in, and send them out again.

"Chief, I would like to have full power available for the next twenty-four hours. In case we should come adrift, I intend to back away from the pier and anchor." I pointed astern to the openings in the two breakwaters: "We may even have to go outside. It will be a risky maneuver and only used as a last resort. So, when you get that Full Astern bell, give it all you've got."

"You shall have it," the Chief said, moving towards the door. "I'll go below now and start things rolling."

The Commanding Officer of the military department, a Naval Reserve officer, had been listening closely. He stepped forward. "Captain, any help I can give, just let me know."

I thanked him and suggested he stay on the bridge. "You may need to give orders to the troops. Use the public address system here. I suggest that you have some of your men patrol the lower decks to prevent unauthorized opening of watertight doors by the troops. The medics should be ready to render first aid."

From the bow and stern came the whine and crank of windlass and capstans as lines were sent ashore and hove taut in such numbers as to resemble a veritable spider web. A fitful breeze had sprung up and dispersed the heat wave. The backdrop of the steep mountains against which the city nestled stood out starkly against a watery, saffron-colored evening sky. Outside the wheel house, I felt the first raindrops on my face.

"What's the idea of the old man cutting off shore leave?" able seaman Jones grumbled. "It's Saturday night and I've got a date."

"Yeah, my heart bleeds for you, sucker," the bos'n interrupted, noting the amused grin on the others' faces. "We've been in port a whole week and you've been ashore every night, spending your dough and all you could borrow on that dame."

"Aw, have a heart, bos'n. I gotta go tonight."

"Listen, chump," the bos'n growled, jerking his thumb toward the wheel house where a face was framed in one of the windows. "See that guy up there? He's got a date with a girl named Jane, and it ain't gonna be no picnic. Now quit bellyachin' and grab that line."

"But, look, bos'n..."

"Shaddup!"

Jones fell into sullen silence at the articulate command, a command backed up by two hundred pounds of bone and muscle.

Daylight broke a colorless gray that Sunday morning. Lowhanging dark and ragged scud raced across the sky. Vicious blasts of the rising gale shook the ship, driving the rain in pelting sheets across the decks. Under the direction and force of the wind, the ship rode the face of the pier, the screech of protesting metal against tortured concrete producing an earsplitting crescendo. All hands were on-station, huddled against the bulwarks. The gangway had been taken in and all hull-openings and bulkhead doors were closed to insure watertight integrity. The engine telegraphs were on 'Standby.'

The phone shrilled in the wheelhouse. "The eye will pass over Kobe about noon, that's the latest dope," the radio operator reported excitedly.

The ship rode high on the flooding tide, all mooring lines taut as fiddle strings. Hull and superstructure towered above the pier sheds. It was certain that these low buildings could not serve effectively as a barrier when the cyclonic circulation resulted in the abrupt reversal of the wind direction.

It had almost stopped raining. Suddenly, the wind was down to a whisper. The thundering silence was broken by the clear tones of the wheelhouse clock, striking eight bells. It was noon. Typhoon Jane was right on time.

Overhead, a break in the flying scud revealed a layer of fleecy white clouds, centered by a small patch of clear-blue sky. The eye of the storm was above the harbor. In the ominous quiet, the voice of the second mate rang out from the wheelhouse door. "Here she comes, Captain!" as he pointed southward.

Nearby headlands, visible moments before, were blotted out by an impenetrable yellow and gray curtain of torrential rain. In the port wing of the bridge, I braced myself. Stinging rain and savage blasts of wind slammed against the hull as I watched the ship being pushed away from the pier as if impelled by a giant fist.

A rapidly widening strip of water appeared between ship and pier as lines stretched and rendered around mooring bitts sweating small milky drops of natural lubricant mixed with water under the agonizing stress of holding twenty-one thousand deadweight tons of ship against the monstrous impact of a 120 mile per hour wind.

Wind-driven spume, whipped off the crest of waves in confused action, mingled with the rain to fill the atmosphere with vaporized moisture. The air was rent asunder by the demoniacal fury of the gale shrieking in the rigging in concert with the strumming and rhythmic slapping of cordage.

Rain, driven in horizontal sheets, rattled against the tin roofs and sides of the pier sheds and warehouses to the thundering accompaniment of roaring seas smashing across the nearby submerged breakwaters. Above this brutal uproar faintly rose the bellows of whistles sounded by ships adrift. Over the harbor communications network came frantic, futile appeals for help. Tugboats, enveloped in black smoke belching from their stacks, their hulls barely visible in the turbulent waters, maneuvered vainly against an overwhelming force.

Mooring lines carried away fore and aft. Heaving lines snaked out against the wind. Soldiers and dockworkers dashed out from the pier sheds to haul the heavy lines ashore again and secure the frayed water-soaked ends with a strange variety of knots and hitches. From the stern came a report of a freighter adrift. "She is bearing down on us, Captain," the mate in charge reported over the phone.

Drifting broadside to the gale, a collision with the WEIGEL's exposed stern seemed inevitable. On the bow of the helpless craft, men were seen struggling frantically with the anchor windlass. "Will that damn anchor never let go?" I swore under my breath, my hand on the general alarm.

To my relief, there came the rattle of the chain in the hawsepipe as the anchor hit the water with a splash, followed seconds later by the other anchor. Fetching up, with both chains standing out nearly horizontally, the vessel slewed around and came to rest a hundred yards across the WEIGEL's stern. A collision had been averted, but any hope of backing out, as called for by our contingency plan, was now frustrated. I rang the engine room. The muffled voice of the Chief Engineer came on. "Chief, you can relax now, our chances of moving out are gone," I said, describing the incident briefly.

"Very well, " he replied. "We'll keep her ready in case the situation changes."

The lash of the storm forced great masses of water across the now completely submerged breakwaters and, further augmented by a maximum highwater stage, raised the water level in the inner harbor to unprecedented heights. A short, vicious sea began to break against the end of the pier, which was soon completely awash. Boxes and crates drifted out of the pier sheds. Soldiers and longshoremen waded waist-deep in the choppy waters covering the pier apron in an attempt to recover what they could. Trembling under the combined might of wind and sea, the ship strained at her lines, surging back and forth under the onrush of the raging sea. "Bow here," the First Officer answered the feeble ring of the phone.

"Walk out both anchors until they reach bottom," I ordered.

The ship steadied somewhat as the anchors came to rest, buried on short scope in the mud. Lines, weakened under hours of intolerable strain, continued to carry away, frayed ends dangling from the chocks whipping in the wind, the remaining lines stretching perilously to the breaking point. Pier personnel struggled valiantly to secure hawsers to cleats and bollards only momentarily exposed to view in the heavy wash of the surflike breakers that rolled across the pier apron.

Darkness descended as the afternoon wore on. The dimness in the wheel house was relieved by the faint glow of the compass binnacle lights and the engine telegraph dials. The luminous radar scope threw a circle of brightness on the over head. The sweep, a thin finger steadily moving across the plan position indicator, cast a pulsating reflection on the second mate's features, as he scanned the radar picture. The hitherto solid mass of rain clutter illuminating the scope had broken up into small, ragged portions, an unmistakable sign that the storm was moving on. A steeply ascending pressure line recorded on the barograph confirmed that the worst was over. Heavy rain was still falling, but the wind was down. The ship lay quietly, her mooring lines hanging slack. The slap of a moderating sea against the hull was audible in the sudden stillness.

Typhoon 'Jane' had come and gone!

"Typhoons are hell, ain't they, pal?" the bos'n said to Jones, with a wink at the seamen who were picking up the slack in the lines to heave the ship back against the pier.

"Yeah," Jones mumbled. He grinned slyly, ignoring the ribbing. It was only the shank of the evening, and the night, with its pleasures, was still young.

A survey revealed that most ships had come through unscathed, with the exception of the drifting freighter, whose engines had been down for repairs, and a troop ship whose hull was punctured. Within days, the harbor was cleared of shipping and the WEIGEL was dispatched to Yokohama for further orders. It was kept a closely guarded secret.

As the result of a brilliant strategy, American forces commanded by General Douglas MacArthur had taken and secured the port of Inchon on the northwest coast of the Korean peninsula. An expanding operation which had split the North Korean forces, now on the defensive, required replenishment of munitions and sustenance. USNS GENERAL W. WEIGEL, along with twenty other transports, steamed out of Yokahama.

Once clear of the harbor, the ships formed a convoy of five columns headed by the WEIGEL, the guide ship. Our destination was Inchon. On board was the convoy Commander, a Navy Captain, and his staff consisting of an Executive Officer, Communications Officer, enlisted Signal Corpsmen and a Marine guard detachment. The speed of the convoy was fourteen knots, held down to match the slowest ship in the group. No Naval escort had been provided. The convoy proceeded at an appropriate distance from the Korean coast to avoid possible gunfire by hostile forces believed to be still in control of certain areas between Seoul and Inchon.

Throughout the trip, I remained on the bridge, taking short naps on a cot in the chartroom. When the seabuoy was sighted at the entrance of the main ship channel, the convoy Commander ordered the convoy to slow down to disband and proceed in single file. It was daybreak and the beginning of the ebb tide. Many of the buildings in Inchon that I had known were badly damaged. Throughout the night, an American warship, anchored in the northern reaches of the harbor, was lobbing shells into enemy positions.

Following debarkation of troops and discharge of cargo, WEIGEL returned to Yokohama for redeployment. In the last months of 1950, the port of Wonsan on the northeast coast of Korea had been secured by U. S. Forces. Heavily mined by the Communists, U. S. mine sweepers had cleared a channel to permit amphibious landings.

As the ship approached the port, a Navy chief petty officer came aboard. He pointed out the entrance to the channel and said, "As long as you stay within the confines of the dangerbuoys on either side, you will be safe."

Georgia.

Janet.

Having landed troops and equipment there, a second mission involved an amphibious landing at Iwon, an open roadstead with clear beaches and no mines. It was considered to be enemy territory and the farthest point reached on the northeast coast of Korea. The landing was unopposed. Upon the completion of these missions at the end of the year, the WEIGEL returned to San Francisco. I was granted leave and had the rare pleasure to enjoy the Christmas holidays in the circle of my family.

IN THE MILITARY SEA
TRANSPORTATION SERVICE

Reporting for duty in February 1951, I took permanent command of USNS GENERAL NELSON M. WALKER.

Built in 1944 in Alameda by the Bethlehem Shipyard as a P2 class vessel, the ship was powered by two turbo-electric plants with a cruising speed of 20 knots. She became my favorite ship. At the end of World War II, the Army had converted the WALKER to a dependent carrier, featuring such amenities as lounges for enlisted men, lounges for officers, recreation rooms, children's playrooms and a well-stocked ship's store selling cigarettes, candy, clothing, cosmetics and a variety of other goods. Now under the control of the Military Sea Transportation Service, the ship continued as a dependent carrier for a year.

The outbreak of the Korean War had taken the world by surprise. The Security Council of the United Nations had met in emergency session and had voted unanimously to oppose the attempted takeover of Southern Korea by the Communist forces of the North. Thus the Korean War became a United Nations action in which twenty nations participated.

Being closest to the scene, it was inevitable that the limited American forces stationed in Japan should bear the brunt of the attack. There was a gradual introduction of military contingents of other powers, primarily air force personnel and equipment, as well as detachments of foot soldiers

U.S.N.S. GENERAL NELSON M. WALKER.

and medical teams from smaller nations. Transportation of men and material by water once again became a vital factor.

Following numerous trans-Pacific runs as a dependent carrier, the WALKER was withdrawn from that service in December 1951, for conversion to an austerity troopship. A ninety-day contract was awarded to a shipyard in Seattle. The family drove up in our new 1951 Chevrolet sedan to join me. We rented a furnished house in West Seattle and sent the children to school for the duration. We enjoyed weekend trips in the surrounding countryside.

In a local maritime publication, I came across an ad by a marine surveyor. The name seemed familiar. A phone call established the fact that he had been the chief mate in the steamer MONTPELIER in 1925 who had helped me in the study of navigation when I had been on board as an Able Seaman. We enjoyed lunch and a visit together.

Upon completion of conversion and repairs in April 1952, the WALKER sailed from Seattle with a full load of troops and war material

Carolyne, wife and mother, 1952.

bound for Yokohama. Having completed her first outbound lift under the austerity program and while on her return voyage to San Francisco, we received a message to prepare the ship for a voyage around the world with United Nations troops.

The news generated a current of excitement among all hands. It had an appeal which prompted those who had applied for annual leave to cancel their requests. The proposed itinerary included calls at Balboa, Canal Zone; Canal transit to Cartagena, Colombia; thence to San Juan, Puerto Rico and Norfolk, Virginia; across the Atlantic to La Pallice, France and Bremerhaven, Germany; to the Mediterranean and Piraeus, Greece and Izmir, Turkey; thence via the Suez Canal to the Aden Protectorate for refueling; across the Indian Ocean to Colombo in Sri Lanka (still known as Ceylon), also for refueling only; on to Pusan, Korea and Yokohama, Japan; and, finally, return to San Francisco.

Weeks of intensive work resulted in the expansion of our chart allowance by one hundred and twenty-five charts and a dozen or more of sailing directions. While other ships had carried United Nations troops to

Master, U.S.N.S. GENERAL NELSON M. WALKER, 1950.

Korea, the WALKER was the first West-Coast-based ship and the first austerity trooper to be employed in a lift of this magnitude. I regarded it as a high adventure and a priceless opportunity to render a service of the highest order in the interest of the Military Sea Transportation Service, the Navy, the Defense Department, and the Nation. This awesome task evoked in me the firm resolution that nothing would be left undone to make this voyage an unqualified success from beginning to end.

In May 1952, the WALKER departed on the initial leg of the voyage.

Still on board from Korea were 260 Colombian troops, veterans of the Korean War bound for Cartagena, Colombia; Puerto Rican troops, also veterans of the Korean War, bound for San Juan, Puerto Rico; and 346 U.S. Army personnel to debark at Norfolk, Virginia. They were joined in San Francisco by 1,100 U.S. Army troops destined for La Pallice, France.

Following a smooth passage, we arrived at Balboa in the Canal Zone and moored at Rodman Naval Base to lift 1,500 Puerto Rican troops for debarkation at Bremerhaven, Germany. Having been stationed in Panama for a year's training, these troops had acquired dependents, 253 in number, to be transported to Puerto Rico and debarked there, while their husbands and fathers sailed on to Europe. It was an arrangement that held all the ingredients of an explosive situation, as we were to find out.

As an austerity trooper, the ship had nothing to offer in the way of the fundamentals for a dependent life, however limited. A waiver had been issued for this special and brief operation, the ship being momentarily provided with cribs, bedding, high chairs, baby food, and children's life preservers.

The following day, amidst the gloom of dark and rain-swollen clouds, the vessel left Balboa with a load of 3,723 persons on board and gained the Atlantic side after a nine-hour Canal transit. The heat was oppressive, the night dark and wet. The silence was broken by the wail of fretful children as the vessel moved along through the murky gloom of low-hanging clouds, the bridge watch and lookouts alert.

By daybreak, no change in the weather had taken place, neither celestial observations nor terrestrial objects had afforded a fix, as the WALKER proceeded at dead reckoning, sounding for bottom. Eventually, a break in the clouds revealed a distant prominent hill, topped by the ruins of a building. It was identified as La Colima de la Popa, the Pope's Hill, most prominent landmark described in the sailing directions. It served as an initial landfall.

At noon, the ship entered Boca Chica, entrance to the historic harbor of Cartagena, where a pilot boarded the ship. With him came a representative of the U.S. Naval attache, who offered his services as interpreter and his welcome advice regarding the conduct of a ceremonious welcome awaiting the ship and the home-coming troops.

Moving up the channel, the WALKER was greeted by blinker signals from units of the Colombian Navy. Lining up for the approach to the pier, the welcome committee was composed of the Governor of the State, the

Minister of the Interior, Minister of Education, Mayor of the City, Captain of the Port, the Commander In Chief of Colombian Naval Forces, and other dignitaries. This group occupied a central position on the pier. To the right and left, a military band, detachments of soldiers, marines and police were drawn up in formation.

Streaming towards the pier from all directions was the general populace and the inevitable hawkers displaying their wares of stuffed baby alligators, swagger sticks, rattles, and other gimcracks. The Colombian detachment was lined up on the promenade deck, ready for debarkation, while the boat deck and forward well deck was occupied by Puerto Rican and U.S. troops. The shouting and general huzzaing was deafening. The troops were throwing coins and cigarettes onto the pier to be pounced upon by the multitude, even the military detachments breaking ranks occasionally to pick up a coin or cigarette.

The climax came when a group of adolescent school girls dressed in white and headed by their teachers marched in formation onto the pier. The appearance of so much feminine pulchritude was the signal for the troops on board to go wild with enthusiasm, causing the guards to lose control. With troops surging into the restricted areas, the successful mooring of the ship was momentarily in doubt.

Some semblance of order was restored when the band on the pier struck up the Colombian National Anthem, followed by the National Anthem of the United States. With the ship finally moored, the welcoming committee, escorted by the Assistant U.S. Naval Attache, boarded the ship and, following introductions, retired to the Master's quarters for refreshments and a brief respite from the uproar of the crowd on the pier.

After a suitable interval, these gentlemen took their leave and returned to the pier to observe the debarkation, which was accomplished without a hitch. In late afternoon, the vessel departed, heading through Boca Chica for the peace and quiet of the open sea.

San Juan, Puerto Rico, was the next port of call. Here the detachment of Puerto Rican veterans of the Korean War and the 253 dependents of the 1,500 Europe-bound Puerto Rican troops were to be debarked.

Standing in for San Juan Harbor, we picked up the pilot and entered the channel, where the boarding party came aboard. It was learned that the scheduled one-day layover was cancelled. The ship was to depart immediately upon completion of debarkation.

Ashore, large crowds had assembled in the streets leading to the waterfront. They followed as the vessel slid by, slowly heading up the channel towards the pier, the Puerto Ricans on board waving and shouting enthusiastically, elated at seeing once again the familiar sights of their homeland. Suddenly a voice came over the public address system in clear and crackling Spanish: *"Attencion, Attencion!"*

A hush fell over the ship. One did not need to know the language to understand what was being announced. The 1,500 Puerto Rican troops were getting the word about the imminent turnaround of the ship, and no shore leave. The voice broke off, leaving for a brief moment a void of dead silence, to be broken by a roar of anguish from a thousand throats under the impact of the message.

It was a scene of despair mixed with monumental anger and resentment. Giving full rein to their volatile Latin temperaments, the troops were venting their feelings, shouting and throwing their arms heavenward in dramatic gestures of distress.

About a city block away, a wide street leading into the area of debarkation had been roped off. Pressing against the rope were relatives and friends of the troops and a crowd of onlookers held back by a cordon of police. The sight aroused fresh emotional outbursts among the troops, climbing everywhere for a place of advantage to see and be seen, waving hats, handkerchieves and towels. As the ship was being maneuvered alongside, a soldier jumped off the fantail, swimming towards the pier, followed by shouts of approval from his compatriots.

He was helped out of the water by members of the military police. One man having set the example, others followed suit. They were picked up by a picket boat or the M.P.s on the pier. With the vessel alongside, the troops began to bombard the M.P.'s with G.I. cans, lids and garbage. Others managed to gain the pier apron, only to be apprehended by the M.P.'s and returned to the ship. A great deal of credit was due these men, few in number, who in the face of great provocation, showed restraint in their difficult task. None of the escapees was handled roughly when returned to the ship.

Amidst this ongoing tumult, debarkation began. At the foot of the gangway was the Mayoress of the City, greeting each of the 264 returnees with a hug and a kiss. Red Cross workers were present to help in the processing of the dependents. Again, there were heartbreaking scenes. In complete abandonment to their emotions, women swooned and were carried away in litters, their offspring looking on in puzzled wonder, or terrified to tears, too young to fully understand the significance of these dismal scenes.

With the last person and last draft of cargo ashore, lines were let go and the vessel moved out into the stream, heading down the channel. A total of three hours had been spent alongside the pier. Packed with action, these few hours had seemed an eternity. As the ship moved along, the crowd ashore again followed from street to street, waving a last farewell to those on board. The troops were more subdued now.

By the time Morro Castle was abeam, the uproar had subsided, and the troops on deck gazed silently at this famous familiar landmark in an attitude of resignation and dejection, their eyes hot with unshed tears. Long before the coast of their homeland had faded in the distant haze, most of them had gone below decks. Fatigued and wearied by the physical strain of clinging for hours to precarious perches and positions of advantage, waving and shouting, and exhausted by the emotional strain resulting from their disappointment, they sought the dubious comfort of their bunks and the final solace of sleep.

Few of them turned out for the evening meal. Peace and quiet once again settled on the ship as she gained the open sea on a course to Cape Hatteras and Norfolk, Virginia.

AROUND THE WORLD
IN NINETY DAYS

When I first examined the itinerary of the proposed trip around the world, I noted that June 28, 1952 was the scheduled arrival day in Bremerhaven, Germany. It was also my mother's eighty-second birthday. The possibility that she might be able to see the ship's arrival that day was an electrifying thought, and I wrote to her of my impending visit.

Being right on schedule, I wrote to her from Norfolk, confirming my arrival date. I also wrote a letter to the commanding officer of the MSTS office in Bremerhaven, soliciting his assistance in helping my mother to be there that day. She took up temporary residence with friends in nearby Bremen to be on hand for the great event.

Loaded with provisions and water and fueled to capacity, the WALKER left Norfolk for La Pallice and Bremerhaven. It was early June 1952. Borne along on the bosom of the Gulf Stream, the WALKER reeled off 20 knots without her plants fully extended. Nearing the continent, the brown sails of fishing smacks appeared more and more frequently, and trawlers attached to their gear in pairs made frequent course changes necessary.

On the seventh day, a bright sun rose out of a cloudless sky, throwing into sharp relief a thin black line, the west coast of France. Ordinarily a turbulent body of water, the Bay of Biscay, historic battle ground of the

French and British Fleets, was smooth and glassy this time of day. The WALKER, her forefoot cleaving the golden path laid down by the ascending sun, entered the bay. Sliding past the ancient fortified fishing harbor of La Rochelle, the ship headed for La Pallice, a deepwater port capable of accommodating deep-draft vessels, but more famous for the concrete submarine pens constructed by the German Navy during World War II.

In the hazy distance behind the low-lying shore stood ancient windmills, medieval towers and fortresses of the Napoleonic era, old historic landmarks, reminders of the glory that was once France's. The pilot pointed out the famous Isle D'Aix where Napoleon, defeated at Waterloo, had been held prisoner by the British. On that bright and sunny morning, I was conscious of being in the presence of history. In my mind's eye, I saw the famous painting of Napoleon on the maindeck of the British ship of the line "Bellerophon," awaiting exile to the island of Elba. Unadorned, stripped of all the trappings of power, he stood with his right hand tucked characteristically into the front of his grey greatcoat, a solitary solemn figure. With a feeling of awe I surveyed the scene where he, at the height of his power, controlled the destiny of nations and men.

Now we were secured to the pier, and French stevedores were engaged to unload the ship. Returning from a two-hour lunch break, they resumed their work. Observing their rather lackadaisical attitude and fearing a delay, I voiced my apprehension to the U.S. Army officer present. He replied, "They have had a two-hour siesta and a lunch fortified with plenty of red wine. You can't hurry these people."

It was late that night when the cargo gear was secured, and with hatches battened down, the ship went to sea. The news of a planned reunion with my mother on her eighty-second birthday had spread throughout the ship. Joining the ship's officers in the day room for a last cup of coffee, I casually expressed my concern about our late departure and the possibility of not arriving in Bremerhaven on June 28 as scheduled. One of the engineers smiled, "I think we can make it; we might be able to squeeze another turn out of her."

I thanked him and went to the bridge for a last look before turning in. The British fleet and units of the NATO fleet had been reported to be on maneuvers in the English Channel, so it was advisable to favor the French side of the Channel and avoid any mishaps in case of low visibility. Apparently a lot of other ships had the same idea, and traffic was heavy.

Mother and son.

In time, the WALKER eased across the Channel to Dover, to pick up a British North Sea pilot to guide the ship through the minefields, not yet fully cleared. Passing Goodwin Sands, the ship's company was vouchsafed that rarest of all sights—a three-masted ship under full sail. A bark, running free before the wind, her canvas bellying out on the fore, main and spanker, only her jibs hanging limp in the halyards, deprived of wind by the great foresail. A bone in her teeth, she stood out sharply in the light of the late afternoon against a dark green sea and creamy whitecaps, a painter's, photographer's, and sailor's delight.

At daybreak on June 28, we arrived at the mouth of the Weser River, and a river pilot came aboard. A rare day in early summer, the scenery lay bathed in brilliant sunshine. All along were dikes to prevent flooding of the rich soil in the lowlands where fat cattle were grazing. The fields and orchards gave testimony to the industry of those who till the land and never venture forth to follow the lure of a sail slowly drawing away to disappear below the distant horizon, beckoning others to follow, beckoning...beckoning!

At the edge of the fields, the red tile roofs of substantial timbered brick dwellings and barns were partially hidden by stately oak and beech. A gentle breeze carried the aroma of meadows and ripening fruit. It was noon when the ship arrived. As a military band played lively tunes, we moored at Columbus Quay. Mother emerged from a car as the gangway went up. Assisted by a member of the boarding party, she came to the embarkation deck. Following a separation of more than twenty years, it was a tearfully happy reunion, the scene illuminated by popping flash-bulbs and the clicking of camera shutters.

Seated in my quarters, a waiter brought up a birthday cake, compliments of the ship's baker. Someone had designed a birthday greeting on a piece of framed silk, which bore the signature of many of the crew members. She was indeed "Queen for a Day!" In late afternoon, other family members joined us. I spent a three-day weekend visit at the family home in Bad Pyrmont. A spa of international repute, this lovely, peaceful community, devoid of any industrial establishments as military targets, had been spared the destruction of saturation bombing in the last years of the war.

Relatives and friends came from far and near to greet me, and take part in the festivities Mother had scheduled for the weekend. I did not receive any of the official photos taken on the embarkation deck. Again, it was the ship's company that came through with some amateur snapshots recording the memorable events of the day.

With the first half of the around-the-world voyage completed, the WALKER left Bremerhaven in early July 1952, bound for the Mediterranean and the Far East. A small detachment of Dutch troops had been embarked, consisting of two officers and 59 men. They were a mix of Caucasians and Colonials from the Dutch possession of Surinam. All spoke or understood English.

With the ship practically empty for a week, the crew took full advantage of this opportunity to prepare the troop compartments, messhalls and washrooms for the upcoming lift of Greek and Turkish soldiers. The Dutch officers volunteered their troops to take part in the work. They swept compartments, inspected and changed defective bunk bottoms.

1952 Family Reunion with, left to right, Niece, Mother, Sister, Brother-in-Law.

Visibility along the coasts of France, Portugal and Spain was low—at times, zero. The WALKER sounded fog signals during periods of low visibility, in accordance with the International Rules of the Road. Curiously, not one of the many ships we met every day was heard to sound their fog signals or were observed to do so—when we momentarily sighted them—by the white plume of steam escaping from the whistle on the foreport of the stack. Perhaps it was the old saying, "One blast on the whistle equals one bucket of steam."

Fortunately, the weather cleared as the ship rounded the southern end of the Iberian Peninsula and entered the Straits of Gibraltar, the crossroads of the world since history was first recorded. The passage was made during hours of darkness, numerous tiderips, overfalls and heavy traffic in both directions calling for caution and watchfulness.

Family Reunion to celebrate Mother's 82nd birthday, June 28, 1952.

On one of my frequent tours of inspection, I was accosted by one of the Dutch Colonials who said, "Captain, when we came on board, we had not expected to be put to work. We thought the crew would do everything."

I replied, "When you were ashore in your barracks, I am sure you were required to keep the place clean, sweep the floors and make up your bunks for the daily inspection."

"Yes, sir, but this is different...."

"No way. This ship is your barracks now and you are not on a pleasure cruise. It requires organization of a high order to handle a full load, as you will find out. It is official policy that embarked troops be employed to functional advantage on a daily routine in which there will be guard details, mess details, garbage details, head details and such other details as determined by the troop commander."

I thought I had put the idea across. But as the soldier turned away, he looked across his shoulder questioningly several times. I had the feeling that he had not fully comprehended what I had said and was still trying to sort things out.

In late July 1952, a pilot boarded the ship outside the breakwater of

Family Reunion, June 28, 1952.

Pireaus, harbor for Athens, Greece. The ship was maneuvered alongside a seawall, adjacent to which was a large flat and barren piece of ground, enclosed by a whitewashed stone wall on the street side. A single gate afforded access. The place was tidy and well swept.

The enclosure was crowded with relatives and friends of the soldiers about to embark. A brass band rendered martial music as the detachment, commanded by a lieutenant colonel, embarked without delay, passing through an honor guard of Greek sailors at the foot of the gangway. The crowd remained orderly, curiously silent and passive during this brief period of embarkation. There was no display of emotion on either side. The troops had stowed their packs and stood on deck, waving their caps to their departing relatives, who slowly filed out of the compound and went about their business with hardly a backward glance. In less than an hour, the show was over.

En route, it had come to my attention that some members of the ship's company desired to be granted liberty at this port. Personally, I favored the idea, although it was against the rule to grant liberty on an eight-hour layover. I considered it unthinkable not to afford the men a chance to visit this world of the ancients, the cradle of western civilization where Socrates, Demosthenes, Homer and Plato had once held sway. It was an opportunity that, for most, might never come again.

Following consultation with department heads, it was decided to make an exception and grant liberty until 1500 hours to all who could be spared from their duties, so they could tread this hallowed ground. While for some this had no appeal, their preference lying in the direction of a cold glass of beer, I could state from personal observation that the Acropolis was alive with WALKER men, with cameras clicking furiously in all directions.

Promptly at 1600 hours, the ship departed amidst the din of whistles from all ships in the harbor. Not a soul was in the compound or on the seawall to wave a last farewell to the Greek soldiers. Of all the men on liberty, only two failed to make the ship. They were flown to Izmir, Turkey to rejoin the crew.

During the night, the ship made her way through the passages formed by the numerous islands dotting this part of the Mediterranean, arriving at the Izmir pilot station at daybreak the following day.

EN ROUTE WITH UNITED
NATIONS TROOPS

The harbor of Izmir was formed by a long and narrow bay and designed to accommodate only shallow-draft coasters and medium-
sized vessels. Along a seawall, a set of flat barges was moored to breast
off the WALKER to keep her in suitable depth while serving at the same
time as platforms for the embarkation of troops.

As soon as the ship was secured, accompanied by the Commanding
Officer of the Military Department aboard (COMILDEP), I met the
boarding party on the embarkation deck and conducted them to my quarters. Following introductions and exchange of information relative to official procedures during our stay in port, the ranking member, a Colonel
in the U.S. Army, dismissed the boarding party. Staying behind, he said,
"What I am about to pass on to you is for your ears only and should not
be a topic of casual conversation with others. Both of you, of course, are
acquainted with the protocol of military etiquette which, as a matter of
form, nominates the senior officer present to be the troop commander of
all military personnel embarked, regardless of nationality. He appoints
officers of the various contingent aboard to such administrative functions
as guard details, mess details, etc., for the duration of the voyage.

"The Turks on board are of brigade strength, making their Commanding Officer the senior officer present. Greeks and Turks have been bitter

enemies and at each others' throats for centuries. The Greek Army General Staff was adamant in their refusal to have one of their officers, in this case the Lieutenant Colonel of the Greek detachment, serving under a Turkish officer of higher rank. It was a tough, three-cornered situation among the U.S., Greek, and Turkish General Staffs, and it took some tough negotiations to come to an agreement satisfactory to all concerned.

"The solution was to carry the two officers, ranking members of the General Staffs of their respective armies, as Lieutenant Colonels on the passenger list, to be restored to their rightful ranks upon arrival in Korea."

Turning to the COMILDEP, he added, "This will be mostly your responsibility, hopefully. I do not anticipate any difficulties likely to come up on this last leg of the voyage."

It was not hard to guess how the situation would play itself out. Each of these gentlemen had the privilege of appointing a lower-ranking officer. Thus the Dutch Captain drew the guard detail, and his assistant, a Lieutenant, became the troop Mess Officer. These functions were primarily supervisory, the real work falling to senior non-commissioned officers selected from the various contingents on board.

Although it was still early in the day, a crowd of onlookers watched with quiet interest the mooring of the vessel. In time, mounted police and a company of footsoldiers cleared the area, as trucks carrying an advance party arrived. The soldiers marched in single file and quickstep onto the barges, where they were checked off and boarded the ship. The troops lost no time in making themselves at home. They were in high spirits, the foredeck resounding to the beating of drums, the plaintive wail of flutes and the twang of a stringed instrument. Groups of men formed circles and, with arms linked across shoulders, engaged in a shuffling dance, accompanied by the music and the rhythmic clapping of hands by onlookers. They seemed tireless and pursued their activities well into the night.

A U.S. Army Major had been assigned to the ship to maintain liaison with the local command. He informed us that the local provost marshal and his aide would take us on a tour of the city. Besides myself, the invitation included the Chief Engineer and the COMILDEP.

I soon discovered that neither of the officers spoke English. Since none of us spoke Turkish, there were some difficulties in communication. I learned that the aide, a young lieutenant, spoke a passable German he had learned while training with the German Army years ago. Thus a three-way conversation took place, the senior officer describing the sights we were to see to his aide, who translated it to me in German, to be passed on to my companions in English.

A walking tour through the city streets included a visit to a mosque, a theater, the local waterworks and a final jeep ride to a hill above the city to see the remnants of an ancient Roman fortress and a view to the back country in the direction of Ephesus, reputed burial place of Mary and the Apostle Paul. It was a peaceful, pastoral scene, sheep grazing on the hillside, a shiny stream below and, in the distance, the ruins of an aqueduct dating back to the Roman occupation. A delicious lunch of seafood and fresh vine-ripened apricots and grapes on a restaurant's outdoor terrace concluded the day.

Displayed above the entrance to the restaurant, I noticed large pictures of three persons. Having followed events of historical significance during my school days, I recognized the face in the center. Turning to the Lieutenant, I said casually, "I see there a likeness of your national hero, Kemal Pasha Attaturk." The Lieutenant passed it on to his superior. They both smiled and nodded their heads vigorously. Little did I know that what I had considered an innocuous remark would have some unexpected consequences.

During the night, on a grassy slope behind the seawall, a giant floral piece had been deposited. Representing the Turkish flag, it was composed entirely of blood-red roses for the field and white roses for the Star and Crescent. A local florist had presented the ship with a large wreath of palm leaves with multicolored gladiolas in the center. It was displayed aboard in the main foyer.

Behind the seawall, a large crowd had assembled, many of them relatives and friends of the departing soldiers. In a festive atmosphere, they had baskets of food to sustain themselves. Fruits, ice cream, cakes and other delicacies were being sold from elaborately decorated little carts by vendors doing a brisk business.

On the left was the honor guard of an infantry company in full battle dress, presenting arms with the arrival of each body of troops. A military band rendered martial music, most of it limited to one particular tune characterized by a curious swing and lilt. All troops coming within hearing distance would take up the refrain, singing the words with fervor and elation. A large Turkish flag had been draped over the rail on the foredeck, a Greek flag over the rail aft, and the Dutch, not to be outdone, displayed their national colors amidships.

On the embarkation deck, I was approached by the liaison officer who said, "Captain, you must come ashore. There is a delegation of students up the street who want to meet you." I followed him and was met by a group of young men carrying a flag and a large picture.

A spokesman, speaking in halting English, handed me a large photo depicting the grim visage of Kemal Pasha Ataturk. "We present to you and the troops on board this picture, with our best wishes, to accompany you on the task ahead."

I thanked them and acccpted the picture on behalf of the ship and all aboard. I suspected that this episode was the result of my having recognized the likeness of their national hero above the restaurant on the previous day. Walking back, I held the back side of the picture toward the ship, thinking no one, least of all the Greeks, needed to know what I was carrying. Said the Major, "Better turn the photo around for the Turks aboard to see." Reluctantly, I followed his advice and ascended the gangway to the frenzied applause of the Turkish troops viewing their idol, soldier, statesman, emancipator, benevolent dictator and venerated founder of the modern Turkish Republic. The Greeks were not exactly silent either, but probably for different reasons.

Embarkation continued until late afternoon. A strong wind had sprung up, raising whitecaps in the bay and pushing the ship up against the barges. At the time of departure, three tugs arrived to take the ship away from her moorings. They were low-powered vessels and, the wind having increased, there were moments when the scheduled departure of the ship was in doubt.

Eventually, after much backing and filling, the WALKER reached deep water and, amidst the deafening din of the ships' whistles in port, headed for the open sea. Once clear of the harbor, the ship was joined by a Turkish destroyer as an honor escort to Port Said, Egypt.

The following morning, in the charge of a British pilot, the WALKER, second in line of a convoy, entered the Suez Canal. Although moored to the bank for several hours to allow other vessels to pass, the ship entered the upper part of the Red Sea at daybreak the following morning and, having discharged the pilot, continued her voyage.

The heat in the Red Sea was unbearable. The temperature of the sea water stood at 96 degrees Farenheit. In the shade of the deck houses, it was 94 degrees Farenheit. With the sun beating down from a brassy sky on the ship's steel hull, dccks and superstructure and her underwater body warmed by the seawater, the WALKER soon became like an oven and neither ventilation system nor fans were of any help. In addition, the ship's interior became permeated with a peculiar sharp and acrid odor. It was determined to stem from the particular brand of cigarettes the troops were smoking. This, plus the exudation of some four thousand humans, caused the ship to float along in an effluvium which was an insult to the olfactory nerves and defied description.

In late afternoon, a threatening cloud appeared on the horizon. Soon a violent rainstorm burst over the vessel, each raindrop containing a piece of the Sinai Desert. When the squall had receded, the exterior of the ship was covered with mud, which, under the heat of the sun, soon turned to dust. Introduced into the blower system, it found its way into every nook and cranny in the ship's interior, presenting a nice problem in housekeeping.

It had always been my custom, after passengers and troops were settled, to invite the ranking troop commander and members of his staff to my quarters for coffee and cake, an invitation to be extended later to the unit commanders. Such meetings were always attended by the COMILDEP and the department heads. I had extended the courtesy to the Dutch officers earlier in the voyage. It was now time to follow through.

The dilemma was that an invitation to one and not the other would be considered an insult by the one not invited first. Since both Greek and Turkish commanders were of equal rank on the passenger list, I extended the invitation through the COMILDEP to both. They came. Their demeanor was courteous, but they avoided eye contact with each other and spoke only through their interpreters. I carried most of the conversation, hoping they were comfortable, would enjoy the trip, the weather, the food and our limited amenities, etc.

Arriving in Aden in the late afternoon of August 5, 1952, the ship was directed to anchor for the night. A moderate wind, bearing dust and sand, blotted out the horizon to seaward. A rising feeble moon served to accent the dark sinister aspects of the night, where everything seemed shadowy and without substance.

At daybreak, the ship moved to mooring buoys and took on fuel through a submarine pipeline. Departure was set for 1600 hours that day, the harbor Master stating that a later departure might be seriously hampered by the diurnal northerly sandstorm, expected to blow with considerable force.

While ashore in the afternoon to sign for the fuel and clear the ship, I was given a jeep ride through the sere and forbidding looking countryside, and I made a brief visit to the city. At the appointed time, the ship got underway with the Norther just beginning to blow. Having cleared the buoyed channel, we moved out into the Indian Ocean, into a dark and shapeless world, the atmosphere filled with dust, the sinking sun a blood red and distorted fiery ball. The sea was in a rough and confused state and the WALKER made sloppy weather of it, being tossed about in a rather nasty corkscrew motion. There was no beating of drums or dancing that night.

The following day, the sea subsided and once again the decks of the ship were in a reasonable state of equilibrium. In the ensuing days, there was a daily lineup of the Turkish troops on deck for inspection. The Brigade Executive Officer, a Major accompanied by Company Sergeant, would walk along slowly, frequently stopping to slap a soldier's face severely, for whatever reason. Small in stature, this pip-squeak martinet often had to reach high to administer this particular style of instant discipline, while the soldier stood rigidly at attention, staring straight ahead, never moving a muscle.

There were some problems in housekeeping and sanitation. The Turkish soldier is obedient, willing, cheerful, patient and accustomed to an exacting discipline. When properly instructed, he will carry out orders faithfully and to the letter. It was the lack of adequate numbers of interpreters and the ingrained habits of centuries that combined to raise obstacles. With a naive trust and willingness to learn on the one side and patience coupled with tact and forbearance on the other side, most problems were solved satisfactorily and amicably.

On a dull and rainy day, the ship arrived at Colombo to fuel and, within hours, left on the last leg of the trip. So far the voyage had been unclassified, but on this last stretch the vessel was under radio silence and routed by the Naval control Shipping Organization to Pusan, Korea, the final destination.

In the last days of the voyage, I invited the various unit commanders and members of their staffs to my quarters for a last farewell. I no longer regarded it necessary to observe the punctillio of the first meeting and had them up separately this time, starting with the Dutch officers, then the Greek Commander and, last, the Turkish Commander. In a less restrained atmosphere, I thanked them for their cooperation and praised their troops for their good behavior under sometimes trying conditions. The traditional Captain's dinner was served the evening before arrival.

On August 21, 1952, the voyage came to an end in Pusan, Korea. A reception committee composed of U.S. officers of Flag rank, United Nations officials, members of President Synghman Rhee's cabinet and Flag officers of the Republic of Korea (ROK) Army and Navy greeted the arrivals. A band was playing, welcoming speeches were made and flowers were presented to the debarking unit commanders. President Syngman Rhee, surrounded by his bodyguard, arrived shortly to welcome the troops. As the last in line, he shook hands with me, repeating the last sentence of his well-rehearsed speech: "If you don't fight the Communists here, you will have to fight them in your own backyard some day."

In retrospect, the worldwide voyage had actually begun in Pusan, Korea with Colombia and Puerto Rican troops on rotation to their homelands, and ended this day in Pusan, with the largest United Nations troop lift ever to be landed, to continue and finish the fight.

In the space of ninety days, the WALKER's stem had cleaved the waters of the Pacific, Caribbean, North Atlantic, the North Sea, the Mediterranean, Indian Ocean, Philippine Sea, South China Sea, East China Sea, the Yellow Sea, and the Sea of Japan. She had called at 15 ports, steamed 34,575 miles and transported a total of 17,907 persons without a mishap. It had been a voyage of rich experiences for me, the ship's company, as well as the United Nations unit troops commanders, their officers and men.

THE LAST DAYS AFLOAT

For the remainder of 1952, the WALKER resumed routine operations to Japan and Korea, carrying troops of all services of the armed forces.

The valiant ROK divisions in their advance to the Yalu River had been badly mauled by massive Chinese forces and were decimated to the point of ineffectiveness as combat units. Replacements were mostly young, inadequately trained recruits. To restore the combat effectiveness of the ROK divisions, these replacements were first integrated in the U.S. Army for training, that is, for every American serviceman, there was one ROK recruit attached to his unit. It was called the Buddy System.

In early 1953, voyages to the Far East continued, with a gradual shift away from Yokohama to Sasebo, a former Japanese Naval Base, and to Pusan and Inchon. In March, the WALKER was assigned to a naval task unit composed of three ships. The WALKER's mission was to transfer U.S. troops from guard duty at a prison camp on Koje Island to Inchon. Steaming in formation as the last in the convoy, the WALKER's officers had, in effect, a refresher course in signaling, darken ship, station keeping and other evolutions.

As the result of prolonged negotiations over a period of two years, an armistice was signed at Panmunjom in July 1953, ending three years of fighting. A demilitarized zone was established, and, under the watchful eyes of neutral observers, limits were imposed on replacement, for troops on rotation. In the ensuing months, the WALKER continued to carry troops to Inchon. Neutral observers were on hand to check on the number of troops debarking. On the UN side was a Swiss and a Swedish Army officer, On the Communist side a Pole and a Czech officer. The UN observers allowed me to take their pictures. The Communists declined my invitation to pose.

The Year 1953 came to a close, and so did my active service afloat.

REPRISE

Personnel administration in the maritime industry preceding the era of enlightened labor relations involved the simple elements of hiring and firing. Along with the introduction of civilian marine personnel in the Naval Establishment came the necessity of defining the terms and conditions of employment for seagoing civilian employees of the Navy.

Foremost was a clarification of the position of the civilian shipmaster in command of United States Naval Ships (USNS). Here is how his position was described in the operating manual:

> "The master's authority emanates from maritime law, navigation laws and responsibilities assigned to COMSTS. He is responsible for enforcing all laws of the United States and all applicable orders and regulations of the United States Coast Guard, the Navy and COMSTS."

Elsewhere, Navy Civilian Personnel Instructions (NCPI) provided the legal basis and authority for implementing a policy objective:

> "To assure the highest possible living and working conditions aboard civil service manned ships, consistent with maritime practice and the public interest...and to provide regulations governing personnel in civil service manned ships which will attract and retain superior crews and assure efficient administration of civilian marine personnel."

A statement of basic premises and policy amplified the objective by declaring:

> "Because the Military Sea Transportation Service is engaged in operations in support of the Armed Forces of the United States, standards of performance and discipline typical of the naval forces must be maintained among civilian marine employees."

This concept was tempered by the concluding statement:

> "To administer the civilian marine personnel program in accordance with Navy standards of personnel performance and disciplinary traditions while conforming as closely as appropriate to current conditions and practices in the maritime industry."

Reconciliation of these concepts based upon blending industry practice with naval standards posed a formidable task for the USNS shipmaster.

During my years afloat as Master I had adhered to these precepts as closely as possible. I had been in command of eight ships and in retrospect I like to believe that an imprint of my administration was left in every ship. Needless to say not everyone liked my style. Be that as it may, I neither aspired to play the heavy nor the role of a Goodtime Charley. From the day I stepped on board I set the tone by my own conduct. I spoke quietly and in a moderate tone when discussing affairs of the ship with the ship's company, civilian or military. When I felt like cussing it was against a problem, never against a person. I recall the day when a junior watch officer made a blunder, not a serious one but an embarrassing one. Noting his discomfiture, I chose to ignore it and said nothing. A redfaced young man later related the incident to his fellow officers: "I made a stupid mistake. The Old Man never said a damned word. Boy, I never felt so bawled out in my life."

It is a truism that the Master lives in a glass bowl. His every act is observed and evaluated; his every word is heard, embellished and variously applied to the situation of the moment. I discouraged loose talk and gossip, horseplay and practical jokes as potential sources of trouble. Gambling aboard ship was a known fact. Trying to stop it was a difficult if not an impossible task. Taking an occasional walk through the ship in the late evening the face of a lookout at the end of a passageway would disappear. "Hey, fellows," he'd whisper, "ditch the cards and the dice, here comes the Old Man."

I knew I could not stop the gambling, but I devised a method to curtail it. I often received letters from the wives of crewmen complaining that their husbands had failed to leave an allotment or had not sent money home when paid enroute. At various ports of call I arranged with the Army Post Office (APO) to send a clerk to the ship with money orders to give the men the opportunity to send money home. At least that much would not fall into the hands of the gamblers.

My office door was always open. Some men came to me with personal

Reunion with old playmates.

problems. Merely listening but giving no advice, I often sent them away feeling better.

One night a strong wind came up, and saltspray encrusted the large pilothouse windows. "Have the windows cleaned," I told the officer on the morning watch as I went below for a moment. When I returned shortly, the windows had not yet been cleaned.

"I had to send the A.B. on an errand" the watch officer explained. I noticed the ordinary seaman of the watch standing in the corner.

"Get a bucket of water and wash the windows," I ordered.

"I can't do it, I am afraid of falling off" he quavered.

"You what?..." I broke off as I felt my anger rising.

There was a catwalk on the forepart of the pilothouse with a substantial hand rail and a sliding safety belt. I recalled the days when I had been aloft battling canvas in a fullblown gale, and here stood this nincompoop riding the gravy train telling me he could not do the job because he was afraid of falling off?

"I don't want to see you aboard this ship next trip."

He wasn't.

The voyage had been uneventful and without incident. My relations

Carolyne in Germany.

with the department heads and the military contingent aboard had been cordial throughout. I was left in command of USNS GENERAL N.M. WALKER until detached for duty on the staff of Commander Military Sea Transportation Service, Pacific.

Carolyne.

ON THE STAFF
OF COMMANDER MILITARY SEA
TRANSPORTATION SERVICE
PACIFIC

The position of Port Captain, MSTSPAC, was open as the result of the incumbent's retirement. I had always regarded the billet of Port Captain as the peak of a career at sea. Yet it was not easy to leave a ship and "hang up the suit," as the saying goes. Following a lengthy debate with myself and Carolyne, it was decided that I should apply for the job. It proved to be a wise decision, in the light of later events.

My application was accepted, and I took up my duties early in 1954. The position carried the classification of Supervisory Transport Specialist, G.S.13, with the title of Port Captain. I had three assistants with deck officer's licenses and a secretary-typist. The duties of the Port Captain's Branch are set forth in the job description, excerpted here:

> "The position is the Port Captain, Vessel Operations Division under the very general supervision of the Director Vessels Operations Division.

"Duties are handled on own initiative. The incumbent must have a thorough knowledge of ship's administration and operation in order to make an accurate analysis and evaluation of the needs of the ship.

"The incumbent is required to be an experienced Licensed Master Mariner.

"Serves as staff advisor on technical matters pertaining to the operational efficiency and material condition of USNS ships. This includes advice on the utilization of personnel, allocation and areas of responsibility among various departments aboard ships, operational efficiency of these departments, problems and problem areas that arise and recommendation of solutions to same, overall administration aboard USNS ships and other complex and technical matters of a varied and diversified nature.

"...Furnishes technical advice concerning ships' movements which involves consideration of tidal and weather conditions and which require familiarity with harbor conditions and prevailing marine practices. Acts as technical advisor to Office of Counsel in litigation involving MSTS ships carrying DOD cargo under MSTS charter or shipping contract. Furnishes technical advice in the field of vessel construction (Deck Department items), ship operation, ship capabilities, maritime customs, navigation, and seamanship.

"...Maintains liaison between masters, deck officers, and staff headquarters. Provides advice and assistance to Masters of USNS ships on all types of problems. Advice is provided to Masters on command and COMSTS policies and procedures regarding operations of ships, personnel utilization and practices. Serves as troubleshooter and expert in solving problems. Problems are often resolved by personal visits to ships.

"...Maintains information on licensed deck officers, giving due regard to their technical abilities and competence to fulfill administrative and operational requirements of the particular type of ship.

"...Administers the night relief officers' pool, in addition serves as representative on the Marine Board of Examiners, when appointed, serves on various boards and committees, e.g. space board, habitability board, beneficial award committee. Formulates recommendations to higher authority concerning policies and procedures affecting Deck Department personnel and operational matters aboard USNS ships. Makes special studies and carries out special assignments as

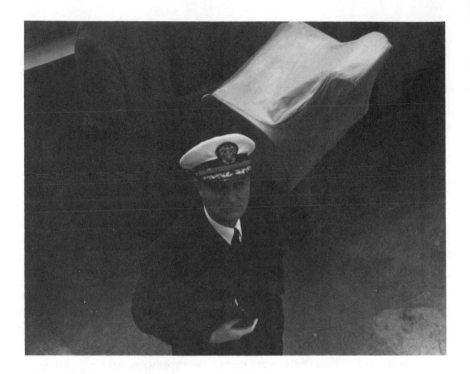

Master U.S.N.S. NELSON M. WALKER

required in the field of ship operations and civilian marine personnel, e.g. recommendations for revision of manning scales. Maintains record of Coast Guard Annual Inspections and of the requirements of the Coast Guard. Certification of Inspection issued to each ship.

"...Attends ships arriving, sailing or shifting berth in port as representative of the Operations Office. Observes and reports in detail any damage sustained by ships, tugs, or any harbor structure during in-port movements. Collects records and disseminates port facility data. Carries out special assignments involving travel to other localities. For example, reports on harbor facilities, geographic peculiarities and other matters of interest in connection with the establishment of new ports or the addition of ports not previously visited by MSTS ships. Schedules presailing fire and boat drills.

"Observes and evaluates proficiency of crew and condition of equipment, Deck Department gear and appurtenances, personnel and related matters affecting the seaworthiness of ships.

"Coordinates with the Readiness Assistant the assignment of Deck
Department personnel to training courses. Represents the Operations
Office during underway training and safety.

I took up these duties with gusto and enthusiasm, entering upon a
phase in my career that was both interesting and challenging.

The principal customers of MSTS had been the Army, Navy, Air Force
and the Marine Corps. To fulfill the transportation requirements of these
shipper services, MSTS had operated a nucleus fleet of dry cargo ships,
passenger ships and tankers. MSTS operations had reached its peak in the
mid-1950s. The wars were over, with the exception of minor flareups
throughout the world, but the Cold War in Europe was still very much a
reality, and national security demanded extraordinary steps to safeguard
the Western World.

The concept of the Distant Early Warning Radar System (DEW Line)
became reality when men and material were landed in the North Polar
Region in over-the-beach operations around the clock. MSTSPAC military and civilian crews undertook the formidable task of logistic supply--
nothing short of a miracle--to construct the DEW Line, which, when
completed, extended across the entire Arctic border of North America.

The assault on the North Polar region was carried out simultaneously
from the Pacific and the Atlantic Coasts. MSTSPAC ships landed men
and material at Point Barrow, Alaska. Under the leadership of the Washington, D.C.-based Commander of the Military Sea Transportation Service, a US Naval and MSTS Task Group undertook the formidable job of
charting a supply route through the legendary Northwest Passage and
opened up the ice- choked Bellot Strait leading into the western approaches. It was not only a supply line but also an escape route for MSTS
ships which found themselves blocked by ice across the usual routes out
of the Arctic.

The achievement of a long-sought, practical deep water passage across
the North American Continent was the result of years of experience in
polar logistics and the joint cooperation of the military and civilian personnel engaged in the task and supported by the governments of the
United States and Canada, the Navy, Army, Coast Guard, Merchant Marine, and elements in the private sector.

It was a Canadian icebreaker, followed by three U.S. Coast Guard
cutters, that led the first fleet of supply ships through the newly charted
channels. The conventional fleet of MSTS had been augmented by a

number of small cargo vessels with ice- strengthened hulls. For maintenance and resupply of the DEW Line, six such ships were stationed at the Mackenzie River Delta in the Canadian Northwest. They were later turned over to the Canadian Navy.

Upon completion of that project and to allay the specter of an upcoming reduction in force (RIF), the management cast about for other worlds to conquer. As the result of rapid developments in the field of science and technology, there arose a demand for more ships of varying types manned by skilled crews. To meet this new situation, headquarters at MSTS, Washington, D.C. created a Special Project Section responsible for the procurement of ships and crews available to Government agencies for research projects.

A number of ships of new design were constructed and put in service to engage in oceanographic research, including explorations in the Antarctic by the National Science Foundation, Others conducted a South Pacific Survey and Island Ecological Studies.

Foremost in this new scenario was the ongoing interest in space exploration, in which MSTS ships assumed responsibility in tracking and recovering missiles. Two MSTS ships of the Victory type were stationed at Port Hueneme, California, specially equipped with helicopter pads and hangars for missile recovery. A third Victory type ship served as a telemetry ship for tracking missiles. These ships were under the operational control of the Navy's Pacific Missile Range. USNS HAITI VICTORY was the first civilian-manned ship to recover, at sea, a satellite--DISCOVERER XIII--which had re-entered the earth's atmosphere.

MSTS had now become the largest operator of ships from the National Defense Reserve Fleet, as well as foreign bottoms under charter, a strong link in the logistic chain supporting the interests of the United States, the United Nations, and the Free World. It was an exciting and challenging period. In the course of time, the names of prospective masters and deck officers came to my desk for evaluation and recommendation to higher authority.

In the selection of a crew for a ship assigned to a special mission, first consideration was given to the professional competence of the prospective Master, since he would carry the full burden of responsibility for the success of a mission. Such competence was not limited to the technical operation of the ship--including navigation, piloting and ship-handling-- but also included to a large degree the proper administration of personnel.

Certain difficulties could be anticipated, stemming from poor crew morale for which the discomfort of adverse climatic conditions and the lack of adequate recreational facilities en route and in outports could be held responsible. The bringing together of many different and varying personalities in the close association inherent in shipboard life produces the stresses and strains responsible to a large degree for the upheavals and disruptions often observed in ships not engaged in routine operations.

Although any actions on my part were limited to the deck department, I kept a close eye on the composition of a ship's company. Remembering the searing experiences of my first command in the USAT WILL. H. POINT, I did not hesitate, when necessary, to comment off the record or to point out potential trouble spots.

LCDR—USNR active duty for training.

LIFE ON TERRA FIRMA

Since coming ashore, I had applied for Annual Active Duty for Training (ACDUTRA). On my own time, I took required Navy correspondence courses. Additionally, every Wednesday I attended evening classes at an Officers' Training School on Treasure Island in San Francisco Bay, then controlled and administered by the Navy. As the result of these activities, I rose to the rank of Lieutenant Commander in the Naval Reserve. I also joined the Propeller Club of the United States, Port of the Golden Gate, and the Mariner's Club of California, associations useful to me for keeping my finger on the pulse of the maritime community.

Other extra-curricular activities included participation in the restoration of the Cape Horn windjammer BALCLUTHA. A fullrigged ship, she was launched in Scotland in 1886. Throughout the years, the ship had wandered the world's oceans in the trades of her day under the British, Hawaiian and ultimately the American flag. Operating under several names and ownerships, she was last known as the PACIFIC QUEEN. With the elimination of sailing ships in commercial trade, she wound up on the mud flats of Sausalito in San Francisco Bay. Slowly deteriorating, she was saved from the ship breakers when the San Francisco Maritime Museum Association bought her in 1954 to be restored to her original state and serve as a museum ship on the San Francisco Embarcadero under her original name, BALCLUTHA. From its inception, the project of restoration captured the imagination and interest of the entire Bay Area community. Foremost in getting things underway were members of the shipbuilding industry and their unions of metalworkers, shipwrights, carpenters, cordagemakers, shipfitters, electricians, plumbers, painters and many others. They were joined by men and women, private citizens not necessarily connected with the maritime industry, who came down to scrape, varnish, clean, or push brooms for the fun of it. All work was voluntary. Materials were donated by manufacturers, ship chandlers, and other purveyors.

A major problem arose when it developed that an essential craft was missing, riggers with experience in sailingship rigging. The shortage was acute and resulted in many newspaper ads calling for men with expertise in that field to come forth and lend a hand. Along with others, I responded to the call and spent Saturdays and some Sundays at the old ship. Many of the group had in their youth served before the mast in Cape Horn windjammers. We set up standing rigging, rove running rigging, bent, set and furled sails as required. Some brought their own tools, tools that had gathered dust in attics and basements--marline spikes, prickers, fids, serving mallets, palm and needle--to practice once again the long unused but not forgotten skills, generally described as marline-spike seamanship.

It was a time when old shipmates met again and new friends were made. We were the crew that manned the ship, under tow from the shipyard, for delivery to the museum site. General interest soon waned. Not so on the part of the rigging gang. About forty of us formed a club named "Friends of the Balclutha." The purpose was to continue rigging work as needed. On the fun side, we met monthly for lunch to preserve our association, retain old and make new friends.

Our emblem at these meetings was a framed picture of a life ring. On the upper part appeared the logo, "Friends of the Balclutha"; in the center was a picture of a ship under full sail; immediately below it were the crossed tools of seamen, marline spike, serving mallet; and a ball of spunyarn. Across the lower part of the life ring appeared our motto: RIGGERS NON MORTIS, an appropriate and pithy pun suggested by one of our members.

Inevitably, as time went on, the group dwindled to a few individuals and the meetings were discontinued. The emblem was donated to the Maritime Museum and became a part of the exhibits in the BAL-

CLUTHA, in memory of those who had served to the last and then joined many others in their celestial Snug Harbor.

To keep the family together, I purchased a two-room cabin in the Santa Cruz Mountains near my early stamping grounds to serve as a retreat for annual vacations and weekends. For a modest stipend, we obtained membership in a nearby swimming pool. The children had married and a first grandchild, a boy, had joined the family circle.

I recalled the lodgings we'd taken during an early visit to Germany in a rural inn in the Black Forest area. The room was richly decorated in the prevailing peasant style of the region. Fortunately, I had a photo of the room and, upon our return home, I determined to add a master bedroom to our cabin, a duplicate of what we had seen in the Black Forest Inn.

It became a weekend family project. I acted as architect and carpenter and, with the help of Janet and Brooks who sawed lumber and drove nails, the project got underway. The exterior was of the local board-and-batten design. For the interior, we used tongue-and-groove knotty pine. A beamed high ceiling added to the overall appearance. Georgia, the artist in the family, decorated the interior, using the photo as a guide. When we were done, we took pride and joy in our accomplishment.

From a secondhand store in the area, I purchased a dresser with a plate glass mirror hung in a carved frame of a lyre design. Because the mirror was partly clouded, I negotiated a low price for the piece. Back at the cabin, I cleaned off the dust and dirt of many years and removed many coats of varnish to see what was underneath. It proved to be of fine wood and solid construction. I stripped and sanded the exterior and applied a new coat of clear varnish. With antique fittings on the drawers, it became a showpiece in the room. A wooden bedframe and headboard received the same treatment.

The cabin served us well in the ensuing years. Things were going our way and we were embarked upon an enviable lifestyle. But--whom the Gods envy, they will destroy--disaster struck in the fall of 1958. Returning from a weekend visit to the cabin, Carolyne complained of seeing spiderwebs on the windshield of our car. I assured her that the windshield was clear, but she insisted. En route, through a remote mountain area, she sustained a massive vitreous hemorrhage. Because of the severity of the affliction, and with no immediate help available, she lost her eyesight.

Back at home, I immediately applied for and was granted emergency leave. Words are insufficient to describe our anguish and despair when we learned that there was no possibility of recovery. In time, we received a visit from the State Teacher for the Adult Blind. A distinguished woman, herself blind and highly educated, there was an instant rapport between these two women, both of whom were on the same cultural and educational level.

For children who are born blind, the process of education begins while they are infants and continues through enrollment in schools for the blind, where they receive an education equal or superior to that which the public school system can offer. Many go on to college and as adults are fully prepared to enter the business world for gainful employment. Never having seen the outside world, they do not encounter the debilitating problems of those who lose their sight in midlife and must move from a world of light to a world of darkness. For some adults, blindness is a gradual process that affords timely steps to deal with oncoming problems. In Carolyne's case, the loss of sight which occured practically overnight without advance warning proved a devastating shock.

During my emergency leave, I gave Carolyne maximum support, feeding her, reading to her and leading her around the house, feeling this was a necessary duty. The state teacher came frequently to instruct her in mobility and the use of the white, red-tipped cane. She started her reading and writing Braille. In time, she admonished me not to do too much for her, lest the progress toward functioning independently be impeded. I felt I could not refrain from helping Carolyne in the face of her daily misery. Carolyne had always been an outgoing and gregarious person who loved people and enjoyed their company. "I thought our friends would rally around us, but nobody rallied" was her complaint.

The children had established their own households and moved away, so they could do little to help. Brooks, still a ward of her aunt Carolyne, had earlier requested and received permission to live with her mother's family in Washington State for awhile. When she heard of her aunt's misfortune, she returned, saying, "It would not be right for me to be away, now that Aunt Carolyne needs me." I gave her high marks for the decision. While still in high school, she found time to read the daily paper to her aunt, and she performed other helpful duties. However, following graduation, she declined an offer by the Veterans Administration to pay her tuition for a college education and, at age eighteen, chose to marry a classmate and establish her own household.

I had long since returned to work. Friends, acquaintances, and even

Brooks

neighbors gradually dropped away, probably not knowing how to cope
with the new situation. A cleaning woman we had employed for years
continued to come once a week. I engaged a part-time housekeeper to
give Carolyne breakfast and lunch and stay with her in the afternoons. An
elderly black woman, a native of Texas, she was very sympathetic and
supportive. We missed her greatly when she became ill and had to leave
our employ.

We joined the California Council of the Blind and took part in their
meetings and conventions. We entered a new world of men and women
who, as a group, dealt with their handicap as a matter of course. With
courage, cheerfulness and competence, they successfully competed with
the outside world. As a support group, they filled the void created for
both of us by the retreat of our former circle of friends and associates.
Once again, Carolyne enjoyed the company of her peers and found an

Ingeborg

outlet for her energies by taking part in their activities as best she could.

A daily routine now included listening to novels by well-known authors, recorded on platters and provided as a free service by the State Library. Several times a week a volunteer came to read to her. In spite of all this, the scourge of boredom continued to be a problem for which there seemed to be no solution.

One day, our cleaning woman, a person well along in her middle years, confided to Carolyne that she had enrolled in the Berkeley Evening School for Adult Education to obtain a high school diploma. She had experienced some difficulty in reading and pronunciation of difficult words. Carolyne, as a former teacher, immediately offered to coach her on the days she came to clean. Knowing that a part of the curriculum included the mandatory study of American History, I supplied the books and at times looked up information on various subjects. Following graduation, our cleaning lady proudly showed us her high school diploma. We complimented her upon her achievement. Smiling brightly, she said, "I done good, eh?"

We were startled but agreed that she had indeed "done good."

At the state teacher's suggestion, Carolyne attended Arts and Crafts classes at a newly opened Orientation Center for the Blind, making simple artifacts such as ornaments and jewelry. It was not a noteworthy success, but it did get Carolyne out of the house and in contact with other people. Then something went awry. When I picked her up one afternoon, I found her in a state of agitation and angry tears. "I'll never go back to that place," she said.

Somehow, she had been channeled into an adjacent establishment called Workshop for the Blind. "They want me to make brooms and dusters to be peddled to householders. I am not going to do it!" she declared angrily. It was a severe setback to her morale.

Immersed in my duties at the office, I found some escape from her problems serving MSTS, a burgeoning organization. I also realized that at the rapidly approaching age of seventy, I would reach compulsory retirement age in the Federal Service. Thus in April 1965, I found a letter on my desk, as required by existing regulations, informing me that, a year hence, on the last day of the month of my birth, I would be retired. It was a shock, in spite of the fact that I had known it was coming. I had formulated no firm plans regarding future activities during the upcoming leisure days.

In the ensuing year, Carolyne continued to accompany me to many social functions. She moved with ease about the clubrooms, using her white cane, and enjoyed the sociability of the moment. On an evening prior to my official retirement date, my former shipmates and staff personnel threw a farewell cocktail party for me at the Fort Mason Officers' Club in San Francisco. In addition to the many cards and letters, I received an unexpected honor when I was presented with a Certificate of Achievement and a 26-year service plaque.

On Friday, April 29, 1966, my retirement became effective. At the close of the day, I took one last walk through the halls and offices where I had spent so many happy days in a position I had always considered to be the most productive and rewarding part of my professional career. Through a side door, I quietly faded into the waning day, avoiding a last encounter lest I lose my carefully guarded composure. The sound of the door closing behind me symbolized the end of my professional life. Shaped by a chain of events composed of interacting forces more often than not beyond my control, it had run its course.

At an early age, I had been confronted with the necessity of making decisions entailing far-reaching consequences. Foremost in a series of events was the acquisition of U.S. citizenship and the firm resolution to continue the pursuit of a career at sea. In the course of time, I served under more than twenty shipmasters, men of varying degrees of expertise and accomplishment. As collective role models, each and every one contributed something. I learned from their successes as well as some of their failures.

Fortified by a formal education in the German school system, augmented by a U.S. high school equivalency test, further enhanced by an affinity for foreign languages, I found no difficulty in learning English. In America, I pursued no organized course of language study, I simply absorbed English by reading newspapers, magazines and books--and by osmosis.

In my early days in California, I had the good fortune to be befriended by an American family of substance. George S. Beadle became my mentor and role model in the use of good English. From the day I met him, first as an employer and later as my father-in-law, I clung to every word and phrase he used. I also quickly adopted the mores and usages of society governing the conduct of daily affairs in the early decades of the century.

Mr. Beadle--I could never bring myself to call him father and always addressed him as Sir--was a gentleman of the old school, punctilious in the observance of the etiquette and the niceties of an era long gone. It was a time when men still wore hats and doffed them in the presence of members of the opposite sex. In mixed company at table, men rose when ladies left, and rose again when they returned, and remained standing until they were seated. In the company of others, Mr. Beadle was unpretentious, his choice of language fastidious, his manner invariably courteous. In the business world, he was experienced, and a worthy foe of anyone who tried to best him.

All these were valuable bits of knowledge that enabled me to pursue a career and a way of life from which I extracted the utmost in satisfaction. I successfully met the challenges of administrative work while serving as port captain on the staff of Commander Military Sea Transportation Service Pacific. That dreaded bugaboo, "paperwork," the bane of many a good sailorman, held no terrors for me. To the contrary, I welcomed the opportunity to express myself in official reports I was required to submit to higher authority during the last years of my service ashore.

THE PLEASURES
OF RETIREMENT

I had retired from the job, but not from life. Most seamen I had known had come from the land. At the end of a life at sea, they returned to the land from which they had come to live out their remaining years.

In a modest way, I followed in their footsteps. I cultivated a large portion of our rear garden, raising an abundance of flowers, fruits and vegetables. Yet, in time, I felt the need for outside activities. Part-time work as a cargo surveyor and occasional appearances as a witness in court for legal firms trying cases in admiralty law, served to keep up my interest in maritime affairs.

Throughout the years I supported Carolyne in her attempts to deal with the problems of life in a world of darkness. Because of her keen interest in the affairs of The California Council of the Blind, she had been elected vice president. The accomplishments of this remarkable group accustomed to deal with their handicap with courage and determination was a decided stimulus. Fluent readers of Braille and gifted speakers, their eloquence revealed an intellect second to none. In all their activities, formal or recreational, they were sustained by an uncommon zest for life. However, the stress of ten years of sightless life took its toll, and Carolyne succumbed to a heart ailment. A good marriage of thirty-eight years had come to an end. Her family, her friends and the community suffered a

Backyard farmers *(photo taken when Janet was a child).*

grievous loss. She had been advisor and counselor to the young and the old, the blind and the sighted. Carolyne gave unstintingly to those who came with troubled hearts, and they went away refreshed and imbued with new courage.

In accordance with her wishes, she was cremated and her ashes placed in the family plot on a verdant western slope facing the Golden Gate. I spent the ensuing months settling her estate and taking care of bequests she had made to her children, other family members, and her friends.

A year passed quietly and I felt the need for a change of scenery, to sort things out and get back on an even keel. Winter was approaching and I recalled the days of my boyhood, the landscapes of the Franconian forest in deep snow, the rich aromas of Christmas trees lighted with flickering wax candles, and the warmth of family visits. I planned a leisurely trip of several months, to roam the old familiar trails in the

Edna

woods, to call on remaining relatives and renew acquaintance with former schoolmates and playmates.

I had kept in touch with former office associates. Edna had continued as secretary to the new port captain, and he relied heavily upon her experience to carry him through the initial phases of a job he apparently found bewildering. To the men afloat she became known as "Captain Edna." During the working years of our association, we had developed high regard and respect for each other, a feeling which, upon parting, had turned to affection and compassion. Although the Military Sea Transportation Service was still very much a going concern, there were indications of change. The consolidation of several office branches resulting in staff reduction was being considered. The possible abolition of the port captain's position was a persistent, dark rumor. Contemplating the lonely years ahead, Edna and I thought of marriage. She accepted my proposal and, in laying plans for the future, we each decided to pay what might well be a last visit to the lands of our birth, Canada and Germany. She retired from government service at the end of the year.

When I returned from Germany in early 1969, I called in the family and informed them of my intention to marry Edna. The news was received with acclaim. My daughter Georgia said, "I could not attend your first wedding but I plan to be present at this one." She and her husband Danny accompanied us to Reno, Nevada, where we obtained a marriage license. This was followed by a religious ceremony at the hotel where we had taken quarters. At the wedding dinner, Georgia asked, "Do you mind telling us where you're going on your wedding trip?"

"To Death Valley," we replied.

"Death Valley? Isn't that a peculiar place for a honeymoon?"

"Might be. Neither of us has been there before. Anyway, this is the best time of the year to go. Moreover, at times it's more fun to do the odd, rather than the conventional thing, don't you think?"

Following a week's stay exploring that wondrous place, we drove on to Texas to visit with former shipboard associates from the military department. Through their good offices, we secured on the return trip a one-week stay at a 3000-acre ranch in West Texas, with quarters in an old building that was once a stagecoach stop.

We rode horseback every day to observe the abundant wildlife, the muletail deer, pronghorn antelope, quail and other birdlife. We had a wonderful time. We then settled down to a domestic routine which was interrupted one afternoon in late 1969 by the telephone. "There is someone on the line," Edna told me, "who says he knows you and wants to talk to you."

The caller identified himself as a former deck officer with MSTS. I had known him briefly. He informed me that he had married, quit the sea and joined an organization specializing in ship charters. I listened patiently as he related the purpose of his call. It appeared that his company had chartered a ship of German registry to the United States Government, to carry construction machinery and material to Micronesia via Honolulu.

The ship's second mate had been hospitalized and the Captain and first mate had declined to take the ship to sea shorthanded. Attempts to fly in a replacement from Hamburg, Germany were frustrated by a merchant marine officers' strike in that country. Unless the ship put to sea by 5 p.m that day, the time charter would expire and the ship be off-hire. It was imperative that a replacement be found who could speak German and would be interested in taking the job. "I knew you were retired and that you spoke German, so I thought of you," he said.

I hesitated as I tried to absorb the information he was providing. Overhearing part of the conversation, Edna urged me to do it. "Take it, take it, it will be a wonderful trip for you," she said.

Reluctant to leave her alone in a big house for what might be several months, I said, "Hold on now, and let's not go overboard on this until I can find out more about it."

I could feel the sense of urgency in the caller's voice as he pressed on. "If you can go as far as Honolulu, I am sure we can get a replacement from Hamburg by that time," he said. He continued, "If we can agree upon a price for your services, we are prepared to fly your wife to Honolulu and return, with a return ticket for you to the U.S."

I felt this was an acceptable offer. We agreed upon the conditions mentioned and the sum of three hundred dollars for the run, payable on the day of arrival in Honolulu. With my sextant, my license and some clothes, I boarded the vessel and, within moments, found myself headed once again through the Golden Gate into the open sea beyond.

Although I had often visited the Hawaiian Islands in the pursuit of my calling, Maui had always been off the beaten path but not forgotten. Perhaps, some day, I'd thought. That day came after I stepped ashore at Honolulu, where I was met by Edna and a company official who handed me a check for three hundred dollars. A long dormant desire to re-visit Maui and retrace my steps into the past came to life. We were able to engage a room in a private home in neighboring Hana, and we settled in for a week.

Experience had taught me that nostalgic visits to places of long ago were fraught with disappointment. Fortified with that knowledge, I hoped to avoid disillusionment. We rented a car and drove the narrow, winding road to Kipahulu. From the high promontory, we took the heavily overgrown zigzag trail leading down to that old favorite spot, the clear, translucent freshwater pool, fed by a high upstream waterfall, and separated from a pounding ocean surf by a rocky beach.

To rest again on the small grassy plot shaded by a small grove of young coconut trees, that haven of rest many years ago for a group of forlorn foreigners destined to await the end of a war in this remote spot;

to let the scenes of the past drift across my mind, towering Haleakala Crater; to hear the shouts and the crack of whips of the cane-wagon drivers; to smell the heavy, sweetish odor of molasses; to hear once again the sounds of the Hawaiiian language from the lips of young friends, than which there is no more melodious sound in all the world; to sleep, perchance to dream... I awoke with a start to the touch on my shoulder. "You've been asleep, dear," my wife said. "It's time to go."

I sat up, hearing the surf pounding the rocky beach. It had broken through and allowed saltwater to flow into the pool. Shivering in my wet bathing trunks, I surveyed the familiar scene. The deep pool fed by small waterfalls cascaded over shiny black lava rocks. On the far side, the high arch of volcanic rock that had served in its day as a diving board. All seemed the same, but not quite the same.

The water had lost its sparkle; the pool was dark; yellow scum had collected in the eddies. The grassy plot, our resting place fifty years ago, had been taken over by an impenetrable jungle. Slowly, we made our way to the top of the bluff. I cast one long backward glance. From the distance, it was still the lovely picture I had never forgotten, but the Kipahulu I had known was no more. Above the cavernous hollow of the old dismantled sugar mill, the stack still stood, crowned by a tuft of grass, weathered and gleaming against the backdrop of the verdant slopes of Haleakala. What price nostalgia?

The following day we took our leave from the only persons we had met who remembered me and my companions, the elderly Japanese couple and their daughter who had served the plantation owners as houseman and housekeeper. On the voyage from San Francisco to Honolulu, I had written an article relating my early experiences on the Maui plantation, 1917-1919. I finished it during our brief island stay and, upon returning to Honolulu submitted "Maui Revisited After Half a Century," along with a group picture, to a Honolulu newspaper, which bought it for thirty-five dollars.

Upon our return to California, we again took up life in our neo-Victorian home in lower Piedmont, essentially a residential community with fine homes and gardens bordering on the sprawling City of Oakland. The region was the terminus of transcontinental railroads and highways coupled with an outlet into San Francisco Bay, the vast Pacific Ocean and the lands of the Far East.

Sitting on a gentle slope, backed by a spacious rear garden with lawn, shrubbery and trees, the place was an oasis, a refuge and playground for city wildlife, and a resting spot for flocks of migratory birds who found abundant sustenance in the rich insect life. Nesting places in large trees offered protection from predators. Here many species of birds thrived and fulfilled their destiny. It became a fascinating pastime for us to watch through our rear windows, affording a full view of the garden, the comings and goings of our feathered habitues! Camera and field glasses were always at hand at this observation post.

Western robins, thrushes, scrubjays, hummingbirds, mourning doves, brown thrashers, a rare goldfinch, nuthatches and the ubiquitous rowdy English Sparrow were the most common visitors. Casual visitors included a pair of golden-winged woodpeckers, extracting worms and larvae from a dead peartree stump or feeding on the ground.

Lately, there had been a marked increase in the number and variety of our backyard guests. Small furry animals began to join the bird population, obviously in retreat from their former habitats as the flatland communities took on a cosmopolitan complex in which the roar of construction machinery and the rhythmic pounding of pile drivers heralded the destruction of residences and gardens to make way for highrise buildings, drab parking lots and ribbons of freeways.

Green belts and parks disappeared under the onslaught of an ever-increasing population. Creek beds, lush with vegetation and the homes of innumerable small creatures of the animal world, were being ruthlessly denuded and deeply scarred by that man-made ogre, the bulldozer. Lifegiving water became encased in culverts and storm drains. Dust filled the air as monstrous clamshells bit into the earth to excavate building sites. There was no headlong flight into the woods and meadows of the back country; rather, a gradual withdrawal to remaining residential areas as yet untouched by the hand of industrial developers. Thus our garden had now become a haven for small displaced creatures of nature. A pair of dun-colored, beady-eyed squirrels with bushy, bright orange tails found food and shelter in our giant Monterey pine and large Redwood tree. Another furred stranger, a pointed snout leading a fat pear-shaped body, waddled across the lawn: a female possum obviously heavy with young. A less-welcome skunk occasionally left his odoriferous calling card.

It is the law of nature that the wild of field and forest prey upon each other, but, ironically in this peaceful environment, domestic cats were the greatest menace. A small heap of feathers was all that remained of some

Nordic Race, Badger Pass, 1974.

hapless nestling, tragic evidence that peace and security were illusory even in this tranquil retreat.

A number of grandchildren had joined the family circle. We enjoyed the visits of infants and youngsters and, as they grew up and approached their teenage years, they came to enjoy our hospitality and the comforts of their ancestral home and garden. Their first question always was, "Grandpa, can we go down into the basement?" Filled with an overflow of odds and ends and the repository of many memorabilia I had gathered over the years, the basement held an everlasting fascination for the small fry as well as for their elders.

Among my many possessions of windjammer days was a small ball of spunyarn. In times of stress, I would go down and sniff the aroma of Stockholm tar, the sailor's perfume, to relive again the days when, as a youngster, I had tarred down the rigging, fought galefilled canvas aloft or dodged foam-crested combers smashing across the maindeck weather bulwarks.

The ensuing years were filled with all sorts of activities, adjustment to a new marriage, the pursuit of long-neglected hobbies, family visits and travel abroad. I had learned of the opening of a ski-school in Yosemite

The author on Bachelor Butte, Bend, Oregon, 1983.

Valley headed by a retired ranger and a former member of a U.S. Olympic Ski Team. Cross-country skiing was their speciality. With rented equipment, I took up the long forgotten practice of skiing.

The floor of Yosemite Valley was in deep snow. Selecting a meadow with the magnificent backdrop of El Capitan for my first attempt in sixty years, I soon knew that I had never been away. A passing ranger, using my 16mm camera, obligingly recorded my performance, falls and all.

During the week I took basic and intermediate training. I had taken pains not to reveal my age, then seventy-five, lest the school decline to take me on. The annual Nordic Race was scheduled for March of that year. With some trepidation I queried the ranger. "Do you think I would be allowed to enter the race?"

"Sure, it's open to all comers from toddlers to centenarians."

The race was a free-for-all over a marked course. Anyone completing the run within a specified time was declared a winner. Joining a mob of some four-hundred skiers, I completed the distance within the allotted time and as the oldest participant received a pair of metal ski poles as a prize. "Congratulations on having changed your sea-legs for ski-legs," said the instructor.

Edna was more at home on skates. After several attempts with rented skates, it did not come up to her expectations. Said one of the instructors, "If she can skate, she can ski."

At age sixty-six, she joined me on the ski trails for several years. Yosemite National Park, easily reached over an all-year open highway, remained our winter playground for years to come, to ski and enjoy the company of the friends we had made there.

Yearly visits with children and grandchildren who had moved to the states of Oregon and Georgia became routine. Never content to wither on the vine, we took cruises to the Caribbean, the Mexican Riviera and Alaska. We also managed to squeeze in an occasional trip to Europe. Most memorable was a visit to England, Holland, Germany, and France.

Years earlier I had met Captain Friederich Krage, a retired German shipmaster, then temporarily residing in Washington State. Like me, a charter member of the Square Rigger Club founded in San Francisco in 1965 and a former Cape Horn windjammer sailor, we had much in common and enjoyed swapping yarns of our early seagoing days. As Master of a German merchant ship during World War II, he had the distinction of being the first German shipmaster to successfully run the British blockade of the coasts of occupied France and the English Channel.

His exploits in the early years of the war included a long voyage from Japan by way of the Pacific and Atlantic Oceans with much needed war material for the Nazi regime. German raiders were active in the South Pacific, notably Polynesia under French rule, sinking allied ships and retaining their crews as prisoners. It fell to Fred Krage to relieve the raiders of their human cargoes, mostly French, and deliver them to their homelands. It was a long and difficult voyage with an increasingly restive crowd aboard. Eluding enemy surface and submarine forces, he succeeded in reaching Bordeaux, France. A spokesman for the prisoners called on Krage and thanked him for the fair and humane treatment they had received enroute. It was followed by the traditional accolade of

"Three Cheers" by the departing crowd.

On another voyage he was not so lucky. Intercepted by air and surface forces near his destination, he scuttled his ship in accordance with his secret orders and with his crew spent the rest of the war years behind barbed wire. He confided to me that as a last act he unlocked the ship's brig, housing a political prisoner wanted by the Nazi regime. "I could not have it on my conscience to let this man perish with the ship. I set him free and gave him a choice to go down with the ship or take his chances with the rest of us."

To be in Hamburg and not call on this doughty old sailor was unthinkable, and so I met again with this remarkable man who, at 83, had recently recovered from an auto-pedestrian accident. As a resident of Woerman Haus, a retirement residence for shipmasters and officers, he had reserved a guest room for me. We spent the day cruising in legendary St. Pauli, visiting old and new bistros, paying no heed to the flight of time. As a last stop, we entered a place named "Zillertal" after an alpine village. Certainly an incongruous transplant from the Southern mountains to the Northern flatlands, it featured the traditional Octoberfest brass band with the musicians in lederhosen, calf-length socks and feathered hats. In time, we were joined by two young couples, tourists from Sweden. It was a pleasant encounter. When the band struck up a tune I could not resist the urge to take a few turns on the dance floor with the comely Swedish lasses.

But, "All things must come to an end," said the waitress as she served a last beaker of suds. It signalled the imminent closure of the establishment pursuant to a city ordinance designed to protect the merrymakers in general and the local citizenry in particular. The waitress didn't say who was presently being protected. Guided by a faint rosy glow in the east, we found our way to our quarters. But it was "rise and shine" again for a late breakfast. Reminiscing about the past, our conversation touched on the bark Obotrita in which both of us had served at separate times.

"Come to think of it," said Fred, there is a fellow nearby who was an able seaman in the Obotrita, probably at your time 1911 to 1913."

We met for lunch and immediately recognized each other. "I remember you as the young fellow with the violin," he said.

I recalled his insistence that I learn to box the compass and steer the ship. He had also shown me the craft of putting a ship in a bottle, the traditional souvenir to bring home at the end of a voyage.

Visiting old friends. Hamburg, 1972. Left to right: George Anlauf, the author, Fred Krage. Painting of five mast Preussen in back.

Fred and I spent the last hours downstream at the Elbestrand in Blankenese where arriving and departing ships were saluted by loud-speakers, followed by music and the dipping of the city colors. Finally and regretfully we said *"Auf wiedersehen,"* each holding the unspoken thought that "We must do this again sometime." We did not meet again.

The next day a cab took us from Gare du Nord in Paris to our hotel. A relic of the Napoleonic era, it had seen better days. Probably refurbished in the days of the last empire, the walls of the wide winding interior stairway were decorated with fading paintings of gentlemen and ladies in court dress, the latter in flowing white robes and the generous decolletage of the times. There was a pervading aura of history about the place. The bellhop deposited our bags on the floor and handed me the room key, a massive iron affair consisting of a headpiece, a shank and a beard, much too large for any of my pockets. I left the monstrosity with the concierge.

We spent the day strolling along the Champs Elysee, visiting Napoleon's tomb and climbing the Eiffel Tower. Following a restless night in a bed not designed for comfort, we took in the customary sights, including the Notre Dame cathedral, and went for a walk along the banks of the

Seine. We saved the afternoon for a visit to the Louvre. At the entrance of the building, our ears were assailed by the highpitched sound of young voices and the tumult of running children. It seemed as if all the schools in France had selected this day to introduce their students to this natural treasure. Sadly we turned away.

The evening found us wandering in the Place Vendome. A large hotel diningroom looked inviting and we decided to have dinner. There wasn't a soul in the place. The maitre d' inquired, "Does monsieur and madame have reservations?"

"Non," I offered in my best French.

Following these preliminaries we were seated and enjoyed a delicious, albeit solitary, dinner. The place was still empty when we left. We realized then that it was the custom in France to have dinner at a late hour, often extending past midnight. Nevertheless it was past our time and we felt the need to retire. Having retrieved the room key, I soon saw that I couldn't handle the capricious arrangement of lock and key. The concierge came, failed and left. A big fellow whom I took to be the house dick appeared with a large assortment of keys on an iron ring. Next came a man probably carrying the same set of keys. Our hopes rose when we noticed his mechanic's dress. He quit after many attempts and departed mumbling to himself. There were neither chairs nor settees in the hall, and we were about to go down and lodge a complaint with the management, when a beardless youth ascended the stairs. I had seen him in the diningroom helping the waiters. As an apprentice waiter he was known in the trade as Piccolo. He inserted a table knife into the key slot, opened the door, and stood back: "Voila."

In my astonishment I forgot to tip him.

We tumbled into bed and slept soundly. In the early morning hours we waved a last goodbye from aloft to the green fields below us.

THE CHALLENGES
OF RETIREMENT

Home again, but there was no one to greet us. As the years had passed, our outside contacts had become fewer and fewer. The family had grown and now included a number of great-grandchildren. Because of distance, travel expense and other considerations, they visited less frequently. For years, we had held open house, entertaining friends at dinner and offering our hospitality to anyone who needed a night's rest. In our less formal lifestyle, backyard barbecues took the place of formal dinners.

With the passage of time the truth dawned upon us: we had outlived most of our contemporaries and faced a future of loneliness and isolation, alone in a big house and grounds we could no longer maintain without outside help. The prospect of selling the house, leaving behind half a century of memories was an agonizing thought, haunting sleepless nights.

Not far away we had observed construction of a development advertised as a "Retirement Residence for Independent Living." When it was completed and opened for public view, we took a tour of the premises. The manager, a charming lady, asked us to stay for lunch. We were impressed by the spacious public rooms, the elegance of the furnishings and the attractive decor. The persuasive slogan, "Independent Living" coupled with the thought of being in the company of folks in our age bracket, led us to decide to take an apartment by the month.

The sale of the house and the disposal of long-cherished possessions was a heart-wrenching experience leaving us emotionally drained and physically exhausted. Once settled in our new surroundings, we soon discovered that not all our expectations would be realized. The quality of food and diningroom service could at best be called mediocre. We were at a table with three ladies of advanced age, one about to celebrate her hundredth birthday. Altogether, their conversation was limited to trivialities. What we had expected to be a period of relaxation and enjoyment in the company of others became an unfulfilled wish. Observing groups of other residents we had the feeling of being outsiders. We made a few acquaintances but soon realized that we quickly became a sounding board for their troubles. We tried to be sympathetic listeners but found it advisable to curtail close contacts. Before long we knew that the seductive slogan "Residence for Independent Living" had led us to a situation we had not foreseen.

Under the pressure of a changing economy and an aging population, the character of the establishment underwent sweeping changes. Standards of admission were lowered. Basic services were expanded to accommodate the aged and incapacitated in need of support services now provided by newly installed extended care facilities.

An increasingly high rent began to take the better part of our combined income leaving us with the bleak prospect of having to do without the amenities of life we believed we had earned. It meant a substantial curtailment of the pleasures of dining out, traveling and visiting relatives and friends. We knew we were paying for services we neither needed nor wanted.

More and more the place took on the character of a nursing home, catering to the unfortunates no longer in full control of their lives. They filled the public rooms and clogged the limited capacity of elevators not designed to handle such crowds. Their testiness and irritability became an embarrassment to other residents. The scenes, day and night, of ambulances hauling people away, many of whom did not return, added to our depression and strengthened our resolve to seek a change.

The quest of independence from institutional restraints and the resumption of a lifestyle involving choice of association, habitat, travel and return to the enjoyment of our own fleshpots occupied every waking moment. With luck we found an affordable apartment in the area of our choice. Everything we needed was within walking distance in surroundings we had known for years. Now at ease, we settled down to a life of peace and relaxation. At age ninety-seven and eighty-seven, respectively, our health is good and holds the promise of an enjoyable future. We value and appreciate the professional care, the friendship and compassion of medical practioners who, as a support group, are beyond compare. We remain in touch with family and friends and with the outside world. No longer plagued by the stresses of uncertainty our outlook on life is one of confidence and repose.

Mindful of the fact that our days are numbered, we look to the future with composure and face the certainty of the end, whenever it may come, with serenity.

END

Epilogue

It is a truism that the accident of birth and the influence of early environment are the agents forming the human psyche. It starts in infancy and early childhood when parents exert dominance that continues into adolescence. Looking back, I realize that my parents were temperamentally two totally different persons, the products of dissimilar circumstances and social backgrounds.

Father, as a brewmaster, had reached the peak of his profession. In a position of some prestige in certain circles of the business world, he and mother enjoyed the pleasures of an active social life. This agreeable life style eventually came to an end in the secluded little Bavarian village where the fortunes of the hotel enterprise they had embarked upon depended upon short seasonal periods. Stagnation followed with limited contacts with the outside world. Life soon reached an impasse. In the face of developing adversities, father remained calm. He was quiet, not given to much talk. His principal maxim, *"Nur die ruhe kann es machen"* ("Easy does it"), had carried him through life. He was willing to wait it out.

Not so, mother. Chafing under the boredom of a dead-end existence, she would rail bitterly against a future that seemed to hold no promise. Her favorite word in the dictionary was "ambition." Although I was doing well in school, she worried about my prospects. I often became the oblique target of her exhortation, "To succeed you must have ambition." Another of her favorite sayings was, "Always be the hammer, never the anvil," a phrase she had lifted from a popular novel. It was inevitable that these admonitory warnings would lodge in my subconscious throughout my life.

With the approach of adolescence, I graduated into a fascinating world full of promises in which everyone was my friend. I survived this age of gullibility and, carrying a few scars, entered the real world engaged in the struggle for existence in a field full of challenges. In the face of uncommon adversities as the result of unforeseen developments, I was confronted early on with the necessity of making decisions with far-reaching consequences without the benefit of mature counsel. In the growing-up process I acquired a degree of self-reliance and self-confidence, qualities that helped me when facing an uncertain future.

The end of World War I sounded the death knell of the commercial sailing ship and the end of an epoch in marine transportation. Attempts were made to resume operation of sailing craft that had survived the war. Restricted to the transportation of bulk cargos over long distances with low freight rates, the windjammers that had carried the commerce of the world around the globe gradually faded into oblivion. Those of us who had endured the hardships of a profession in which there was no place for the weakling or the fainthearted, who had fought canvas aloft, above a wildly plunging hull, or had manned the braces, standing waist deep on decks awash with a boiling sea, continued to pursue our calling in steamships, for we were bred to the sea and forever a part of it.

Today, there are not many of us left. We are a vanishing breed who witnessed the era of magnificent squarerigged ships which, laden with valuable cargos, delivered manufactured goods to the far corners of the earth. They were manned by officers and men endowed with fortitude and the willingness to endure the harshness and austerity of a training period lasting several years and designed to qualify the aspirants to future better positions. At the end of the rainbow were relatively comfortable jobs in a burgeoning steamship business.

In retrospect, and with time dimming memories of early experiences, life at sea was a rewarding experience, replete with events ranging from the sublime to the ridiculous with various shades of pathos. From time immemorial, the perils of the sea engendered a kinship among seamen of all nationalities. When in distress, help came to save lives in the highest tradition of the sea, regardless whose colors fluttered at the gaff. Regretably, this humanitarian aspect was interrupted twice this century, when seamen found themselves on opposite sides of conflicts not of their making.

Throughout the years I have carried with me vivid memories of events, some mundane, others of high drama. I shall never forget the thrill when, still a mere stripling of fifteen, I was ordered to take the wheel for the first time as a qualified helmsman. Grasping the spokes of the steering wheel with a firm grip, I took control of the ship yawing to the push of a quartering sea as she plunged ahead under full sail, driven by a boisterous northeast trade wind through a purple sea flecked with whitecaps. Steady as she goes. It was a moment of exultation best portrayed by a well-known quotation:

> "Lives there a man with soul so mean
> While still a lad in early teen
> Has never felt the thrill
> Of matching wits with wind and sea
> While at the helm of noble craft
> With all sails set
> Obedient to his lightest touch
> He briefly was the master of his ship."

So ends the saga of one man's life afloat and ashore. The maritime nations of the world still operate different types of sailing craft said to be training ships. Still a magnificent spectacle, the squareriggers under full sail have become status symbols of a romantic past.

I leave this tome to posterity which, besides my immediate descendants and their rising generation, includes close to a hundred persons, residents of record in the United States of America who bear my family name.

Afterword

by C. Cameron Macauley

As one who has been "on board" since Captain Friz first laid the keel for this volume, he has asked me to add this personal Afterword. It is, for me, a signal honor.

My first impressions of the Captain, when we met nearly two decades ago, have steadfastly endured. He is keenly alert, analytical, circumspect, able to size up a man or a circumstance and distill its essence succinctly.

Those qualities shine through in this engrossing account of nearly a century of life upon and around the earth's oceans. The many episodes he shares here are treasured personal memories, particularly intriguing to seafarers and of considerable interest to the general reader. Historic events--two world wars, the Great Depression, the Korean War--spring to life through the eyes of one who was actually there, of one who endured and survived them.

Author Friz writes well. His clarity displays his depth of understanding about the things he writes. This gift is all the more amazing in that English is not his native tongue. I am reminded of another author and Master Mariner who wrote little until he retired from his life at sea. Joseph Conrad, a Pole, also chose to write in English, which was an acquired language for him as well.

You may never have the opportunity to sail on a full-rigged ship. In Liverpool Buttons and Homeward-Bound Stitches, however, you can get so close you can smell the salt water spray.

APPENDICES

COMMANDER
MILITARY SEA TRANSPORTATION SERVICE, PACIFIC AREA
33 Berry Street
San Francisco, 7, California

MSTSP-24-Cy
Ser 240045

1 0 SEP 1952

From: Commander, Military Sea Transportation Service, Pacific Area
To: Captain Ottmar Fris, Master
USNS GENERAL N. M. WALKER

Subj: Appreciation of performance of duty

1. During my year and a half in this Command, your performance of duty
has come to my notice many times, and I can recall no occasion on which
I was not pleased by the reports I received. I have come to take it as
a matter of course, as have officers of my Staff, that a ship under your
command would be so ably administered and well sailed that there was complete confidence in the successful performance of her mission.

2. You have produced that feeling of confidence by your loyal devotion
to duty, your untiring efforts and by your professional excellence, all
of which I consider to have been in keeping with the highest traditions of
the sea.

3. You have earned my commendation for an excellent performance of duty,
but I could not relinquish this Command without also expressing my appreciation for your services.

HARRY SANDERS

Letter of commendation and appreciation signed by Harry Sanders,
Rear Admiral. USN, COMSTSPAC

DEPARTMENT OF THE NAVY
MILITARY SEA TRANSPORTATION SERVICE, PACIFIC AREA
FORT MASON
SAN FRANCISCO, CALIFORNIA 94129

ADDRESS REPLY TO COMMANDER
MILITARY SEA TRANSPORTATION
SERVICE, PACIFIC AREA
NOT TO THE SIGNER OF THIS LETTER
REFER TO
P-23

7 January 1966

Captain Ottmar H. Friz
958 Rose Avenue
Piedmont, California

My dear Captain Friz:

I wish to offer my felicitations upon the occasion of your retirement 30
December 1965 from Military Sea Transportation Service, Pacific Area,
after having completed more than 25 years of service with the U. S.
Federal Government. A retirement certificate attesting to your service
is enclosed.

Your record of service dates back to August 1924 and includes assignments
with the Department of Commerce, the Department of the Army and the Department of the Navy. These assignments include, among others, Second Officer,
First Officer and Master of large transports. Upon your transfer from the
Army Transport Service to the Military Sea Transportation Service, Pacific
Area in March 1950, you became a member of that select group of employees
known as the "MSTS Pioneers" who shared in the creation and success of our
organization. You were appointed as Supervisory Marine Transport Specialist (General) on the staff of Commander Military Sea Transportation Service,
Pacific Area, in September 1954 and served in the capacity of Port Captain.

I have noted with interest the many letters of appreciation and commendation
which appear in your official records and which attest to the excellent
manner in which you carried out your duties. The wholehearted cooperation,
loyalty and devotion to duty you have consistently demonstrated may permit
you to feel justifiably proud. I wish to take this opportunity, on behalf
of the U. S. Government, and particularly the Military Sea Transportation
Service, Pacific Area, to express my appreciation for the service you have
rendered and to wish you many enjoyable years in your retirement.

Sincerely yours,

Wm. D. IRVIN
Rear Admiral, U. S. Navy
Commander Military Sea Transportation Service,
Pacific Area

"Think Safety—Talk Safety—and Sell Safety"

Letter of Retirement
William D. Irvin Rear Admiral, USN, COMSTSPAC

MILITARY SEA TRANSPORTATION SERVICE
PACIFIC AREA
Certificate of Achievement

is awarded to

CAPTAIN OTTMAR H FRIZ

for

Meritorious achievement in the performance of duty while serving on the staff of Commander Military Sea Transportation Service, Pacific Area, as Port Captain from 1 December 1953 through 29 April 1966. By your deep concern in all matters affecting the efficiency and performance of the command, you consistently arrived at sound decisions. Your professional skill and integrity in dealing with the officers and men of assigned ships gained you the respect of everyone. Your conscientious application to all problems associated with ship operations and the cordial relationships you established are a credit to you. Your conduct, loyalty and devotion to duty have been in keeping with the highest traditions of the United States Navy. Upon your departure I wish to extend to you my personal appreciation for a superb job. Well Done!

Given this 29th **day of** APRIL. **19** 66

Wm. D. IRVIN, Rear Admiral, U. S. Navy
Commander Military Sea Transportation Service
Pacific Area

12ND MSTSP 1650/2 (1-63)

Certificate of Achievement
William D. Irvin Rear Admiral, USN, COMSTSPAC

1 April 1966

Dear Captain Friz:

I write this letter with deeply mixed emotions.
Happy for you as you approach your retirement; the anticipation of being able to devote your full attention to
your loving wife and family; and being able to accomplish
the multitudious tasks you have been putting off for so
many years.

On the other hand, I'm apprehensive and deeply sad-
dened by the knowledge that we will be losing a stalwart,
honest, trustworthy, and an exemplary leader. In spite
of the cliche that no one is indispensible, it will be
extremely difficult, if not impossible, for the command
to find a replacement with your superb qualities. - - I'm
not writing these things to flatter you, Captain, I mean
them most sincerely!

I shall always treasure the invaluble advice and assistance you have rendered to me for so many years. Your
cool, calm, collected approach to even the most exasper-
ating situations has been a source of deep admiration and
inspiration to me. Paramount amoung all your wonderful
qualities is the integrity with which you have always conducted your business and personal relations with us. So
you see, Captain, I just don't know how they will find an
adequate replacement for you!

Since all good things must come to an end, you can,
with complete confidence, terminate another phase of a
highly successful career with the knowledge of having accomplished the task in a truly outstanding manner. This
is not just my opinion, Captain, it is the concensus of
everyone who has ever had the extreme pleasure to be associated with you.

Naturally, we all wish you many happy years of retirement life.

Most sincerely,

Letter of Farewell
R. E. Landry, Master, MSTSPAC

TO MY FRIENDS AND SHIPMATES AT SEA AND IN PORT

The 30th of April 1966 marks the day of my retirement from fifty-five
years of employment in the maritime industry. The last twenty-five years
were in ships of the Army Transport Service and the Military Sea Transportation Service. During this time many of you have been my shipmates, others
have known me as Port Captain during the last thirteen years of my tour of
duty on the staff of COMSTSPACAREA.

I leave a position from which I have derived the utmost in pleasure and
satisfaction and in which I have been richly rewarded by your friendship and
goodwill. The Bay Area remains my home and I want you to know that I shall
never be farther away from you than the nearest telephone or the price of
a postage stamp.

Goodbye my friends, adios amigos, and God Bless you.

O. H. FRIZ

Letter of Farewell
O.H. Friz, Port Captain, MSTSPAC (Ret.)

                                          Cam Rahn Bay
                                          South Vietnam
                                          19 May 1966

Dear Capt. Friz:

    Your farewell message was received in the mail at this port.
At this moment all personnel are aware that your retirement is
definite and not a rumor. As I passed this message from person
to person I observed something which I would like to pass on to
you.
    The comments of all those persons who know you had a sameness
to them, there were no mixed feelings regarding your retirement.
Each and every person made some favorable remark expressing their
regret over your retirement and also their respect for you from a
professional as well as personal standpoint.
    Sailors are not especially noted for their tact and diplomacy
but rather for their bluntness. There can be no doubt of their
sincerity. So I pass it on to you in the hope that you will accept
it as a tribute from those who have known you, worked for you and
I might add, some of those who have known the "feel of your lash".
    I will take this moment to thank you again for your constant
assistance and encouragement from the time I first became a member
of MSTS. I have deeply appreciated your confidence in me.
    Goodby Captain Friz. I pray for many years of happiness for
you and your wife, years of good active retirement for you, while
at the same time reliving and enjoying the memories of a proud,
happy and a most successful career.
                                          Sincerely

                                          (Signed) G. C. McCoy

                                          Letter of Farewell
                              G. C. McCoy, Master, MSTSPAC

TRAINING COURSES

U. S. Maritime Commission, Visual Signaling Certificate

Sperry Gyroscope Co. Inc. Operation of Gyro Compass Equipment

U. S. Naval Supply Center, Shiploading and Storage

Department of the Navy, Radar, Maneuvering Board, Radar Navigation

Department of the Navy, Industrial Relations Institute

Department of the Navy, International Law

Department of the Navy, Orientation to Command

Department of the Navy, Organization for National Security Fleet Air Defense Training Center, CIC Techniques and Duties

GLOSSARY

ACLU—American Civil Liberties Union

ACDUTRA—Active Duty for Training

APO—Army Post Office

ATS—Army Transport Service

COMSTS—Commander Military Sea Transportation Service

COMSTSPAC—Commander Military Sea Transportation Service Pacific

COMILDEP—Commander Military Department

CONUS—Continental United States

CPO—Chief Petty Officer

DEWL—Distant Early Warning Line

DOD—Department of Defense

IRO—International Refugee Organization

LCVP—Landing Craft, Vehicle, Personnel

LCM—Landing Craft, Machinery

LST—Landing Craft, Tanks

MSTS—Military Sea Transportation Service

MSTSPAC—Military Sea Transportation Service Pacific

NCPI—Navy Civilian Personal Instructions

POW—Prisoner of War

RIF—Reduction in Force

ROK—Republic of Korea

S.F.P.E.—San Francisco Port of Embarkation

USSB—United States Shipping Board

SERVICE RECORD AFLOAT

Ships Of German Registry
OBOTRITA, ex FAVORITA, bark, built in Denmark, 1892
Deck Boy 1911-1913
BLANKENESE, ex NICOLAS WITSEN, ship, built in Holland 1898
Ordinary Seaman 1913-1917

Ships Of American Registry
GENEVA, brigantine built in Benicia, California 1892
Able Seaman 1917
COLUMBIA, fourmast schooner, built in 1898
Able Seaman, 1919
ADMIRAL SCHLEY, passenger, twin screw
Able Seaman 1920-1921
SANTA MONICA, steam schooner, built in 1902
Able Seaman 1921
LURLINE, passenger and cargo, built in 1908
Quartermaster 1924
SEQUOIA, lighthousetender
Helsman 1924
GUIDE, Coast and geodetic Survey snip
Bos'n's Mate 1924-1925
MONTPELIER, ex BOCHUM, cargo
Able Seaman 1925
PRESIDENT ROOSEVELT, passenger and cargo, built in 1922
Able Seaman 1925
AMERICAN MERCHANT, passenger and cargo, built in 1918
Able Seaman 1926

CASTLE TOWN, built in 1918, cargo
Third and Second Officer 1926-1927
DEMOCRACY, ex JUPITER, built in 1917, cargo
Third Officer 1928
SUTHERLAND, built in 1918, cargo
Third Officer 1929
TASHMOO, built in 1918, cargo
Third and Second Officer 1931-1932
Built for the United States Shipping Board (USSB) and sold or leased to Charles Nelson Co. and Nelson Steamship Co. San Francisco, California 1926

Tanker Service, Standard Oil
R.J. HANNA, Third Officer 1929
S.C.T. DODD, Second and First Officer 1929-1930
DISTRICT OF COLUMBIA, Second Officer 1930-1931
H.M. STOREY, Second Officer 1931
J.C.FITZSIMMONS, Second Officer 1931

Key System Ferries
HAYWARD-SAN LEANDRO, Seaman 1938-1939
YERBA BUENA-TREASURE ISLAND-PIEDMONT-SIERRA
NEVADA, Second and First Officer 1939-1940

Public Vessels Of The United States
USAT. TASKER H. BLISS,
ex PRESIDENT CLEVELAND, troop transport
Built in 1921, Third and Second Officer 1940-1942
USAT. FREDERIC FUNSTON, troop transport
Built in 1942, Second Officer 1942-1943
USAT. BARBARA C. Steam Schooner, cargo
Built in 1920, First Officer 1943
USAT. CHARLES P. STEINMETZ, troop and cargo
Built in 1943, First Officer 1943-1944
USAT. WILL H. POINT, ex WEST CAMARGO, cargo
Built in 1919, Master 1944-1946
USAT. CHATEAU THIERRY, Hospital Ship
Built in 1920, Master 1946
USAT. GENERAL A.W. GREELY, troop transport
Built in 1945, Master 1946-1949

USAT. YARMOUTH, troop transport
   Built in 1927, Master 1945-1946
USAT. ADMIRAL W.S. SIMS, troop transport
   Built in 1944, Master 1947
USAT. GENERAL D.E. AULTMAN, troop transport
   Built in 1945, Master 1949
USNS GENERAL WILLIAM WEIGEL, T-AP 119, troop transport
   Built in 1944, Master 1950-1951
USNS GENERAL N.M. WALKER T-AP 125,
ex ADMIRAL H.T. MAYO, troop transport
   Built in 1944, Master 1952-1953

REFERENCES

Hamburg's Segelschiffe, 1795-1945   J. Meyer
International Maritime Dictionary   De Kerchove
A Glossary of Sea Terms   Bradford
The Reader's Digest Great Encyclopedic Dictionary   Funk & Wagnalls
The United States Navy's Military Sea Transportation Service   Gano
Samuel Beadle Family   Walter Beadle
The Friz Family Heritage Book   Beatrice Bayley Inc.
Balclutha's History
      U.S. Department of the Interior, National Park Service
My Love Must Wait   Ernestine Hill
History Of WWI   American Heritage
US Army Ships and Watercraft of WWII   Glover
Great Passenger Ships of the World   Kludas

Port Captain, MSTSPAC, 1954.